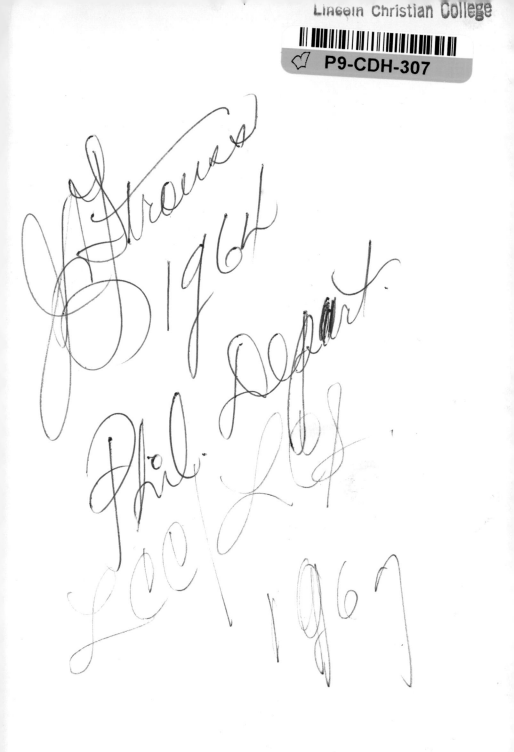

# THE NATURE OF MAN

*In Theological and Psychological Perspective*

# THE NATURE OF MAN

*in*
*Theological*
*and*
*Psychological Perspective*

EDITED BY

SIMON DONIGER

**HARPER & BROTHERS, PUBLISHERS**

**NEW YORK**

THE NATURE OF MAN

*Library of Congress catalog card number: 62-9566*

TO SEWARD HILTNER

# ACKNOWLEDGMENTS

The editor wishes to express his thanks to the authors of the articles which were published exclusively in *Pastoral Psychology:* Chapters 3, 6, 7, 9, 10, 12, 13, 17. He is particularly grateful to the authors of the following articles which originated in journals other than *Pastoral Psychology*, and to the editors and publishers of these journals for permission to include them in this volume:

"The Psychoanalytic View of Human Personality," by Edith Weigert, M.D. Reprinted from the *Journal of Pastoral Care*, Vol. 6, No. 4, Winter, 1952.

"Know Thyself: The Biblical Doctrine of Human Depravity," by James I. McCord. Reprinted from *Interpretation*, April, 1949.

"Existentialism, Psychotherapy, and the Nature of Man," by Paul Tillich. An address delivered at the Conference on Existential Psychotherapy in New York City on February 27, 1960, and published simultaneously in the June, 1960, issues of *Existential Inquiries* and *Pastoral Psychology*.

"Niebuhr and Rogers on the Nature of Man," by Carl R. Rogers. Published in *Pastoral Psychology*, June, 1958. Reprinted from The Chicago Theological Seminary *Register*, January, 1956, No. 1. The discussion by Dr. Loomer, Dr. Horton, and Dr. Hofmann which follows was written especially for *Pastoral Psychology*.

"The Nature of Man," by Carl R. Rogers. Published in *Pastoral Psychology*, May, 1960. Reprinted from the *Journal of Counseling Psychology*, Fall, 1957.

"Emotional Maturity," by Franz Alexander. Published in *Pastoral Psychology*, March, 1950. Reprinted from the November-December, 1948, issue of the *Mental Health Bulletin* of the Illinois Society for Mental Hygiene.

"Theology and the Understanding of Children," by Randolph Crump Miller. Published in *Pastoral Psychology*, June, 1952. Parts of this article, originally written for *Pastoral Psychology*, were condensed into *Education for Christian Living* by Randolph Crump Miller, published by Prentice-Hall, Inc., in 1956.

"The Human Situation: A Feminine Viewpoint," by Valerie Saiving Goldstein. Reprinted from the *Journal of Religion*, Vol. XL, No. 2, April, 1960. It was originally presented at the week of work in August, 1959, of the National Council on Religion in Higher Education, of which Mrs. Goldstein is a Fellow.

"Human Nature Can Change: A Symposium," by Harold Kelman, M.D., Frederick A. Weiss, M.D., Paul Tillich, and Karen Horney, M.D. Published in *Pastoral Psychology,* October, 1960. Reprinted from the *American Journal of Psychoanalysis,* Vol. XII, 1952.

"Hope," by Karl Menninger, M.D. This is the Academic Lecture read at the 115th annual meeting of The American Psychiatric Association, Philadelphia, Penna., April 27-May 1, 1959, and published in *Pastoral Psychology,* April, 1960. Reprinted from the *American Journal of Psychiatry,* December, 1959.

"The Immortality of Man," by Margaret Mead. This is the seventeenth Garvin Free Lecture delivered in Lancaster, Pennsylvania, on December 3, 1956. The discussion by Dr. Tillich, Dr. Horton, and Dean Homrighausen which follows was written especially for *Pastoral Psychology.*

"A Theology for Modern Man," by William Hamilton. Reprinted from *Interpretation,* October, 1957.

# CONTENTS

ix

PART THREE

## MAN'S PROBLEMS AND POTENTIALITIES

# FOREWORD

SIMON DONIGER

THE beginnings of this book go back to more than a decade ago when we first began publishing the journal, *Pastoral Psychology*, under my editorship. As I stated in a prospectus prepared at the time for the consideration of our Editorial Advisory Board, "The purpose of this new journal is to bring to ministers some of the insights, understandings, and skills of dynamic psychology, psychiatry, and the other behavioral sciences, in a way that has immediate and practical application to the minister's work and within the religious framework of the minister's point of view." Thus, the immediate purpose of the journal was practical, functional, and mainly operational. At the same time there was a deep awareness that, important as this practical emphasis was, just as important was a consideration of theory, and particularly theoretical considerations regarding the nature of man. For it was obvious to all of us that the concept of the nature of man that one holds very largely determines how one feels about man's dilemma, what one does about it, and how one goes about doing it. To quote from the same prospectus again, "We mean to deal with practice in a way which elicits relevant theory and does not exclude it. We believe in the importance of theory as a base for intelligent practice, but we hope that this theory will evolve and grow out of practical working content."

It was natural that with such an awareness of the importance of theory regarding the nature of man, every issue of *Pastoral Psychology* from the beginning of its publication contained some important discussions bearing directly or indirectly on this theme by theologians and pastors on the one hand, and by representatives of the behavioral and social sciences (psychiatrists, psychologists, anthropologists, sociologists, educators) on the other. As a matter of fact, there was a constant and continuing dialogue in *Pastoral Psychology* on this theme—a dialogue that revealed inevitably some basic differences, but also striking and significant similarities. It became obvious that it was important to formulate these differences as well as these similarities in a way that would, so to speak, put them side by side; thus, they might be studied, evaluated, compared, and when possible, synthesized more thoroughly and profoundly than could be done through individual articles. More important, it was felt that by such a formulation, this dialogue which was but a beginning would be furthered and continued. That was the genesis of this book.

It was originally intended that the book be made up exclusively of articles that had been published in *Pastoral Psychology*, but a scrutiny of these materials revealed a kind of bias—a bias that was inevitable in terms of the particular function of the journal. Accordingly it seemed wise to supplement these materials with articles from other journals—journals which did not necessarily emphasize the kind of relational approach between psychology and religion that *Pastoral Psychology* stressed. As Seward Hiltner expressed it in a personal letter at the time when we were struggling with the choice of these materials, "Our function in the journal has been to try to relate psychology and theology on a functional and operational level. . . . *All* of our materials, properly enough, attempt to deal in one way or another with the relationship between psychology and theology . . . but to have only such materials would very greatly limit the value of such a book. It would not be a fair picture." The several articles in this book from journals other than *Pastoral Psychology* are the result of a search to overcome this bias and to present a more nearly complete and fair picture of the various concepts of the nature of man from the point of view of both theology and psychology. We are immensely indebted to these other journals, and to the authors of the articles, for their gracious permission to reprint these. We are, of course, no less grateful to the authors whose articles were printed originally in *Pastoral Psychology*.

We have divided the book into three sections: Part One, Views of Man's Nature; Part Two, Good and Evil in Man; Part Three, Man's Problems and Potentialities. The three parts include an approximately equal number of contributions from theologians, philosophers, and educators, on the one side; and from psychologists, psychiatrists, psychoanalysts, and other students of personality, on the other side. Each has been chosen for its merit in illuminating some aspect of the central theme.

The Preview by Seward Hiltner (pp. xiii-xxi) will afford the reader a brief orientation to the articles as a group, their relationships to one another, and their importance for the central theme of the book.

The concluding chapter, "The Dialogue on Man's Nature," is an essay written especially for this volume by Seward Hiltner. With his usual perceptiveness and deep insight, Dr. Hiltner analyzes the relationship between theology and the behavioral sciences, past, present, and future; the false assumptions which once stood as roadblocks in the way of co-operation between theologians and behavioral scientists; the growth and development that have taken place within both groups during recent years; and the still greater growth that must take place before a genuine dialogue and a real working together can eventuate.

I am deeply indebted to Dr. Hiltner for the synthesis he achieves for the book through this concluding chapter, as well as for his invaluable help in the selection of the material making up the major part of the volume. It is a great privilege for me to acknowledge this debt and to dedicate the book to him with deep affection.

My expression of indebtedness would indeed be incomplete if I did not at least mention the invaluable aid which my editorial associate, Helen MacMaster, has given me in the preparation of this manuscript.

# A PREVIEW

## SEWARD HILTNER

THE essays in this collection, as will at once be apparent to the reader, do not all have the same understanding of man. There are real differences in point of view, in method, in context, and in assumptions, among them. Pure agreement would be both premature and sterile. At the same time, the reader will also notice that the volume contains little or nothing of the radical argument about whether theology seems worth anything to psychologists, or psychology is of any value to theologians.

Every theologian herein represented has done some serious study of the modern psychological disciplines; and every psychologist has at least some sympathetic comprehension concerning the purposes of the theological enterprise. This does not mean that the theologians are blowing trumpets for psychology, or that the psychologists all go to church weekly. It does mean that much of the controversy about man's nature that sometimes takes place between two groups of this kind is absent from the present volume—made impossible because each has a more accurate and more sympathetic knowledge of the other than is often true.

The reader will find genuine differences of conviction here. The answers given to the question of man's nature are not uniform. But we believe there is more agreement, or at least sympathetic understanding, in the way the question of man's nature is put than is ordinarily true. No theologian herein denies the relevance of direct observation of man to the proper understanding of man's nature. No psychologist who writes here argues that man's nature may be understood regardless of the larger context in which man exists. Thus we believe that what the authors of this book approach even though they do not reach—a common way of asking the question about man's nature, that includes crucial agreements concerning both method and context—gives promise of better understanding tomorrow of the nature of man.

## Part One: Views of Man's Nature

Side by side at the very beginning of this section we have placed
two articles by Edith Weigert and James I. McCord. As much as is
possible in short compass, each of them expresses, in non-technical
language, the basic viewpoint of his discipline, as he understands
it, on what is crucial about man's nature. Although Weigert is ap-
preciative of theology and McCord of psychology, each of these
articles attempts to articulate a position from within its own brand
of study.

What strikes this reader in Weigert's article is its focus on trust
in relation to content, and its emphasis on development in relation
to method. Man, we might paraphrase Weigert, is the creature who,
to become himself, must experience trust. When circumstance pre-
vents this, the need to trust is simply driven underground but
persists; and special help is needed to bring it back and aid its exercise. Methodologically, Weigert moves from infant to adult developmentally. The child has a future and the adult, a past; if one does
not look, developmentally, both ways, he fails to see the nature of
man who is infant, child, and adolescent, as well as adult. Weigert
is of course not unaware that many kinds of abilities and capacities
must be developed if one is to be a human being. Yet when she must
state what is most crucial and decisive, this lies within the general
area of relatedness, and is seen specifically as capacity to trust. By
implication, that which fosters the capacity to trust what is trustworthy is aiding man to find his true nature. The man whose capacity to trust has been driven underground is to that extent not truly
a man.

McCord's discussion moves directly out of one of the biblical
teachings that is most misunderstood in the modern world, the
"depravity" of man's nature. His analysis is dynamic. What was the
Bible trying to say when it talked of man's depravity? What this
meant, McCord argues forcibly, is not that every man is as bad as
possible but that "all men are sinful and that their sin extends to
the whole of their nature." Thus one may speak of man's "true nature" as created by God, in which man is capable of "fellowship
with God." When man does not use, or misuses, that capacity, the
reason is sin; and man is then "denatured" in relation to his true
nature. In that state man is in bondage, severed from fellowship

with God. From it he may be released only by the redemptive power of God, which is the good news that Christian faith proclaims. To be redeemed is to be restored to man's true nature, of which the highest capacity is fellowship with God.

It is of interest that Weigert's principal positive term is "trust" and McCord's is "fellowship," that Weigert's main negative term is "loss of trust" while McCord's is "sin." Each of them allows for three kinds of "nature" in man: first, his true and original created nature (for Weigert, capacity to trust; for McCord, "a little lower than the angels"); second, his denatured nature (for Weigert, the capacity to trust going underground; for McCord, sin's making fellowship impossible); and third, his restored true nature (for Weigert, through therapeutic procedures and the "miracle of redemption"; for McCord, through Jesus Christ as agent of the redemptive power of God).

Both interpretations are realistic. Both are dynamic. Both combine a preliminary pessimism with an ultimate optimism. Yet they are far from being identical. McCord's account is not developmental in the sense of Weigert's. If the capacity to trust is returned in Weigert's man, will he simply increase his capacity to sin in McCord's sense? Are parents and culture, in Weigert's account, the "Satan" of McCord's? In McCord's view, since men sin with their highest endowments, are the distinctions Weigert makes about capacity to trust not taken seriously? The differences in emphasis should at least be noted. They are suggested here not as negative comments, but lest any reader prematurely amalgamate them unconscious of the remaining differences.

To continue in sharp and precise fashion just the kind of similarity-and-difference dialogue that has been suggested above as a result of reflection on the Weigert and McCord articles, the reader may turn to the discussion of Paul W. Pruyser. Professional psychologist, but able lay theologian, Pruyser continues just the kind of dialogue I have been recommending. How do theology and psychology see stability and change in man's nature? How do they view optimism and pessimism? The look back, and the look ahead? The old man, and the new? To ask such questions now, says Pruyser, is to present but a sketch. But a portrait, he argues, is possible if we persist.

No single article can possibly do justice to the richness and complexity of Paul Tillich's understanding of man's nature, especially since this theme is, as David E. Roberts noted, "clearly central" in

Tillich's entire thought. The present chapter, nevertheless, in addition to being representative, has two additional virtues. First, it discusses the relationship between the "existential" and the "essential" in the nature of man. Second, in considering the essential and the existential in psychoanalysis, as well as in philosophy and theology, it presents a possible structure by which these disciplines may bring together their respective insights into man's nature.

Tillich's understanding of man is, like all aspects of his thought, on a "boundary." Although he does not believe a completely objective or neutral interpretation of man to be possible, he believes that the sciences and philosophy should go as far as they can in delineating those aspects of man's nature that are capable of rational, empirical, and objective investigation. On the other hand, Tillich believes that the quality of religious commitment is ultimately determinative of one's understanding of man, and therefore that any view of man professing both ultimacy and objectivity is at least partially mistaken.

Any reader of the symposium by and about Carl R. Rogers and Reinhold Niebuhr will certainly be convinced that no millennium of harmonious accord has yet been achieved between psychology and theology, or at least between this particular psychologist and that particular theologian. This symposium grew out of Perry Le-Fevre's success in originally persuading Carl Rogers to do a review of Reinhold Niebuhr's book, *The Self and the Dramas of History*. We were then able to submit the Rogers review to three theologians of somewhat different perspectives, all of whom were already familiar with Niebuhr's thought. The resulting discussion turned out to be mainly about Niebuhr's understanding of man, and only incidentally about Rogers'. However, the concluding comment by Rogers helps to make up for the latter deficiency.

Despite the differences among their own views, all three of our commentators on Rogers-Niebuhr suggest that some of the apparent differences between Rogers and Niebuhr are the result of misunderstandings potentially capable of resolution through clarification. However, all of them warn against any attempt to make a facile accommodation of these views which, even after misunderstandings are cleared, continue to represent many kinds of significant difference.

## Part Two: Good and Evil in Man

The chapter by Howard L. Parsons is especially provocative not only because it protests against what it regards as the prevailing theological pessimism about man's nature but also because it makes use of many modern psychological data and views in doing so. The general form of Parsons' argument is philosophical, but its themes and concerns are theological. Since "naturalism" tends to be a negatively loaded word to most theologians, its advocacy by Parsons is unlikely to receive a sympathetic hearing from them. On the other side, psychologists are likely to be puzzled by having this label placed on the implications of some of their findings.

Whether or nor the reader agrees with Parsons' total effort, what ought to be noted especially is his attempt to introduce a developmental and dynamic dimension into the very definition of man's nature. What emerges in man is not, Parsons states flatly, "entirely of man's doing or in his control." And yet Parsons wants us to agree that, even though the source of creativity transcends man, it is "still quite natural." The deepest need of man's nature, Parsons argues, is "for love and growth." That is, so to speak, man's original nature. Disorders and deviations from this are "not innate in man's nature." To recognize this fact, Parsons believes, is to have both a true picture of man's nature and more adequate motivation for discovering and living our true nature "rooted and grounded in love." Parsons' attempt to see man's nature developmentally should be recognized as an attempt to transcend the dichotomy between "essential" and "existential."

The commentary upon Parsons' article by the late Willard L. Sperry, all too brief as it is, is nevertheless of unusual significance partly because Sperry himself belonged in some sense in a "liberal" tradition from which he believed Parsons extrapolated too far. Sympathetic as Sperry was in his later years to the need for theology not to view man too optimistically, he nevertheless felt that "a credible doctrine of man" could be achieved these days only out of the encounter of the "old and new" orthodoxies with "our conventional liberalism." It was, he concluded, precisely a "credible doctrine of man" that Protestantism needs most desperately.

The short article by Carl R. Rogers contains, nonetheless, a characteristically clear discussion of his own grounds for regarding man as "basically trustworthy." That this view is not a sheer superficial optimism will be clear to any careful reader. But it does stand radically against granting any "innate" status to man's destructiveness. Since Rogers sets his view, although with some appreciation, against those of Sigmund Freud and Karl Menninger, it would have been helpful if brief articles from them on the point at issue could have been found and printed here. Unfortunately, that was not possible. The material is available in both Freud and Menninger, but not in sufficiently brief compass for this volume. The chapter by Menninger in the next section speaks indirectly to the issue as raised by Rogers, and the article in the former section by Paul W. Pruyser, a close associate of Karl Menninger's, does also.

Mainly through an analysis of different forms and qualities of conscience, Noel Mailloux, who is both psychologist and Roman Catholic priest, considers the contributions that psychology can make to our understanding and living in the moral dimension. His discussion is, therefore, a psychological prolegomenon to moral theology or Christian ethics. The person who has a "neurotic" or "infantile" conscience is not to be characterized as simply bad. Instead, the moralist may now recognize that the person needs help in overcoming a terrible obstacle. If he gets such help, then "self-respect" and "a genuine love relationship with others" both become possible. Moral judgments that have not first considered these factors will, by implication, run the risk of mistake about the extent of the good and evil in man.

The basic thrust of my own article is similar to that by Mailloux in that we both believe modern psychology has at least an important antechamber function in relation to Christian ethics and moral theology. My specific attempt is to show the need for a proper "casuistry" (study of specific cases) within Protestant Christian ethics. A case is presented in which the forces of good and evil, as they appear at first glance, are eventually shown by psychodynamic analysis to be quite different in nature beneath the surface. The main point of my article is that discussion of good or evil in man in general must be both incomplete and inadequate unless it includes specific case analysis of this general type. Although the case analysis does not render ultimate principles, it makes a needed contribution even to the true understanding of such principles.

## Part Three: Man's Problems and Potentialities

This section begins with two able chapters on the meaning of maturity, by Franz Alexander and Elliott Dunlap Smith. The term "maturity" has often been used loosely. A good test of the discrimination with which it is used is to substitute for it the word "ripeness" (to which the metaphor properly links it) and see what happens. What, then, does the "ripe" human being do? And how does he become "ripe"? By this standard both our authors come off very well indeed.

According to Alexander, the person is mature who gives as well as receives, who knows and accepts his own limitations, who adapts flexibly to actual situations, who turns his interest outward productively, who is basically self-reliant rather than dependent, and who is not under compulsion to regress. By this definition, he continues, no one is wholly mature. Yet maturity in a human being is a quality of one's relatedness as well as of his independence.

Smith sees the primary qualities of human maturity as integrity and considerateness. Writing primarily of the transition from adolescent to adult years, he traces the significance of integrity and considerateness both in general and in relation to many dimensions of life: work, marriage, and others. "To have mature integrity . . . one must have the inner courage to think clearly and fearlessly for himself, to hold valiantly to what he thinks, and to do both no matter how widely or bitterly opposed. . . . To be maturely considerate in human relations, one must be truly and feelingly concerned with what others think and feel . . . not merely in relaxed relationships . . . but also when the difference is . . . deep. . . ."

What are man's chances of becoming mature, of becoming, as an adult human being, what (by one or another standard) he ought to become? Especially in theology this question has often been asked as if the answer could be sought for adult males (and sometimes for white, Protestant, Aryan males as well), and then distributed without alteration to the two other great sectors of the human race, women and children. Even now we are only at the beginning of developing a proper Christian theology of the child or a "doctrine of the child" that has lost all traces of being merely a watered-down adulthood. The chapter by Randolph Crump Miller is a genuine

step in the right direction. Part of the nature of man is the nature
of the child. Miller contends that theology, no less than the psychology upon which he also draws, is primarily the attempt to deal
with relationship in its fundamental senses, and that, rightly understood, this is as crucial in the problems and potentialities of the
child as of the adult.

The other neglected part of the generic man, woman, is discussed
by Valerie Saiving Goldstein in what seems to us by far the most
penetrating consideration we have ever seen. Although the author,
with characteristic modesty and no doubt truth as well, gives special credit to Margaret Mead for a number of her points, she seems
to us most perceptive in moving toward a "doctrine of woman"
precisely when she is most original. Very much of contemporary
theological thought, Goldstein believes, has been constructed out
of male experience, and the resulting doctrines (even about love)
fail adequately to interpret the situation for women. This is in no
way to see an "impassable gulf" between men and women, or the
ways in which they examine the world and themselves. But it does
rightly put us on guard lest unwittingly we extrapolate from purely
male experience to the impoverishment of a more comprehensive
understanding of a generic man that includes woman too.·

More easily than a man, Goldstein contends, a woman "may give
too much of herself" and lose her uniqueness. Estimates of the
human capacity to love ought, she argues, to take this into consideration. Similarly, although women too may have "pride" and "will-
to-power," more often their temptation to sin comes, she holds,
through a drifting into "triviality, distractibility, and diffuseness."
All in all, we predict that every reader will be both illuminated and
brought up short by this chapter.

In replying to the question, "Can human nature change?" the
late Karen Horney does give an unequivocal affirmative as potentiality. But since the conditions of change, as she sees them, are
neither easy nor automatic, her view is surely no simple optimism.
This is stressed differently but no less emphatically by the brief yet
incisive statements on what change means by the other discussants:
Harold Kelman, Frederick A. Weiss, and Paul Tillich. Particularly
important in Tillich's discussion of the problem of "man changeable
and unchangeable," and his analysis of what it is in human nature
that *can* change and what can *not*.

The chapter on hope by Karl Menninger is one of very few discussions of this topic from psychiatric or psychological sources. He views hope dialectically. Part of the process of moving toward hope is discarding false, unsound, or unexplored expectations. Yet that movement is also relentless groping toward the bases of sound expectations. In hope there is no sacrifice of truth, Menninger holds. It does not consist in optimism (which usually overlooks false expectations) nor in predictions about expectations. Hence hope is very difficult but absolutely essential. The dialectical nature of Menninger's discussion, plus his seeing hope as attitude moving toward action, offers real possibilities for linking it with hope in the traditional Christian sense.

Also dealing with a form of human hoping is the symposium participated in by Margaret Mead, Paul Tillich, Walter M. Horton, and Elmer G. Homrighausen. However man's potentiality for immortality or eternal life be conceived, it may indeed be, as Mead suggests, that the very nature of the question must be broadened from its usual form.

The last article in this section is "A Theology for Modern Man" by William Hamilton. This is an unusual essay in that it deals with the main themes of Christian theology in short compass and yet with discernment. It suggests the way in which the Christian understanding of man is set within the whole larger context of theology. For that function it should prove helpful to theologian and non-theologian alike.

# PART ONE

*Views of Man's Nature*

# CHAPTER 1

## THE PSYCHOANALYTIC VIEW
## OF HUMAN PERSONALITY[1]

EDITH WEIGERT, M.D.

MY TASK is to present the psychoanalytic view of human personality, and I shall discuss only those areas of psychoanalysis wherein this young science has something to contribute to the understanding of human personality. The centuries-older wisdom of Christian theology will be able to make use of these contributions. By presenting human personality in the light of psychoanalytic biographic development, I hope to be able to show some preconditions favorable to religious experience as well as factors adverse to religious actualization.

### The Modern Understanding of Emotional Illness

Psychoanalysis is a branch of medicine and psychiatry. At the turn of the century medicine had become divided into many specialties, all of which studied the disturbances of the bodily functions on the basis of physics, chemistry, physiology, anatomy, and pathology, and lost sight of the human personality as a total entity. Psychiatry remained closely linked to the neurological study of the central nervous system, and the neurotic and psychotic disorders which could not be understood as dysfunctions of the nervous system were described and classified, but psychiatry had no access to under-

---

[1] Adapted from a lecture presented in Washington, D.C., April 29, 1952, the second in a series entitled "Christianity and Psychoanalysis." The entire series of four lectures and panel discussion was published by the Organizing Committee, Christianity and Modern Man.

standing and treatment of the causes of these illnesses.

By turning research emphasis from the conscious, rational surface of personality to the unconscious, irrational depth of driving motivations, Sigmund Freud outgrew the old psychiatry of description and classification. We no longer see the mentally ill person—nor the healthily functioning person—as a static entity, but rather as in a constant process of adaptation to his environment.

There is a trend toward integration, or wholeness which, if approximated, is accompanied by a feeling of well-being and subjective freedom. But this feeling of wholeness and freedom is constantly threatened. An external disaster may produce an abnormal state of shock, a disintegrating panic. The reaction of grief to the loss of a beloved person can scarcely be distinguished in its symptoms from a depression or a melancholia. In normal sleep the integration of personality is loosened up; in our dreams we are like psychotics, exposed to confused, piecemeal images, which Freud has taught us to translate into rational language. The slips and errors of everyday living remind us how easily the integrating control of our behavior is jeopardized by unconscious motivations. The borderline between normal and pathological personality functions is fluid.

With such an understanding we have lost many of the older prejudices that morally devaluated neurotic and psychotic persons, who had to endure the ostracism of their more fortunate fellow men as well as their misfortune of illness. In the past mankind has not been as merciful toward the victims of emotional disorders as toward people who succumbed, in the battle with nature, to an invasion of infectious microorganisms or to external or internal physical injuries.

Psychoanalysis and psychiatry have pointed out that those highly sensitized persons who succumb to the hardships of interpersonal living—the neurotics and psychotics—are not morally inferior, but deserve the respect and sympathetic understanding of their fellows. By their very suffering they contribute to our growing understanding of interpersonal tragedies and, we hope, also to future insight and unmasking of group and mass psychopathology such as war, revolution, class struggle, and national, racial, and religious prejudice. Just as physiology has learned much from pathology, so the study of the psychologically disintegrated person has given us insight

into the better-integrated functions of the so-called "normal person."
It is true that the reactions to external pressure are far from uniform in human beings. We find some individuals who stand up under seemingly unbearable hardships with surprising equanimity,
and others who break down under minimal provocation. Psychologists who had an opportunity to study human behavior in concen-
tration camps found that only a few persons can stand such an
amount of terror without distortion of personality.

There are constitutional factors which determine resistance to
traumatic experience. We find various degrees of adaptive flexibility.
Man is more or less emotionally resistant and adverse to any change
—he is by nature conservative—particularly to change which threatens immediate satisfactions or the security of future gratifications. A
sudden change from wealth to poverty, from recognition to disgrace,
from peace to war, from supporting relations to isolation, may overthrow the emotional equilibrium. But even the more gradual transition from protected childhood to responsible adulthood, from full
and active life to the limitations of old age, from the freedom of
the bachelor to the obligations of marriage and child-raising, may
reveal a rigidity, an emotional inertia, which defeats the necessary
adaptation to changed life conditions.

However, such rigidity—such lag in emotional adaptability—does
not stem only from constitutional, hereditary factors. It is influenced
by the early development, by the patterns of conflict solutions in
childhood, which acquire the tenacity of habits and interfere with
the processes of integration and differentiation. In order to understand human personality from the psychoanalytic point of view, we
must study the developmental history and the course of disturbances
which interfere with development.

## The Growth of Personality

Man is distinguished from the animals in that he is born in greater
helplessness and must acquire in less than two decades all the tools
for dealing with the complexities of human culture in order to be
successfully integrated with his fellow men. This process of acculturation is far from being always successful. In particular, emotional
maturation frequently cannot keep pace with physiological growth,

and failures of adaptation and integration lead to various degrees of dissociation of personality.

Physiological growth depends upon processes of intake and output. Similarly, psychological development is determined by the intertwined processes of introjection and projection, or, if you will, incorporation and differentiation. Freud called the need for incorporative intake "libido." Libido is akin to the concept of love, and represents the integrative, constructive principle in living. But the destructive principle is just as necessary for our self-preservation as well as for the preservation of wholesome relations with others. Man has the need to destroy evil or to rid himself from danger and damage from within and without.

These needs of intake and riddance find expression in the emotions of pleasure and pain. The infant is pleasurably contented when his needs for food, warmth, comfort, and tenderness are gratified by adequate intake; he is pained and anxious when gratification is not forthcoming, or when he is subjected to some external or internal harm. His emotional equilibrium is re-established only when he gets rid of the disturbing pain, be it hunger, inappropriate temperature, harsh handling, intestinal cramps, etc.

The human infant is helpless and depends for his satisfactions and protection on his family environment. He is the needy recipient of love. His life from the very outset is surrounded by the dangers of death. The survival of the newborn infant would be extremely precarious without mothering care. The revolutionary change from the protection of the mother's womb to outside existence produces a state of emergency in which the nervous system mobilizes all the available bodily functions—blood circulation, respiration, muscle spasms, crying in an uproar of primitive self-assertion—to surmount this initial state of shock.

Such a state of shock is reproduced in later life by any threat to survival, and its approach is then consciously experienced as panic. The propensity toward shock is particularly marked in the early beginning of life because of the helpless dependency of the infant. The tender concern of mother or nurse immediately after birth re-establishes an approximation to the security of the maternal womb. Grave neglect in the mothering function threatens the infant's survival and keeps him on the verge of shock.

## The Need to Trust

Before the child develops any thinking or verbal expression of his emotions he learns to trust, since he experiences without consciousness that his needs for survival, growth, and development fit into his parents' needs to give gratification and protection in mutually adaptive, tender co-operation. This trust, this confidence, which precedes all rational thought processes, seems to me to be the matrix or an early manifestation of religious experience. It grows with the growing individual and transcends the boundaries of the early environment; it embraces the universe of the broadening personality. This propensity to trust exists even when the parents are not trustworthy. In that case, trust is driven underground, hiding behind defenses; but the propensity to trust cannot be abolished in any human being.

When the tender co-operation between parents and child fails, the danger signal of anxiety appears. Anxiety is a mild form of the aforementioned panic which automatically mobilizes energies to surmount the shock arising from a threat to survival. Anxiety as a danger signal is beneficial, since it mobilizes reserve energies to surmount and master emergency. There is no child-raising without anxiety. Every step forward into undiscovered territory is loaded with danger and anxiety. For instance, the child makes his first daring attempts to learn to walk; hesitantly he leaves the protective and supportive arms of his mother; he stumbles, bumps his head, seeks protection again in his mother's arms; and cries as if he would never try again.

Much depends on the mother's tender rapport with the child, which helps him to transcend his anxieties. The mother may be excessively anxious herself; such excessive anxiety interferes with her realistic evaluation of danger and with the child's potentialities for dealing with danger; she may retard his development by coddling overprotection, or she may ambitiously push the child ahead because she is impatient and herself needs the proof of gratifying performance. But in spite of such shortcomings, the child learns to walk sooner or later; he surmounts his anxieties, and glee about the newly gained mastery over reality obstacles and helplessness beams all over him and his mother.

The child's confidence and trust increase—confidence in himself, in others, in life. Gradually the child becomes more independent of automatic pleasure-pain reactions; he develops recall and foresight, and gains therewith a consolidation of his ego and his relations in the family. He is better equipped to meet dangers, frustrations, postponement of gratifications; he learns to modify his needs in adaptation to available gratifications; and the increasing sense of mastery diminishes his anxieties.

After having stressed the beneficial effect of anxiety as a danger signal, I must point out the detrimental effects of excessive anxiety —dread or panic—which do not further intra- and interpersonal integration. "Anxiety" stems from the Latin word *angustus,* narrow. The excessively anxious individual is narrowed in his potentialities, hemmed in. If the mobilization of reserve energy does not succeed in surmounting the danger, the human being finds himself in a state of painful helplessness, and automatic riddance reactions of fight or flight become unrealistic and destructive. Anger, rage, fury, hatred tend to avert the danger by sadistic means (destruction) ; despondency, apathy, exhaustion, stupor tend to avert danger in the opposite direction (that of self-destruction or masochism). Such excessive anxiety reactions are observed where the tender parent-child co-operation fails over a prolonged period or in an excessive degree.

The child may have been unwanted from the start; the parents may not be prepared or they may be preoccupied with their own troubles; they may not have the surplus energies to take on the responsibilities of a youngster. Parents may want the child ardently, but mainly for reasons of their own gratification: to fill the boredom of emotional emptiness, for instance, or to patch up a disharmonious marriage. Under such circumstances the natural rapport of tender co-operation cannot develop optimally. From the outset the child may feel like an outcast, a stranger—for example, he should be a girl and he is a boy, or vice versa.

The child who is unable to fulfill the parents' unrealistic expectations becomes a burden; his needs are not being spontaneously taken care of; and the child suffers an undue amount of frustration and excessive anxiety. A vicious circle arises. The overanxious child arouses parental anxieties, and parental anxieties reinforce the infantile anxieties—sometimes to the degree of panic, since the intimacy between parents and child (and particularly mother and child) leads to an immediate contamination of emotions on the preverbal level, a phenomenon which the psychiatrist calls "empathy."

## The Effects of Parental Anxiety

An atmosphere of excessive anxieties interferes with the development of natural trust. The trusting child is needy, but not greedy; he learns to wait, and to conform; he shows great adaptability to what the parents can or cannot offer him. The greedy child is haunted by excessive anxieties; his protesting rage estranges him further from parents who are unable to meet his needs. The child that cannot trust barricades himself behind self-centered defenses of despair, defiance, or sullen detachment.

I said before that there is no child-raising without anxieties. In a reasonably harmonious family the growing child is constantly guided by small doses of anxiety which, even before the level of verbal communication, arise from parental gestures of forbiddance. In such gestures, and later in words, the parents express to the child their disapproval of behavior or activities that do not conform to parental ideas of the good child.

These ideas depend largely on the cultural traditions in which the parents were themselves brought up. But we all know that there are great changes and discrepancies in our cultural values. Father and mother may not agree at all in their ideas of the good child— and that is very confusing. One or both parents may adhere to certain cultural values with an unbending strictness which betrays their excessive anxiety; so does a constantly wavering attitude or a parental inability to say no when necessary.

The incorporation of parental expectations forms the so-called "superego," which is nearly identical with the layman's term "conscience." (I want to stress that the conscience develops later than the capacity to trust.) If the parental directions which determine the superego give the child ample room for the development of his potentialities, the child feels good, that is, acceptable to his family and later to his fellow men. He can develop solid self-respect, and to the degree that he can respect himself he can also respect others. He should not remain slavishly dependent on parental or other authorities; an overextended dependency is always a sign that the genuine trust between child and parents, and consequently the self-confidence of the child, have remained underdeveloped.

If there is trust between parents and child—if the child trusts parental guidance, and the parents trust the child's fundamentally constructive potentialities—the imitative, automatically conforming co-operation of the dependent child gradually grows into the capacity to collaborate with self-reliance and mutual respect. The flow of communication, mutual understanding, and flexible adaptation open ever-broadening possibilities of integration and development. In this atmosphere of trust the child develops a good conscience, the best guarantee of a progressive maturing process.

If the parental concepts of the good child are contradictory, inconsistent, overrestrictive, or overly permissive (that is, loaded with their own excessive anxieties), not only is the child burdened with their anxieties by contamination, but conflicts arise between his own natural needs and the instructions of the parents. Under such circumstances, due to his dependency on parental gratifications and protection, the automatically conforming child becomes estranged from his natural needs, which do not find parental approval. These needs go underground; they are dissociated or repressed. That does not mean that such needs disappear; they are expelled only from conscious awareness, and they become foreign bodies excluded from the processes of integration. They remain arrested on the infantile level, and cannot participate in the growth and development of the personality.

Whenever such arrested and repressed needs are stirred up by internal or external causes, the specific anxiety of the superego, or the conscience awakens. The analyst calls this anxiety "guilt." The superego, or conscience is the guardian against such anxiety; it reinforces the defenses of repression and dissociation. It keeps the dangerous needs (dangerous because not approved of) out of sight. But these repressed needs, arrested on a primitive level of development, are like naughty children excluded from the company of adults, hammering at the closed door and importunately demanding readmission. Such disturbing demands for readmission are accompanied by excessive anxieties, and the original needs are distorted into importunate greeds which further estrange the child from the parents, who are annoyed by his greed and importunacy.

While the good conscience is a helpful agent in the process of maturing development, the continually bad conscience is like a stone around a person's neck, retarding and impeding his growth and development. From the psychoanalytic point of view, a bad conscience is a man's—and even more a child's—worst enemy. It is not a sign of inner badness; it is the result of a cruel superego, the tragic consequence of failure of tender co-operation and the repression of trust.

When the parents cannot fulfill the child's needs and the child cannot live up to parental expectations, he turns out to be a burden, a liability, and his bad conscience reflects the frustrated reaction of the parents: "You're just a nuisance, a bad child." On the other hand, parents who feel incapable of meeting their child's needs feel guilty, too. Excessive anxiety and guilt intensify the estrangement between parents and child. In order to atone for guilt feelings and to make up for the missing genuine trust, the parents will frequently, by overprotection or overindulgence, squelch the wholesome aggressive and self-assertive needs of the child.

The child's superego, or conscience, which incorporates the parental expectations and standards, not only represses his asocial and antisocial tendencies (which would not develop in the first place if the child felt warmly accepted and wanted), but it may also exclude healthy, constructive tendencies from integration and development. For instance, the child who from early infancy on has been exposed to an unusual degree of deprivation in his need for tenderness and affection becomes estranged from these basic needs. In the gravely neglected or harshly mistreated child the need for tenderness and affection goes underground, since it has too frequently received a painfully frustrating response. Where, in the growing child, you would expect the expression of a longing for tenderness, you meet with anxiety; and when this anxiety reaches excessive degrees, it elicits those automatic defenses which I have mentioned before: rage, anger, defiance, hostility in the active child; or indifference, boredom, apathy in the more passive, despondent child.

The failure of the tender co-operation between parents and child, together with the burden of excessive anxieties and guilt feelings, condemn the child to a degree of loneliness which leaves him inexperienced in the closeness of interpersonal relations. Even if he learns externally to conform to rules and regulations of conventional behavior, he remains fundamentally lonely; and the thin veneer of acceptable adaptation may easily break down in later life under stress and strain, and a neurosis or psychosis may develop under further duress.

Loneliness and the cruelty of the conscience always go hand in hand. The qualms and shame of a bad conscience lead to withdrawal from company; all energies are concentrated on the inner battle with a relentless conscience, to keep vital needs under repression; and unavoidable experiences of defeat in the attempts to live up to superhuman standards increase the danger of desertion, ostracism, hopelessness, and despair.

## The Results of Loss of Trust

There are in the course of development infinite possibilities of regaining original losses of trust. Children frequently have a redeeming influence on their parents. Even embittered or desperate parents who have surrounded themselves with a shell of harshness cannot always resist the emotional appeal of the child, and tender co-operation may be re-established on any later level. On the other hand, there are hurdles in the various challenging complexities of family life which put tender co-operation and trust to the test.

I mentioned before that the excessively anxious child tries to rid himself of his discomforts by anger, rage, or temper tantrums. But such frank expression of hostility cannot find parental approval, and therefore these hostilities are frequently buried in repression. Repressed anger is often transformed into smoldering resentment, and swallowed hostilities overload the organism with indigestible tensions. Psychological conflicts due to the mobilization of excessive anxieties frequently result in psychosomatic disorders such as impediments of respiration (asthma) or disturbances of the digestive tract. The child who suffers under lack of parental acceptance may capitalize on such psychosomatic disorders because they keep the family at his beck and call. Thus tyrannical power is substituted for trust and tender co-operation.

A similar transformation of genuine needs takes place if the child defiantly accepts the idea that he is incorrigibly bad. He gets a bitter comfort out of pointing out that others are just as bad or worse than he; he gets a false pride out of provoking and bullying others; or he tries to attract attention by specializing in mischievousness, since he cannot get attention in any other way. In this need for despotic power the unhappy, isolated child tries to get rid of his unbearable loneliness and helplessness, which accompany his excessive anxieties. But such despotic power is an unsatisfactory substitute for the missing trust and tenderness. It never fills the bill. Therefore the greed for despotic power, in children as well as in adults, is characterized by insatiability and compulsion.

A particularly difficult test for tender co-operation in a family is sexual lust. The borderline between primitive sexual excitement and the sublimated experiences of love, affection, and tenderness is fluid. Overindulgent coddling may arouse sexual excitement in both the child and the adult. Primitive sexual needs exist in budding form from early childhood on; they are expressed by curiosity, voyeur wishes, and exhibitionistic and masturbatory activities— which are harmless if they are not frowned upon by the adults. But if the adults are overexcited or are frightened into excessive shame, the child becomes estranged from his natural impulses and tries to repress them; and under the pressure of shame and guilt the sexual impulses become the more intensified and compulsive. They cause particularly painful conflicts if the child suffers from lack of tender gratifications, if he is emotionally isolated, and if trust in his most vital relations to his early environment is wanting.

The child who is not inhibited in his emotional development and who feels secure in his trust in parental love will learn to tame his awakening sexual impulses and the accompanying experiences of rivalry, envy, and jealousy. Even if the child goes through periods of upheaval, he learns to tune down his possessive, monopolizing passions for the sake of the family harmony in which he has his anchors of trust.

*The Tragedy of Emotional Isolation.* Freud used the Greek tragedy of Oedipus Rex as a symbol of the conflicts that are implied in the child's sexual and aggressive impulses which endanger his adjustment to the family and, if they remain repressed and therefore untamed, his later social adjustment. You may remember that the Oedipus of the Greek tragedy had been a rejected child; his parents had got rid of him in infancy because of a prophecy which threatened them that their son would in the future interfere with their selfish interests. The son, who had grown up completely estranged from his parents, unwittingly murdered his father and took his place in the kingdom and in an incestuous relation to his mother. Oedipus Rex in the Greek tragedy falls from the summit of self-righteous pride in his heroic achievements into the abyss of shame and despair when his tragic guilt is revealed.

This is a deep human truth: the child estranged and uprooted from the nurturing soil of trust can become the victim of passionate conflicts and tragic guilt. Incestuous impulses toward a parent or sibling, and murderous impulses against a rival, are intensified in the emotionally isolated or overanxious child—in a child who is, for instance, irresponsibly seduced, used for the more or less selfish gratification of an older person, or in any other way deprived of the security of tender co-operation and trust. Under such tragic circumstances the child's preoccupation with sexual lust or murderous impulses can become compulsive and insatiable, since sexual lust (like despotic power) is an absolutely unsatisfactory substitute for the original need for trust.

*The Effects in Adulthood.* Such compulsive preoccupations are threatened by intense disapproval, and therefore they are also driven underground into repression or dissociation. But such attempts at riddance do not extinguish the guilt feelings. Like the automatic safety valve of anxiety, the warning signal of guilt can become oversensitized toward needs and impulses from which the individual feels estranged and therefore threatened by their mere emergence. Under the pressure of an intransigent superego the whole area of sex becomes indicted, but the anxious tensions of guilt increase sexual excitement and temptation. Under the threat of an intransigent conscience a child's lonely experiments in masturbation, which are in themselves a harmless release of tension, become linked up with sadistic fantasies of rebellion and defiance or masochistic fantasies of drastic punishing atonement; and these cruel fantasies increase the feelings of guilt. In this way sexual excitement is divorced from the integrating experience of trust and tenderness.

And the shadows of distrust fall on the later experiments in sexual companionship. Only a sexual partnership that integrates sexual lust with respect, tender consideration, and trust can lift the ban of indictment from sexual activities. For the person with a rigidly intransigent superego the sexual partner frequently remains an accomplice in guilt, more hated than loved—hated since he or she leads into hideous temptation, and he or she mobilizes excessive anxiety and guilt. This makes both partners egocentric, possessive, and exploitative. Instead of providing integrative gratification, the relation is marred by the chilling frigidity of a casual conquest or the slavish dependency of a humiliating addiction.

On the other hand, the natural intimacy of sexual contacts provides the potentialities of spontaneous recovery from loneliness and moral ostracism, when the barriers of shame, excessive anxiety, and guilt can be transcended and the obstructed resources of genuine trust can be reopened.

Returning to the development of the child, we see that the child who cannot trust parental love naturally feels threatened by the arrival of a brother or sister rival. Adjustment to the growing family is complicated by envious competition. The more excessive a child's anxiety, the more importunate is his bid for exclusive possession. The self-defeating claim for despotic power gains in importance in proportion to the degree of failure of the trust in friendly sharing and participation.

The child with a cruel superego, lowered in his self-esteem, is frequently very doubtful about his fitness in competition, which looks merciless to him or her. The overanxious boy is called a sissy. (Hamlet felt that his conscience made a coward out of him.) Withdrawal from competition further lowers the self-confidence of the boy or man who is ridiculed as effeminate. Even if a man overcompensates by pretended toughness, his doubt of his manliness may accompany him far into adulthood. Likewise, a girl who distrusts her future value as a woman, her capacity to win a male partner, to bear and rear children, may evade such painful doubts by playing the role of the tomboy or by withdrawing into defiant independence. In heated competition with her male contemporaries, more interested in the prestige of conquest than in the trustworthy depth of a relation, she defeats herself in most natural needs under the pressure of a punishing conscience.

The world of the "as if," of fantasies and daydreams, is a natural playground for the child's testing and probing imagination, and it remains the testing ground for adult planning and striving. But if the growing child does not dare to branch out, to widen his horizon, because of arresting excessive anxieties and lack of trust, this world of imagination becomes an isolating refuge haunted by nightmares of anxiety. Excessive daydreaming of a superman's perfection, of heroic achievements, or of perfect love is substituted for real experiments in living in the process of co-operative adaptation to others. The child remains self-centered and lonely.

The nearer he approaches adulthood, the greater the discrepancies between the inexpensive victories of his self-centered fantasies and the defeats in real living with others. He does not dare to expose his pretentious ambitions to honest competition with his compeers. He cannot run the risk of losing or of revealing real incompetence.

Since he finds that his self-centered, ambitious claims antagonize others, he may learn to outwit and to cheat, to win by hook or by crook. But such hypocrisy, the product of excessive anxiety, does not open up trust or increase self-respect. A fundamentally lonely existence becomes the more barren, dull, and boring the more the aspirations of fantasy are solely spent in pretense. Nor can such loneliness be dissipated by flight into meaningless overactivity. The person who is isolated by repression of trust fails to learn that which makes life really meaningful, namely, spontaneous participation and devotion to someone or something outside himself.

### Our Yearning for Reconciliation and Peace

I said before that on any level of human development the blocked resources of trust may spontaneously open up again. This is an experience totally beyond human efforts of the intellect or of the will; it is an experience which the religious person humbly accepts as the grace of God. Neither the psychoanalyst nor any other human being can produce this redeeming experience, but the analyst may be able to contribute to the removal of impediments of moral and religious self-deceit and hypocrisy, the outgrowth of an intolerant conscience, an intransigent superego. I do not consider deceit or hypocrisy primary needs; they are a defense, like the claim for despotic power or like lust.

In moral and religious hypocrisy we recognize the vestiges of a yearning for peace and reconciliation with the ultimate power, the ground of existence. But the approach to this ultimate authority is laden with the same excessive anxieties and distrust as the helpless child experiences in the relation to powerful parental authority which he does not dare to trust. The excessively anxious child tries to ward off nightmarish dangers by prayer or by other propitiating or atoning gestures. He tries to win the powers of goodness over onto his side in order to avoid desertion, punishment, and the accompanying excessive anxieties. He tries to fight off the black magic by a protective white magic. We recognize in the black magic the hated punishing parent; while the protective, comforting power represents the good, approving, and rewarding parent.

If his hope for genuine trust has become dissociated, given up in despair, the child—and the child in man—will substitute for trust the magic weapon of deceit in order to transform the dangerous punishing authority into a good and rewarding authority. Parents can be outwitted and placated by "as if" performances, apologetic gestures, going through the motions. The child learns the art of hypocrisy; he gets away with murder; he pursues selfish, not permissible purposes secretly, avoiding the disapproval of authority. He appears good and obedient, and often reaches a pseudo peace with a powerful authority.

By such defiant obedience the child—and the child in man—perpetuates the conflict between obedience and rebellion in relation to authority, as well as in relation to the ultimate authority. Although the hypocrite appears good, he does not feel good deep in his heart. The repressed longing for real peace and reconciliation, which seems out of reach, keeps him restless and unsatisfied.

To a greater or lesser degree we are all easily deceived by our own deceitful manipulations of authority. Nothing is more difficult than to be honest with oneself. We are accustomed from childhood on to think in terms of good and bad, black and white. It is important for our sense of prestige and security that we be on the good side; therefore we try desperately to justify ourselves, sometimes by rationalizing argumentation. In such stubborn insistence on self-justification lie the roots of a paranoid development with its ideas of grandiosity and persecution. We all become identified with the role that we play. We really believe in our hypocritical goodness, our self-righteousness, even sometimes in our saintliness.

But this hypocritical conforming adaptation for the sake of opportunistic rewards absorbs an enormous amount of energy and separates us even further from spontaneous sources of trust; how can we learn to trust if we really trust only our hypocritical manipulations of authority, our defenses against excessive anxiety? In adulthood we remain tied to an appalling number of obsessional rituals and devices that stem from childhood days; we remain preoccupied with the unconscious elaboration of the most complicated devices to gain rewards and to avoid punishment.

But, deceived by our own deceit, we frequently are not able to see through our own complex maneuvers, which are sometimes quite enigmatic on the level of consciousness. Whether we are adherents of a church or profess secularized forms of ethical standards, everybody in our culture is more or less restricted in his spontaneity and creativeness by defensive distortions of original needs, and our system of nonspontaneous adaptation is fraught with compulsion and deep-seated anxieties.

If we are fortunate we may be able to carry our precarious equilibrium through our lifetime, and feel quite complacent about our so-called normal adjustment. But under emotional stress and strain this precarious equilibrium may break down, with symptoms of regression to infantile patterns of behavior, distortions of reality, depressions, free-floating or localized anxieties, and the like.

Such intense emotional suffering forces us to review the complexities of our development, and to withdraw from the bustle of distracting activities. As neurotic or psychotic patients we may have to go through the hell of human misery, sometimes reaching out for help by dramatizing this very misery, sometimes withdrawing from all human contact or from trust in life itself. Self-accusation and self-condemnation are signs of our conflicts with ultimate authority. Reassurance does not provide any comfort, although we may cry for it in abject infantile despondency.

Self-punishment plays an enormous role in all psychoneuroses, as if there were an unconscious belief that by self-torture and punishment and suffering we could force a reconciliation with the ground of existence, as a child tries to bribe parental approval. But such reconciliation cannot be forced. Sometimes in the depths of despair a flash of insight breaks through the shells of repressions and defensive distortions and shows, not to our heads but to our hearts, that what we are most deeply estranged from is trust.

## The Function of the Psychotherapist

At this point you will ask me what the psychotherapist can do to prepare for the recovery of the psychoneurotic patient—after I have made it, I hope, sufficiently clear that I share the conviction of the French physician who said about his treatment of a patient, *"Je le pansai, Dieu le guérit"* ("I treated him, God cured him").

I have tried to convey that psychoneurotic suffering is due to arrested emotional development in childhood. No human parents are so ideal, so free themselves, that they could protect their children completely from being tied by such chains. The psychoneurotic adult is bound to repeat in all subsequent interpersonal relations the original conflicts which arrested his development. This repetition tends to maintain the old repressions and the habitual patterns of substitution, as for instance despotic power substituting for repressed affection. This form of repetition compulsion is called "transference" by the analyst. An important lever in psychoanalytic work is this transference—the tendency of the patient to carry over into the relation with the therapist who offers to help him the crippling conflicts with significant persons of his childhood.

We have only a very limited and distorted knowledge of ourselves because of early adaptation patterns and the restrictive influence of the superego, the conscience, which excludes from awareness impulses and needs that caused disapproval by authority and, therewith, excessive anxiety. It is extremely difficult to extricate oneself from one's self-deceptions, particularly in a period of history which, like our present epoch, leaves us so little opportunity for serious meditation. Psychoneurotic suffering and its therapy lead modern man into meditation.

The method of free associations is intended to free the communications of the analysand from conventional patterns of logical thinking and to open up the floodgates of repressed emotions. The analysand can only gradually arrive at greater frankness. At the start, in accordance with his repetition compulsion, he expects from his therapist the same parental disapproval which had caused his repressions, and he meets the therapist with the old anxieties and the old weapons of defense. The more intelligent the patient, the subtler are his defenses. The analysand fights to preserve his comforting daydreams, illusions of grandeur, claims and entitlements of childhood, which should shield him from frightening new experiences.

Frequently the patient tries ardently to seduce the therapist into a conspiracy of repetition; he prompts him to provide the same substitute gratifications which the patient got as a child from the outwitted parent. He tries to manipulate the therapist, to involve him in a power struggle, to repeat with him the never-ending conflict of obedience and rebellion.

The analysand expects magical help, and if he is frustrated in his infantile demands he may break out into anger and rage. By this he may unconsciously intimidate the doctor and thus circumvent the reliving of painful old anxieties, overwhelming for him in childhood, but which he may face today in companionship with his therapist with better chances of mastering them. Because of the old habit of distrust, however, the analysand may withdraw into sulking passivity, apathy, or despondency.

The great opportunity for profitable change in psychoanalysis is given by the fact that the therapist is *not* father or mother or any other anxiety-arousing authority of the past; that he does *not* get involved in transference repetition; and that when he gets transitorily involved in sympathetic identification, he returns to reality and actuality and regains his benevolent neutrality, which keeps him from overindulgence as well as from moralistic prohibition. The therapist refrains from false reassurances as well as from disapproval, although the patient would like to use him as an auxiliary conscience which would spare him the conflicts of his own responsible decisions.

Ideally, the therapist should not allow himself to be flattered, bribed, or irritated, for he should give the patient an opportunity to relive the old anxieties and to find a more constructive way out of them. The habitually diffident and distrustful patient feels compelled to test the doctor out; and it is too bad if the doctor is pretentious, condescending, or artificial, for thus he loses his usefulness for the patient. Only genuine respect and spontaneous warmth for the patient may dispel his excessive fears of being rejected, forsaken, overpowered, or exploited.

Only in an atmosphere free from such excessive fears and defensive passionate involvement may the patient catch up with his retarded and misdirected development. The tragedies of childhood thus relived need no longer bog him down in anxious loneliness and helplessness. He may be able in an atmosphere of trust to get hold of his repressed needs and rechannelize them toward constructive goals. He may, I say, since I am aware that true success does not depend only on our most honest and serious endeavors and limited human skills. The regaining of trust, the integration of wholeness, lie ultimately beyond psychotherapeutic endeavor. In the Christian religion, it is experienced as the miracle of redemption.

# CHAPTER 2

## KNOW THYSELF: THE BIBLICAL
## DOCTRINE OF HUMAN DEPRAVITY[1]

### JAMES I. MCCORD

No OTHER field of theological inquiry has been cultivated quite so extensively in the past two decades as anthropology, or the doctrine of man. Nearly every important contemporary theologian has felt compelled to provide a book, often his most significant, in this area. Moreover, in secular ideologies the doctrine of man has been the determining factor in their interpretations of history. As Emil Brunner has suggested, "The fact that binds together the most influential thinkers of recent generations, those whose thought was capable of determining the thought not only of other thinkers, but of the masses, and through them of determining the whole course of political development—Charles Darwin, Friedrich Nietzsche, and Karl Marx—was this: that each of them gained power, directly or indirectly, over a considerable section of mankind by his view of man, by his 'anthropology.' "[2]

In American theology the dominant movement, Christian realism, is essentially an anthropology. Its unifying center consists in a reappraisal downward of man's capacities and in the rediscovery of man as sinner. In a large measure this has been simply a commentary on brute fact. Human perfectibility is difficult to maintain in the face of the complete breakdown of world order. Unfortunately, however, the value of realistic theology has been limited largely to criticism. When it turned to a positive statement, the results were

[1] This article was written at the invitation of the editors of *Interpretation*, who suggested that all dogmatic or systematic considerations be suspended and that the theme be treated strictly from a biblical standpoint.

[2] *Man in Revolt*, trans. by Olive Wyon (London: Lutterworth Press, 1939), p. 34.

disappointing. Instead of generating a distinctive theology, it lapsed into a sterile neo-orthodoxy or into a vague symbolism[3] which failed to apprehend the depth of the biblical point of view.

When one turns to the Bible for the doctrine of man as sinner, he encounters two difficulties at the outset. In the first place, the subject of the Bible is God and not man. Its theme is "Seek ye first the Kingdom of God" (Matt. 6:33), and its burden is the proclamation of the evangel, "that God was in Christ reconciling the world unto himself" (II Cor. 5:19). The Bible is primarily a message for man, but it does not purport to present a doctrine of man.

A second difficulty arises when one tries to extricate biblical anthropology from the Augustinian interpretation of Paul. While Augustine has had tremendous influence on Western theological thought, it is doubtful that he does justice to the biblical account of the nature of sin on two scores. He overgeneralizes Paul's comparison between Adam and Jesus Christ in Romans 5:12, and in defining the nature of sin as a *privatio boni* he betrays that he was never able to free himself from Neoplatonism. It is generally agreed today that Augustine had two bases for his anthropology, and it is highly probable that philosophical considerations determined his biblical exegesis in the passage in question.

The key to the biblical doctrine of man, then, is not the prehistorical figure Adam, but Jesus Christ, the God-man. The mystery of the Incarnation wherein the divine entered human history and identified himself with human nature discloses to us our true humanity. This does not mean that the humanity of Jesus Christ is not unique or that anthropology is absorbed in soteriology, as Pierre Maury has observed.[4] Rather, in Jesus Christ who was "made . . . sin for us" (II Cor. 5:21) is the depth of man's sin revealed, as in his perfect humanity is seen the victory over sin and death.

The biblical understanding of man begins and ends in God. Man is a "theological being" who is both a part of nature and who transcends nature, but his transcendence always has priority. He is made in God's image (Gen. 1:27), a little lower than the angels

---

[3] In this connection I have not yet seen an adequate answer to A. E. Murphy's penetrating review and criticism of Niebuhr's "The Nature and Destiny of Man" in *The Journal of Philosophy*, XL, pp. 458-468.

[4] *The Christian Understanding of Man*, by T. E. Jessop and others (New York: Harper & Brothers, 1938), pp. 248-250.

(Ps. 8:5), the crown of all creation (Gen. 1:28), with dominion over the works of God's hands and with all things under his feet (Ps. 8:6). As image-bearer he is capable of knowing God and of responding to God's word. At the same time, there is a dialectical tension. He is also a slave to sin, "dead in trespasses and sins (Eph. 2:1). At the heart of human nature it is assumed that there is something radically wrong, that man's nature has been twisted, and that only divine grace is powerful enough to redeem him.

## Sin as Rebellion

The fact of sin constitutes the central problem of the Gospel record. Death itself is only symptomatic of this deeper malady. However, the assumption of the universality of sin in both the Old and New Testaments does not mean that sin originates from nature, that it is a by-product of man's creatureliness. In this respect the biblical view differs materially from other anthropologies. Sin is not a product of the lowest in man's nature but a product of the misuse of his highest endowment, his capacity for fellowship with God. It is not indigenous to man's true nature but contrary to it.[5] Hence sinful man is "de-natured man." This is what Emil Brunner means when he writes: "Sin is never the beginning; it always comes second. Sin always has a history behind it."[6] It presupposes a divine-human relation that has been broken. Both the story of Eden in Genesis and the parable of the prodigal son in Luke illustrate that sin presupposes communion and results in alienation.

Sin emerges out of unbelief and takes the pattern of rebellion against God. It has a deeper dimension than the transgression of a moral code, for its character is both personal and decisive. It is personal because it involves a conception of God's character, and it is decisive in that it represents a definite rejection of God's claim.

Both of these elements are brilliantly depicted in the narrative

[5] "We say . . . that man is corrupted by a natural depravity, but which did not originate from nature . . . it is rather an adventitious quality or accident, than a substantial property originally innate." John Calvin, *Institutes of the Christian Religion,* Bk. II, Chap. 1, par. 11.

[6] *Revelation and Reason,* trans. by Olive Wyon (Philadelphia: The Westminster Press, 1946), p. 26.

of the Fall. God, who is gracious and righteous, creates man, whose origin is out of God's love and whose purpose is to love God. In this man differs from all the rest of creation. He alone can be addressed by God and can respond in communion. He is the apex of creation, but he is not infinite. The prohibition, "But of the fruit of the tree which is in the midst of the garden . . . ye shall not eat of it" (Gen. 3:3), means simply that man is finite, that there are limits about him, and that he is not God. Moreover, man's freedom to obey or disobey the divine command is assumed. But sin arises out of mistrust. Man is afraid to trust the divine destiny and to accept his limits. The rebellion that follows is a decisive act of repudiation, a trusting of self over against God.

As the Old Testament revelation unfolds, the sin of Adam is reenacted in the life of God's people. Again and again they resist God's sovereign will. Yahweh declares unto Moses at Sinai: "I have seen this people, and, behold, it is a stiffnecked people" (Exod. 32:9). Indeed, the conception of sin as rebellion underlies both the covenant and the law, the two unifying principles in the life of Israel.

When we come to the prophets, sin's dominant motif continues to be conceived of as rebellion against God. It has often been assumed that the prophets were interested in the problem of sin primarily from the ethical standpoint, but recent study has shown that they were first of all religious prophets and only secondarily ethical teachers.[7] As religious prophets their standard of judgment was God and not an ethical code, and their conception of sin was basically in terms of a distorted relationship between man and God. In the first two chapters of Amos, for example, the prophet numbers, one by one, the neighboring kingdoms, arraigns them before God's judgment, and specifies the charge of rebellions[8] against God. Hosea indicts his people for revolting against God's covenant, for their unfaithfulness to Yahweh, while Isaiah, picturing the relation between God and Israel in terms of father and son, opens his prophecy with the charge: "I have nourished and brought up chil-

[7] Norman H. Snaith, *Distinctive Ideas of the Old Testament* (Philadelphia: The Westminster Press, 1946) , p. 74.

[8] Professor Snaith, commenting on the prophets' serious view of sin, writes: "Their most characteristic word is *pesha*, the word which is translated 'transgression' by the English Versions, but actually means 'rebellion.' " *Ibid.*, p. 79.

dren, and they have rebelled against me. The ox knoweth his owner, and the ass his master's crib; but Israel doth not know, my people doth not consider" (Isa. 1:2 f.). Micah echoes the same indictment when he declares: "He hath showed thee, O man, what is good; and what doth Jehovah require of thee, but to do justly, and to love kindness, and to walk humbly with thy God?" (Mic. 6:8).

The Synoptics always speak of sin as personal and decisive. The parable of the prodigal son opens with an assertion of self-will: "Give me the portion of goods that falleth to me" (Luke 15:12). Rather than to enjoy his gifts in his father's house and in the freedom of his father's service, the son chooses to affirm his autonomy and to claim the illusory freedom that is a correlate of self-affirmation. In the parable of the wicked husbandmen, the same pattern is evident. The gift of God is freedom in his service, but man denies the claim of God, beating, stoning, and killing God's emissaries, until at last the son himself is slain. Professor Burrows has noted that Jesus never speaks of sin in the abstract, but always of specific sins.[9]

Often it is contended that a new idea of the nature of sin is found in the Pauline literature, an almost gnostic identification of sin and "flesh." But Paul's doctrine of the flesh is quite different from Hellenistic dualism, which held the locus of sin to be the body and promised salvation through asceticism and death. His description of human life is in terms of conflict between two warring principles, the flesh and the spirit. The former represents the natural man, or self (I Cor. 2:14), and is at enmity with God, while the latter stands for the new man made in the image of Jesus Christ (Col. 3:10). To Paul sin is not the negative product of an alien and hostile substance—flesh—but the positive perversion of the relationship between man and God.

The nature of this relationship is set forth in the first chapter of Romans. Paul's aim in this epistle is not to formulate a doctrine of the origin of sin, but to establish two things: first, that sinful man—both Jew and Gentile—is "without excuse"; and, second, that justification and reconciliation come through Jesus Christ. In order to accomplish this, he begins by affirming that man cannot escape God, that he is bound to him even in his sin. God's witness is constant and his claim is never withdrawn. God's revelation of himself in nature,

[9] Millar Burrows, *An Outline of Biblical Theology* (Philadelphia: The Westminster Press, 1946), p. 167.

both external and internal, does not constitute the basis of a theology of nature, as has been supposed; rather, it furnishes the basis of human responsibility, for man "holds down the truth in unrighteousness" (Rom. 1:18). Here Paul is not describing a single act of disobedience but a continuous process that goes on in the life of every man. Man uses his freedom in an attempt to free himself from God and to obliterate all traces of God's presence and sovereignty.

The conception of sin in the Fourth Gospel does not differ materially from Paul's. The affirmation that "the Word became flesh" (John 1:14) rules out any possibility of a gnostic dualism of spirit and matter. The world is the object of God's love (John 3:16/f.), "the world knew him not" (John 1:10). As W. F. Howard has written: "To St. John . . . the world is the mass of mankind mobilized in defiance of the divine purpose. . . . It raises its head arrogantly against the Creator."[10] Men love the darkness rather than the light (John 3:19), and choose evil rather than God. As in Paul, the light that shineth in darkness (John 1:5) constitutes the background of human responsibility. Against the revelation of God man rebels, and he is, therefore, without excuse.

The first characteristic of sin, then, may be summarized in the confession: "Against thee, thee only, have I sinned" (Ps. 51:4). Sin is always viewed within a divine and personal frame of reference. God's purpose for man and his claim upon man are given as the background for responsible existence. But responsible existence entails freedom, and freedom entails possibility, the possibility to misuse the divine gift. The source of sin, therefore, is not in man's contingent existence, but in his will.[11] It manifests itself in self-love and pride, in open hostility and rebellion against God.

## Sin as Egocentricity and Idolatry

The second element in the biblical view of sin is man's enthronement of his ego. Rebellion, the positive negation of God, is followed

[10] *Christianity According to St. John* (London: Duckworth, 1943), pp. 83 f.
[11] Jeremiah mentions repeatedly the "heart" as the source of sin. In Mark 7:21 Jesus declares that "from within, out of the heart of men, evil thoughts proceed," that is, that which defiles a man comes from within. Professor Burrows points out that the heart is the principal biblical word for the seat of feeling and will. *Op. cit.*, pp. 138, 169.

by the substitution of another god—the self. In the Genesis narrative man is tempted to overstep his bounds by the promise "ye shall be as gods" (Gen. 3:5). This insinuation, as Søren Kierkegaard has shown,[12] touches the heart of man's perplexity, for by exalting the self beyond the limits God has decreed, man hopes to resolve the tension arising out of the ambiguity of his existence as both a child of nature and a child of the spirit. He responds by claiming the right to order his own life and to become the center of his own world. His is the sin of Titanism, the usurpation of the divine prerogative, and the result is that man becomes *incurvatus in se,* to use Luther's expression, selfishly turned in toward himself.

Exaltation of the self, however, is but the first stage in a wider pattern. Its correlate is idolatry. The "self-ordered" life fails to mitigate man's anxiety and quiet his fears. Indeed, they are intensified. The contingency of life is accentuated. Man hears the voice of God and is afraid. He seeks stability by projecting his ego into idols, into false gods that he can control. Hence, Paul writes that man has "changed the glory of the incorruptible God for the likeness of an image" (Rom. 1:23). Luther's disjunction, *Gott oder Abgott,* is a valid description of man's psychological processes. His existence demands a principle around which he can organize and by which he can direct his life. He must choose, therefore, not whether he will serve God but which God he will serve, the God who made him or the gods he has made.

It is unfortunate that the word idolatry has all but disappeared from the vocabulary of today, while, at the same time, the concept has been relegated to the science of comparative religions as an obsolete practice once utilized by mankind in the quest for God. The Old Testament writers are one in their insistence that idolatry is quite different from tentative steps toward a clearer apprehension of God. It is second and not first, and must be understood as a distorted replica of the true God. Idolatry represents the attempt of man to achieve his ends through means other than God, and to organize his life around that which is less than God. For the idol makes no absolute claim, and man can control it for his own immediate ends.

[12] *The Concept of Dread,* trans. by Walter Lowrie (Princeton: The Princeton University Press, 1944).

Idolatry symbolizes the short cut that is faith's indomitable foe and is a product of the narrow and limited perspective of man apart from God.

The conception of sin as idolatry furnishes the clue to the meaning of the Second Commandment: "Thou shalt not make unto thee a graven image . . . for I Jehovah thy God am a jealous God" (Exod. 20:46). The image is forbidden precisely because God is jealous, because the image becomes his substitute and rival and not merely because the incorporeal is superior to the corporeal. The idol need not be a sensuous object equipped with magical power—a graven image—for idolatry has a much wider connotation. Any act growing out of man's selfish will is idolatrous. In this sense idolatry is a quality of human behavior.

The Old Testament abounds with illustrations of the various forms idolatry may take. Sometimes it is crude and vulgar, as in the worship of the golden calf in Exodus, the sacrifices to the Moabite god in Numbers, the serving of the Canaanite gods in Judges, and the apostasy of Israel during the time of Ahab and Jezebel. At other times idolatry is more subtle and refined. It consists in trust in foreign alliances (Isaiah) and in indifference to human need and the acquisition of wealth by social injustice (Amos). Paul Minear has catalogued a few of the many types of idolatry listed by the exilic prophets, a list that includes pride in human wisdom, trust in one's beauty, reliance on horses and chariots, immunity to God's demands and vision, and denial of God's reality, power, and control.[13]

In the New Testament the prayer of the Pharisee breathes the spirit of idolatry: "God, I thank thee, that I am not as the rest of men" (Luke 18:11). His is the sin that belongs to ecclesiastical standing and to the moral nature. To Paul ritual and race may also become the elements of idolatry, "circumcised the eighth day, of the stock of Israel, of the tribe of Benjamin, a Hebrew of the Hebrews" (Phil. 3:5)—things to be counted but to be refused in order to gain Christ. In fact, the entire account of the rejection of Jesus Christ is an object lesson in the idolatry of race-ego, the tendency of man to create a god and then to cling stubbornly to it, even in the presence of the living God.

[13] *Eyes of Faith* (Philadelphia: The Westminster Press, 1946), p. 68.

## The Origin and Nature of Depravity

So far in our discussion, sin has been defined as a misuse of man's highest endowment, his capacity for fellowship with God. As such its pattern is, first, that of mistrust and rebellion, and, second, egocentricity[14] and idolatry. From this description several conclusions necessarily follow. In the first place, it is clear that the Bible makes no attempt to explain the origin of sin. In Genesis its existence is presupposed. "The Fall is not occasioned by the transgression of Adam; but the transgression was presumably its first manifestation."[15] The first significant act that is recorded is the occasion of man's sin. This should not be interpreted as the basis of a radical dualism of God and Satan whereby evil becomes an absolute power inherent in the structure of the universe. Throughout the course of Christian thought perplexity over the inability to explain the origin of evil has led many to posit a second power over against God and to interpret history as the arena of their cosmic struggle. Such an interpretation, for example, underlies the Christian gnosticism of Nicolas Berdyaev, especially his conception of the *Ungrund* as the unfathomable abyss out of which both God and man emerge. Edwin Lewis, in his recent book, *The Creator and the Adversary*,[16] espouses much the same position. Rejecting the monistic point of view in which all reality is traced to one source, the will of God, he adopts a philosophy of conflict involving a second principle which goes down to the very roots of existence, a demonic discreativity directed against God's creativity.

Both Berdyaev and Lewis, however, fail to take into account the uniqueness of biblical satanology. Although the idea of Satan developed rather late and undoubtedly has traces of Persian influence, Satan is never depicted in terms of the principle of primordial evil, a Hebrew version of Angra Mainyu. He seems to have been a victim of his own rebellious pride and will to power, and in no sense co-

[14] A form of ego-centeredness is necessary for conscious life and serves in part to define what is meant by free action. Here egocentricity is an aspect of idolatry and is not to be confused with ego-centeredness.

[15] Karl Barth, *The Epistle to the Romans*, trans. by E. C. Hoskyns (London: Oxford University Press, 1933), p. 172.

[16] Nashille: Abingdon Press, 1948.

existent with God. In poetic language in the Prologue to Job, he is described as possessing limited power and operating within definite limits prescribed by God. Moreover, in the light of biblical eschatology Satan's fate is even more sharply defined, since all question concerning his final destiny is removed. Satan is often identified with the serpent in the Genesis story, but the serpent does not stand for evil. He simply misinterprets the ambiguous and contingent situation of man. Instead of explaining the origin of evil he illustrates its presence.

If the Bible does not attribute the origin of evil to an absolute source in opposition to God, neither does it make the source of evil God himself. When God's creative work was completed, the result received divine approbation in the verdict: "Behold, it was very good" (Gen. 1:31). The Bible is seemingly unaware of the dualism implicit in the dichotomic and trichotomic views of man so long popular in systematic theology. Instead of disintegrating man into two substances or three, it uniformly treats him as a unity of body *and* soul, created for responsible existence and good. Evil then enters into goodness and permeates it in its entirety, rather than into a substance alien to the spirit.

The genius of the biblical account of evil lies in the fact that it escapes both of the errors described above, that of absolute dualism and that of ascribing evil directly to God. Sin is the inevitable correlate of freedom and personality, but no attempt is made to ascertain its genesis. To do so would perforce reduce the problem of sin from the level of the moral to the level of nature. In this connection J. S. Whale concludes: "Man's sinful will cannot be explained: it must remain as the one completely irrational fact in a world which God created."[17]

From this study a second conclusion also follows. The Bible does not teach a doctrine of total depravity, in the sense that man is "utterly indisposed, disabled, and made opposite to all good, and wholly inclined to all evil." Despite alleged evidence to the contrary, it is doubtful that Reformed theology has ever consistently maintained such a view. Calvin himself was reluctant to allow that the image of God in man was completely destroyed. In order to vouchsafe man's essential humanity he introduced what Emil Brunner has called the

[17] *Christian Doctrine* (New York: The Macmillan Company, 1941), p. 50.

"doubtful concept" of a relic which remains in sinful men. Again, one can appreciate the flourishing doctrine of common grace in Reformed theology only when he sees it as an attempt to correct the excesses of total depravity. For the evident accomplishments of sinful men in history, the presence of the good, the true, and the beautiful in their lives hardly jibes with the definition cited above. Today, with the revival of Calvinistic theology, there is no doctrine that needs more to be reworked than that of common grace.

The emphasis given to the doctrine of depravity by the Reformers is, from the vantage point of history, understandable. It was a reaction against the optimism of Renaissance anthropology and, more especially, against the humanism latent in Roman Catholicism. Paul, with whom they felt the closest affinity, had faced a similar situation within the context of Judaism, and had met it with the theory of human inability and salvation by grace. But there is a world of difference between human inability as attested throughout the Scriptures and the doctrine of total depravity.

The old doctrine of total depravity has been linked with the theory of original sin in such a way that Adam's sin became disastrously determinative for all mankind, and the *locus classicus* for such a position is said to be Romans 5:12-21. But it seems hardly fair to Paul, not to mention the other scriptural writers, to construct biblical anthropology on this passage alone. For one thing, it is based on dubious exegesis. Paul develops his view of man in the early chapters of the epistle and in this passage he is discussing the extent of Christ's redemptive work. The figure of Adam is introduced for comparison and not to account for sin's origin. Too, it seems strange that the Adamic origin of sin and depravity is not mentioned in the Old Testament, save for the mooted passage in Genesis. Finally, the implication of Romans 5:12 is that death and not sin was transmitted by Adam. The traditional interpretation distorts the meaning of the entire letter, for it tangibly weakens the personal character of Christ's redemption and tends to reduce salvation to a mere bookkeeping transaction.

Again, this doctrine as it has been formulated in history is misleading because it leads to a conception of sin that is static and impersonal. In making the sin of one man decisive for all mankind it results in a crude determinism more closely akin to the *moira* concept of Greek tragedy than to the righteous will of the God and Father of our Lord Jesus Christ. Even Romans 5:12 concludes with the assertion "for that all sinned." To deny this leads to the loss of individuality and to a denial of human responsibility.

Nevertheless, there is a deep insight involved in the doctrine of total depravity that must not be lost. It does not mean that every man is as bad as he can be, but that all men are sinful and that their sin extends to the whole of their nature. We have said that in biblical psychology man is a unity, a total personality created to enjoy communion with God. To say that man is depraved means that his "being-in-communion" has now become "being-in-sin." The source of trouble is the whole personality which was made to be God-centered but is now self-centered. Man's entire nature has been changed from its original purpose to a purpose alien to God. He is apart from God in darkness and perdition, dead in trespasses and sin.

Total depravity, therefore, refers to the consequences of a severed relationship rather than to a substantial defacement. Not something in man but man's being itself is twisted. This is experienced as alienation from God and as subjection to his wrath. The God of love becomes the God of wrath, and freedom in his service becomes bondage to the law. It is also seen in man's spiritual inability. He cannot achieve the destiny for which he was created nor can he originate the love of God in his heart. Even the knowledge that he is the enemy of God and under his wrath is not available to him. It is knowledge that transcends the categories of speculative anthropology. The Socratic injunction, "Know thyself," is impossible apart from Jesus Christ, for man has no basis by which to know until he is known.

That the New Testament shares this serious view of human depravity is attested by the fact that redemption is always conceived as a divine gift, coming down from above. It is a new birth, a destruction of the sinful self, and an implantation of new life in the image of Jesus Christ. Jesus tells his disciples: "Except ye turn, and become as little children, ye shall in no wise enter into the kingdom of heaven" (Matt. 18:3), and to Nicodemus he repeats: "Ye must be born anew" (John 3:7). In II Corinthians 5:17 Paul declares: "Wherefore if any man is in Christ, he is a new creature," while in a moving autobiographical passage in Galatians he confesses: "I have been crucified with Christ; and it is no longer I that live, but Christ liveth in me; and that life which I now live in the flesh I live in faith, the faith which is in the Son of God, who loved me, and gave himself up for me" (Gal. 2:20).

Redemption, therefore, is more than forgiveness. It entails release from the bondage of a world of sin and the impartation of power by which man can reorient his life. That this cannot be done by might or by power is the universal testimony of experience and of the Scriptures. Only the power of God is strong enough to break the circle of self-centeredness that encases man and to restore his original being in relatedness to God. That God has done this in Jesus Christ is the gospel, "the power of God unto salvation to every one that believeth."

# CHAPTER 3

## TOWARD A DOCTRINE OF MAN IN PSYCHIATRY AND THEOLOGY

### PAUL W. PRUYSER

IT MAY be said, with confidence in so elementary and evident a truth, that theology and psychology are different in regard to their objects. Theology is concerned with God; psychology is concerned with man. Can there be a more radical difference than this between the objects of any two disciplines? And with such a striking difference in objects, do not the two disciplines stand far apart?

At one plane of comparison, of course, they do. Even at the highest level of abstraction, or at the last point of reduction, God and man form neither an identity nor do they overlap. The biblical statement that man is made in God's image is certainly a daring and only barely permissible comparison. It hardly indicates similarity, at least not formally. Perhaps it bespeaks an affinity, but then an affinity in image only.

Yet, paradoxically, the more one accentuates, in the spirit of each discipline, the difference between God and man, the more one is bound to imply and sometimes recognize their intimate relatedness. In deep reverence for God's holiness one may feel compelled to call him "the Other"; in just admiration for the intrinsic reality and value of man one will speak of the "self," the "ego," or the "me." This new language, independently developing in each of the two disciplines in order to elucidate the specificity and exclusiveness of its object, also opens the possibility for building bridges. For all these new words are relational terms. They refer to a twosome or a dyad, over and beyond the separateness and the duality. If there were only distinction, and no relatedness, Augustine's *Confessions*

35

would be pointless and James's *Varieties of Religious Experience* meaningless.

Still, someone might say that theology and psychology are basic disciplines, each with its own formalization and conceptual structure, and that they should therefore legitimately continue in separateness. Even if their objects were related to each other in some way, the disciplines themselves, for that matter, need not interact. Why should they, after all? Interaction is usually not without tension, and tension may distract from contemplation and study. Is it not better, then, to avoid such tension?

But theology and psychology are more than basic disciplines. There is also a pastoral theology, even a pastoral psychology, in which man and not God is the object of study and work. In this context man becomes indeed the object of a practical and direct, though not ultimate, concern. And in the borderlands of psychology there is psychiatry, for which man is not an object of study and experimentation, but first of all an object of care and challenge. At this applied level the two disciplines converge on an identical object. And here they *must* interact, in whatever way possible: wholeheartedly, hesitantly, reluctantly, or in anxious or angry avoidance. And here is one place of recognized, open, and demonstrable tension.

Much has been written about the modes of professional interaction appropriate to theology and psychiatry. Some tensions are being resolved, but not without others taking their place. The latter may be due to the fact that one very deep and potent source of tension is often unrecognized because it simply precludes the very interaction which could make it explicit and denotable. That is the tension implied in the continued separateness of psychology and theology as basic disciplines, to which we alluded above. It is the purpose of this article to help resolve various tensions between religion and psychiatry by considering certain aspects of their common object: man. Or, more precisely, by considering some features of the picture of that object as drawn by some religious leaders and some devoted psychiatrists.

It has been said by no less a person than Paul Tillich that both psychiatry and religion are in dire need of an anthropology, or a doctrine of man, without which they cannot fulfill their huge tasks.

No single man, no theological system, and no psychological theory have as yet offered an absolutely and universally valid idea of man in sufficient detail, with sufficient idealism and sufficient realism to satisfy all specialists and all laymen alike. We have piecemeal approaches only, and with these we have to do the best we can.

Theologians have written extensively about man's ultimate calling; they have offered the world some profound ideas of what man should be. They have said far less about what man actually is. What he *is*, is by them described in a single word, which is very meaningful in relation to the ideal notion of man. That word is "sin"; but it tells us very little about the actual workings, the detailed processes, and the day-by-day living of man, other than that all or most of it is sin. It is granted, however, that many a wise pastor or parish priest knows from his daily contacts with real people very well what man actually is. The psychologists and psychiatrists, on the other hand, have written extensively about what man actually is, i.e., how he is biologically, behaviorally, socially; in terms of his feelings, strivings, perceptions, disappointments, his love and hate, and the serious distortions thereof. But they have said far less about what man should be, what he ought to become, or what he ideally is. To be sure, they have a word for it, but that tells us very little. That word is "maturity." It is again to be granted, however, that many a psychiatrist, in the process of liberating a man from his inner distortions, can convey to his patient very well what he ought to be, and what he ideally is to become.

This seeming controversy or paradox may mean that at some level of understanding man, theology and psychology are complementary to each other, and that their continual interaction may bring us closer to a comprehensive and valid picture of ourselves.

Let us now consider the actual psychological and theological pictures of man in broad outlines. What strikes us right away is that both professions look at man with a peculiar mixture of optimism and pessimism. Both of us admit that man can be, and often is, in bondage; but both also acknowledge that man can be much freer than he now is. We perceive that there is a good deal of stability, or even rigidity, in human nature. "We are born and raised in sin," says the one; "we can never depart from the power of our instincts," says the other. But this is to neither of us the whole story; both of us know that man is not as rigid as he sometimes seems. In religion and in psychiatry we are deeply impressed by the changeability of man, and for both groups this is the premise of their work. What use would it be to preach the gospel, or even to announce the moral law, if we did not believe that man can change, or be changed? And what would be the *raison d'être* of psychiatry if we would assume that every man would forever remain the same? Be it in our theories or in our daily practice, but somehow and somewhere and at some time we profess (in word or action) that we have tremendous expectations of man.

Is there any more hopeful, more glorious, more promising picture of man than that described in Revelation? But when we read it, do we sincerely think that we can change that much and that our calling is so high? Yet, sometimes such a miraculous change is wrought on the back ward of a mental hospital when a human wreck, considered totally hopeless, arises as it were from the dead, and for the first time fulfills his human calling. And not by a miracle after all, but by a dutiful application of skill and love, perhaps very rare but exceedingly human. In both professions we practically believe in the impossible (so it seems), and yet, when the results are there, we humbly say that it was no miracle but that it must happen that way. We share an enormous optimism; we dream of a world not yet realized but very well possible and sincerely desirable. And both of us feel that we have to work hard and diligently for such a world.

This is only one aspect of our common doctrine of man. We also share a profound pessimism. We see that not every change in man is a change for the good, and we also see that much of man's stability is actually stagnation, a being stuck in misery, in suffering, in hate, in sin. "Hardness of heart" says the one; "human reality" says the other. Theology found that particular sin is not sufficient to explain man's actual condition and it postulated, long before Darwin, a genetic trait in the whole human race in order to account for his omnipresent misery. Original sin is the genetic condition of man. And so did a well-known psychiatric theory when it formulated some observations into the idea that man is by nature a destructive being with an immense love for himself, at first. From this original condition to a later one of love for one's fellow man and constructiveness toward the world is an enormous step, normally a course of difficult crawling, hesitant passes, falling, and sometimes no stepping or crawling at all. And when all has gone well in the beginning, and for quite a while, one may still fall, and one's fall may be deep. Again omnipresent misery. The systematic thinking of Christianity, particularly Calvinism, and of psychiatry, particularly psychoanalysis, shares a stark realism in that both state emphatically the actual presence and concrete reality of evil. We may use different words, such as sin and suffering and narcissism, but the picture to which these words refer is very much the same.

The mixture of optimism and pessimism with which we describe the human situation is not merely the observer's preference for a mood in which to contemplate; it is the product of perceiving or experiencing an existential duality in man. Theology perceives in man two beings; an old Adam and a new Adam, the condemned and the saved, the wicked and the sanctified, and it acknowledges that this duality creates tension. Life is a struggle between the old Adam and the new, and no life is complete without the mark of an incision or a turning point which distinguishes the old self from the new. The old and the new are distinguished and also connected by a series of supreme human acts which we call choice, decision, conscious realization, commitment, need of redemption, or response to grace. In an entirely different vocabulary, the state of man described by psychiatry is also a duality within a unity: take, for instance, the pleasure principle and the reality principle, or the primary process and the secondary process in psychoanalytic thought. Or the self-in-bondage and the self-in-freedom alluded to in Carl Rogers' system.

The psychiatric picture of man is not complete without the recognition of a transition between the old and the new man, between the infantile outlook and the mature mind. The transition from one to the other means again choice, commitment, loyalty to one, and renunciation of the other. Theologians and psychiatrists alike know from self-experience and observation how difficult such transitions are, and how tenuous any achievement in the new direction is. The old Adam, or the infantile core, stays with us and remains dynamically active even when we have made our choice for a new loyalty. Theology and psychiatry alike profess to the necessity of some fundamental metamorphosis in man without which he does not reach his destiny.

This concept of metamorphosis, whether stated in theological or

in psychiatric terms, implies that man can look backward and forward; back at his old self, which he still is to some extent, and forward to his new self, which he is not yet entirely. Theology has its
words for looking backward: it is repentance and the development of
a need for redemption. It has also its words for man's looking forward: freedom unto the enjoyment of God or living in the Holy
Spirit. The forward look cannot be without the backward look; man
is that creature which looks both ways in order to know what he
must do in the present. Much the same thing happens every day in
the psychiatric interview. Although it may sometimes seem as if the
psychiatrist and the patient look mostly backward, while exploring
the antecedent conditions of a present conflict, the backward look
is really for the sake of a liberation which will allow man to look
forward toward maturity, freedom, and charity as a desired state of
greater happiness and goodness.

We admit that there is a considerable difference between the developmental year-by-year pictures of the child as given by Arnold
Gesell, the stages of psychosexual development as described by Karl
Abraham, and the *Pilgrim's Progress* of John Bunyan; yet, this
should not blind us to the fact that they all conceive of man as a
developing, changing, traveling being, whose present is suspended
between a past which he is not any more and a future which he is not
yet. Theologically and psychiatrically, the present is a moment of
suspense, with multiple forms of bondage and multiple forms of
freedom. No teaching and preaching and analysis can do without
this point of view, implicitly or explicitly.

These are merely some preliminary remarks on certain parallels
to be found in a theological and a psychiatric doctrine of man. Doctrine can be stated in words as well as in deeds; when we speak of a
living doctrine we mean that the spirit of the doctrine becomes
manifest in behavior. The parallels which I mentioned are not always so manifest; yet I believe they are there if one really makes the
effort to look and scrutinize. They do not obliterate the differences
either; yet I believe that our differences are not always found at the
most important levels.

The foregoing statements can be compared to a very rough and
simple sketch of man, drawn by theologians and psychiatrists together. It consists of no more than a few strokes, just enough to sug-

gest some significant features of the object which is intended. It may not remain a sketch but must be developed into a detailed, accurate, and realistic portrait. Such a process will require a multitude of drafts, with major and minor revisions, a multitude of draftsmen, and infinite time.

# CHAPTER 4

## EXISTENTIALISM, PSYCHOTHERAPY, AND THE NATURE OF MAN

### PAUL TILLICH

### Existentialism and Essentialism

In all schools of psychotherapy there are many concepts which have proved more or less useful for directing research as well as practical work, but which are devoid of a philosophical foundation and, consequently, without critical and uniting principles. As a nonexpert in this vast realm of theory and practice, I can only pose the question of a possible philosophical foundation for psychotherapy on the basis of my own thought, in which the existentialist element has a definite place, although I would not call myself an existentialist.

It is an indication that one has misunderstood existentialism if one uses it without reference to its opposite. Philosophical ideas necessarily appear in pairs of contrasting concepts, like subject and object, ideal and real, rational and irrational. In the same way, existentialism refers to its opposite, essentialism, and I would be at a loss to say anything about the one without saying something about the other. The easiness with which the term existentialism and its derivatives have lately become the talk of the intellectual market is because from the very beginning in America, after World War II, the term existentialism was used without reference to its opposite. Indicative for the general situation is the fact that the term essentialism did not even exist in the early discussions of existentialist philosophy. But it seems to me that in a group which seeks for an existentialist psycho-

42

therapy, the implicit reference to essentialism should be brought into the open.[1]

Instead of giving an abstract definition of essentialism and existen-tialism, I will point to an example *par excellence,* the nature of man. One can describe man's essential nature and one can describe man's existential predicament. Both tasks have always been performed, but often the one has tried to eliminate the other. In religious thought, for instance, the view of man's predicament has frequently over-shadowed the view of his essential nature. One can say this of ancient Gnosticism as well as of some forms of radical Protestantism. If man's estranged predicament is so much emphasized that his creative good-ness appears completely destroyed, an impressive but untenable theological existentialism arises. Some theologians of the Reforma-tion period, like the great church historian, Flacius, as well as some recent theologians like the early Karl Barth, have taken this position. None of them would have denied or even minimized the doctrine of creation and with it man's essential goodness, but they did not draw from it the consequences for the doctrine of man. The divine was cut off from the human without "point of contact." Man was seen as a mere object of divine action and man's productive activities in cul-ture and history were devaluated. This is theological existentialism without the essentialist frame in which classical theology had stated it.

But the main stream of existentialist thought was running through philosophy, the arts, and literature. In contrast to the situation in the last three years after World War II when most people identified existentialism with Sartre, it is now common knowledge in this country that existentialism in the Western intellectual history starts with Pascal in the seventeenth century, has an underground history in the eighteenth century, a revolutionary history in the nineteenth century, and an astonishing victory in the twentieth century. Existentialism has become the style of our period in all realms of life. Even the analytic philosophers pay tribute to it by withdrawing into formal problems and leaving the field of material

---

[1] Here the distinction between existential and existentialist should be brought out: "Existential" points to the universally human involvement in matters of genuine concern; "existentialist" points to a philosophical movement which fights the predominance of essentialism in modern thought, be it idealistic or naturalis-tic essentialism.

problems to the existentialists in art and literature.

There are, however, only rare moments in this monumental development in which an almost pure existentialism has been reached. An example is Sartre's doctrine of man. I refer to a sentence in which the whole problem of essentialism and existentialism comes into the open, his famous statement that man's essence is his existence. The meaning of this sentence is that man is a being of whom no essence can be affirmed, for such an essence would introduce a permanent element, contradictory to man's power of transforming himself indefinitely. According to Sartre, man is what he acts to be.

But if we ask whether his statement has not, against its intention, given an assertion about man's essential nature, we must say, certainly, it has. Man's particular nature is his power to create himself. And if the further question is raised of how such a power is possible and how it must be structured, we need a fully developed essentialist doctrine in order to answer; we must know about his body and his mind and, in short, about those questions which for millennia have been discussed in essentialist terms.

Only on the basis of an essentialist doctrine of freedom does Sartre's statement have any meaning. Neither in theology nor in philosophy can existentialism live by itself. It can only exist as a contrasting element within an essentialist framework. There is existentialist philosophizing but there is not, and cannot be, an existentialist system of philosophy. The answers given by existentialists to the questions they raise in their analyses are derived from essentialist traditions. Existentialism is an element within a larger frame of essentialism, and it exists only as such an element, even in its most radical antiessentialist statements. In order to describe the negative in being and life, one must see its impact on the positive. For only through this impact does the negative have reality. There is no existentialist description of the negativities of the human predicament without an underlying image of what man essentially is and therefore ought to be. The cutting power of existentialist novels, paintings, even philosophical analyses of man's predicament, is rooted in the implicit contrast between the negativities they show and the positives they silently presuppose.

But now we must ask the converse question: Is pure essentialism possible? It is possible only if man's searching mind is subjected to a strict censorship, prohibiting all those questions in which man asks about his existence within his world. Plato did not accept such censorship. He was aware of the conflict between the essential and the existential element in reality. And if he talked about the "destiny of the soul," namely, of man's predicament in space and time, he did not use dialectics, but myth. He is the greatest example of a union of essentialism with existentialist elements. In the Middle Ages, existentialist descriptions of the human predicament were present in monastic self-scrutiny and in the penitential manuals for priest-confessors. These manuals contain materials which in many respects are an anticipation of the insights elaborated in the psychotherapeutic schools of the twentieth century. In Protestantism, this concrete material disappeared, but certainly not the question of man's predicament. In philosophy, the problem came to a dramatic height in the conflict between Descartes and Pascal in the seventeenth century. Both men stood in the Platonic-Augustinian tradition, both were creative mathematicians, and mathematics was always the pattern for essentialist thinking. But while Descartes reduced the elements to a minimum, Pascal put them against his own and Descartes' essentialist emphasis.

Ever since, this tension has remained alive, although in the modern period it has been under a definite predominance of the essentialist element. A change took place with the existentialist revolt against Hegel's essentialism in the middle of the last century and with the major victory of the existentialist attitude in the twentieth century. But this victory does not mean that the tension has ceased between the two approaches to reality. And a slight recovery of essentialism seems to be noticeable, especially in the arts within the last decade.

## The Philosophical Matrix of Psychoanalysis

Seen in the background of this development, the question of the relation of existentialism and psychoanalysis can be asked in more definite terms. The term "psychoanalysis" has shared the fate of a large group of important concepts that have grown beyond the limits of their original meaning and in this way have received an increased significance and a growing indefiniteness. This makes it necessary to determine the sense in which psychoanalysis shall be used in its confrontation with existentialism.

Originally it meant a therapeutic technique, a refinement and transformation of earlier techniques. But this was possible only on the basis of a new understanding of the psychological processes which produce both the necessity and the possibility of psychotherapy. "Psychological processes" is a name for processes in the living *Gestalt* which we call "man." No understanding or even description of them is possible without an image of this *Gestalt,* without a doctrine of man in the several dimensions of his being. No therapeutic theory can be developed without an implicit or explicit image of man. But we must go beyond this step. No doctrine of man is possible without a general understanding of the general processes of life, their trends and their ambiguities. And finally, no understanding of life processes is possible without a doctrine of being and of the structure of being universally.

This consideration shows the basis of the question, how is psychoanalysis related to existentialism? The question is two-sided. The psychoanalytic practice is not only dependent on the doctrines of man and of life and of being, but these doctrines are also dependent on the practice of psychoanalysis. Every practical dealing with reality provides experiences which have theoretical impact. This insight is as old as the Gospel according to John when it speaks of doing the truth, and it is as new as Marx in his earlier writings when he fought against the separation of theory and practice. And it is as old and as new as the main emphasis of Nietzsche and the American pragmatists when they tried to reunite action and knowledge. Therefore, it is not astonishing that Freud's analytic practice became the source of ideas which changed the whole intellectual climate of the twentieth century.

Unfortunately, the philosophical matrix in which the psychoanalytic techniques were conceived was rather inadequate to the implications and consequences of their conception. The naturalistic (and in some respect, idealistic) presuppositions of Freud do not fit the immense contribution he has made indirectly to the existentialist analysis of the human predicament. Therefore, it is a justifiable attempt by the different Neo-Freudian groups to overcome this inadequacy and, by doing so, to correct some shortcomings of the therapeutic method which follows from the inadequacy of Freud's philosophical presuppositions. This is what existentialist psychotherapy also tries to do. I believe that such a task is necessary, not only for psychotherapeutic practice but also for the contemporary intellectual situation.

If my philosophical assumptions are correct, an important consequence follows: It cannot only be existentialist, it must also be essentialist thought which provides the philosophical matrix for the psychoanalytic practice. Existential psychotherapy is almost a truism; for disease is one of the central existential concepts. Therefore, let us not talk of existentialist psychoanalysis as such, but of a possible philosophical matrix of psychoanalysis, being aware of the fact that every constructive philosophy and theology unites essentialist and existentialist elements. In order to understand sin, the theologian must understand creative goodness. In order to understand estrangement, the philosopher must understand that from which we are estranged, namely, our own essential nature. This means psychotherapy must remain aware of its dependence on the doctrine of man, on the doctrine of life, on the doctrine of being. As psychotherapy, it cannot create such a philosophy, although it can influence it.

This is a difficult relationship. The problem is the same as it is in all creative functions of the human spirit. Always and inescapably they have a philosophy in their background. We must bring this into the open and subject it to criticism and transformation. On the other hand, all creative functions of man's spirit must contribute to a philosophy which deals with all of them. This mutual dependence of philosophy and the other functions of the spirit produces a perpetual problem. For more than fifty years, I have been laboring under this problem in relation to the philosophy of religion; and I am consoled that now other groups are in the same predicament and will have to labor probably more than fifty years under the same problem. As a group of healers you cannot identify yourselves with a particular philosophy; but you cannot do without a philosophy. Instead of attempting a general answer, I want to give a description of some exemplary situations, thus leading to the next consideration: philosophical problems of psychoanalytic procedures.

## Philosophical Problems of Psychoanalytic Procedures

Naturalism, the philosophy from which Freud came, is, together with idealism, the main expression of an essentialist philosophy. Freud's determinism was his naturalistic heritage, his moralism was his idealistic heritage. And in both he represented the basic attitude of the victorious and "Victorian" industrial society of the nineteenth century. But with the empirical rediscovery of the old philosophical concept of the unconscious, he broke through his own moralism, and with the concept of sublimation, he broke through his determinism. The first, the rediscovery of the unconscious, was the confirmation of the inability of autonomous morals to lead man to his fulfillment. It was the destruction of the philosophy of the "men of good will," which is so rampant in American Protestantism. Freud showed the ambiguity of goodness as well as of evil, and in doing so, he helped to undercut Protestant moralism. This perhaps was the most important existentialist contribution of psychoanalysis to the doctrine of man. Man is not what he believes himself to be in his conscious decisions.

This is the point where Freud is a true existentialist in the sense of all existentialist descriptions of man's predicament. He is certainly not the moralistic idealist he sometimes gives the impression of being, especially in relation to sex. And he is not a determinist either, toward which his naturalistic heritage seemed to push him. I don't look for indeterministic utterances of Freud. They probably could not be found. And they should not, because the traditional fight between determinism and indeterminism is a dead issue. But I look at his concept of sublimation, which philosophically is completely unelaborated.

Sublimation is the act which transforms something not sublime into something sublime. And the sublime is a concept which deserves highest standing in formulating a philosophy of life. The structure of life shows that the sublime is the greatest potentiality of life. It is not a mere transformation of the not-sublime; then it would be only another form of it. But the sublime is something qualitatively new, it demands a creative act—and this means freedom, in a meaningful sense of the word. It belongs to the theories wherein Freud was "behind" himself in that he tried to derive sublime things, like works of art, from nonsublime things like early psychological disturbances of the artists. But the very concept of the sublime requires that such disturbances be looked at as occasions and not causes of the creation of the sublime. This is not an existentialist, but an essentialist question. It refers to man's essential nature and to the central concept in which converge all elements in man's essential nature, the concept of freedom. I do not mean the so-called "freedom of the will" (an obsolete concept), but the power of man to react centrally to a stimulus, by deliberation and decision.

This explains the fact to which Rollo May drew my attention, that in so many of his patients' dreams there appears the necessity of deciding. His patients have not yet lost the awareness that sublimation goes through decision, and that the power of deciding makes men human. This consideration is an essentialist one—although it shows the precondition for the possibility of man's existential self-loss. This should lead to the acknowledgment that biological and sociological methods of interpretation are by no means sufficient in order to explain the drive toward the sublime. The centered act of the centered self is the source of sublimation. This is a basic statement of an essentialist doctrine of man and is as necessary for psychoanalysis as the existentialist insight in the determining function of the unconscious is for morality and religion.

After these examples of existentialist as well as of essentialist elements in which psychoanalysis must find a solid philosophical ground, let me speak of a phenomenon in which elements of both sides are effective. I point to the difference and confusion of existential and neurotic anxiety, of existential and neurotic guilt, of existential and neurotic emptiness. I believe that Freud is partly responsible for the confusion because of his inadequate philosophical foundations which did not admit the distinction between essential goodness and existential distortion. The decisive question here is whether one believes that it is possible to remove by a successful analysis not only neurotic forms of anxiety but also its genuine forms —the anxieties of finitude, of guilt, of emptiness. Of course, no one would deny that a completely successful analysis is highly improbable, but many analysts assert that in principle both forms of anxiety can be removed because there is no qualitative difference between them. They all can be treated as neurosis, capable of being healed. This would include the anxiety of having to die, the anxiety of having become guilty, the anxiety of lacking a meaning of life. This, however, would imply, at least in principle, that the analyst is able to remove from human beings the awareness of their finitude, and consequently their basic anxiety; that he would be able to convince men who have become guilty that they are not really guilty; that he would be able to answer the question of the meaning of life to his patients. But all this is not realistic.

Actually, the situation is quite different. Neurotic anxiety is misplaced compulsory anxiety, and not the basic anxiety about everything being finite. Basic anxiety is anxiety about being bound to the law of coming from nothing and going to nothing. Neurotic guilt is misplaced compulsory guilt feeling and not the existential experience of being guilty of a definite concrete act which expresses the general estrangement of our existence, an act for which responsibility cannot be denied, in spite of the element of destiny in it. Neurotic emptiness is a compulsory flight from meaning, even from that remnant of meaning which makes the experience of meaninglessness possible. It is the expression of an unreflective and unsophisticated understanding of men and life if these neurotic phenomena are confused with the universal structures of existence which make neurotic phenomena possible. No great physician has ever claimed that he can change the biological structures of life; and no psychotherapist from whatever school he comes should claim that he can change the structures of life in the dimension of self-awareness usually called the psychological dimension. But he can assert that he may heal disorders which follow from the relation of men's existential to his essential nature. Here are very obvious reasons why psychoanalysis needs a philosophical matrix.

There are other reasons, some existentialist, some essentialist. I can only point to them. What do norms of thought and action mean in relation to the therapeutic process? For Freud, the "superego" is the name for the consciousness of norms. But the material of the superego is taken from the "id." It has no standing in itself, no objective validity. It has only the power of psychological oppressiveness. The reason for this construction is that Freud did not distinguish the essential structure of man's being, from which norms and principles are derived, and their existential distortion in the images of the superego. Certainly, there are images of destructive power in most human beings; but they are not identical with man's essential nature.

Essential norms, if obeyed, fulfill and give the joy of fulfillment because they represent our own essential being against our existential distortion. Religious commandments, for instance, express a concrete understanding of man's essential nature. The superego gives arbitrary commands and produces unhappiness and revolt. Dr. Hanna Colm writes about the revolt of children, not only against oppressive education, but also against the lack of any direction. This is an interesting confirmation of the assertion that norms and principles are an expression of our essential being. In view of these facts, the distinction between essential and existential elements in human nature becomes empirically verifiable. In spite of this, the general acceptance of the id-ego-superego scheme has blinded many scholars against the distinction of the essential and the existential in human nature.

A further problem is that of the relation between the analyst and the patient in the therapeutic process. A person becomes a person in the encounter with other persons, and in no other way. All functions of our spirit are based on what I call the moral self-realization of the centered self. This is what morality is—not the subjection to laws. The only way in which this can happen is the limiting encounter with another ego. Nature is open to man's controlling and transforming activity indefinitely, but man resists such control. The other person cannot be controlled like a natural object. Every human being is an absolute limit, an unpierceable wall of resistance against any attempt to make him into an object. He who breaks this resistance by external force destroys his own humanity; he never can become a mature person.

This interdependence of man and man in the process of becoming human is a judgment against a psychotherapeutic method in which the patient is a mere object for the analyst as subject. The inevitable reaction then is that the patient tries in return to make the analyst into an object for himself as subject. This kind of acting and reacting has a depersonalizing effect on both the analyst and the patient. The transference phenomenon should be reconsidered in the light of a "philosophy of encounter," in which existentialist and essentialist elements are united.

My last example is the phrase "being in the world" (Heidegger), which plays a great role in existentialist literature. It points to the fact of "being with" in spite of our aloneness in the world. But more important for the understanding of man is that he has the potentiality of having a world in contrast to other beings which have only environment. Man breaks through his environment in all directions; his language is his liberation from bondage to a limited situation. But this freedom is not easy to accept and many people turn back from the openness of their world to the prison of their environment. This is another description of the neurotic withdrawal from reality, and one which shows the neurotic character of many forms of seemingly normal behavior, as in conformism and submission to absolute authorities. Without a sharp essentialist distinction between world and environment, such approaches to the phenomenon of neurosis have no foundation.

Existentialism has discovered many characteristics of man's predicament which are able to provide a philosophical matrix for psychotherapy. But this does not mean that there should be a definitive marriage between existentialism and psychotherapy. It is an alliance which should not be exclusive. Without a powerful essentialist frame the alliance would not hold. It would fall into vagueness and irrelevance, both on the philosophical and the psychotherapeutic side. But it is the task of a philosophical matrix in all realms of man's intellectual life to help these realms towards definiteness, clarity, fundamental principles, and universal validity.

# CHAPTER 5

## NIEBUHR
## ON THE NATURE OF MAN

### A Criticism of Reinhold Niebuhr's
### "The Self and the Dramas of History"

CARL R. ROGERS

WITH DISCUSSION BY BERNARD M. LOOMER, WALTER M. HORTON, AND HANS HOFMANN

I WAS persuaded to read and comment upon Reinhold Niebuhr's *The Self and the Dramas of History* because in my work as a psychotherapist I have become deeply concerned with the self and its place in our psychological existence. My reactions are not intended as a formal review.

As I lay the book down, I find that I am impressed most of all by the awesome certainty with which Reinhold Niebuhr *knows*. He knows, with incredible assurance, what is wrong with the thinking of St. Thomas Aquinas, Augustine, Hegel, Freud, Marx, Dewey, and many, many others. He also knows what are the errors of Communism, existentialism, psychology, and all the social sciences. His favorite term for the formulations of others is "absurd," but such other terms as "erroneous," "blind," "naïve," "inane," and "inadequate" also are useful. It seems to me that the only individuals who come off well in the book are the Hebrew prophets, Jesus (as seen by Niebuhr), Winston Churchill, and Niebuhr himself.

So strong is this impression that I cannot help but speculate as to whether in some sense Niebuhr may be speaking to himself when he says that "religion lends itself particularly to the pretensions of possessing absolute truth and virtue by finite and sinful men"; or when he states that the sin of the self consists of "claiming too much for its finiteness, and for the virtue and wisdom which it achieves in its finiteness." I find myself offended by Niebuhr's dogmatic statements and feel ready to turn back with fresh respect to the writings of science, in which at least the *endeavor* is made to keep an open mind.

But I do not wish my distaste for the *form* of the presentation to cause me, or the reader of these comments, to overlook the major issue toward which the book is directed. Stated in oversimplified fashion, Dr. Niebuhr is wrestling with the fact that the trend of social and psychological science is to make man a creature determined by natural causes, and history an essentially predictable sequence. He dislikes this trend and stresses that man is a free self, transcending natural causes, and that history is an unpredictable affair, growing out of dramatic choice.

I feel deeply sympathetic to Niebuhr's attempt to deal with this problem, because it is one which concerns me sufficiently that I have tried to pose somewhat the same issue for psychologists to consider.[1] I looked eagerly to find what resolution he might have found for this complex and disturbing problem. I did not find it easy to discover this resolution, because the author is much more clear about what he is against than what he affirms. As I understand him, he points in several directions which seem to him desirable. He wishes to remove both the self and history from the realm of the "structures of nature," a realm which can be understood by empirical science. He justifies this by the fact that both the self and history are compounded of freedom and necessity (determinism), and thus they fall outside science, which is "absurd" when it endeavors to discover empirical laws regarding the self or historical events. To me, this seems to be roughly equivalent to telling scientists to stop seeking for orderliness in man's inner nature or in his outer behavior, and I am skeptical that they will pay much attention.

Another thread which runs through Niebuhr's thinking is his tendency to see the universe in terms of contrasting systems in a state of tension. Thus, in the individual there is a tension between creativity and destructiveness, between rationality and faith, between the self as creator and the self as creature, and hence between freedom and necessity. Niebuhr does not seem to recognize that this

[1] "Persons or Science? A Philosophical Question," *American Psychologist*, X, No. 7 (July, 1955), 267-78.

duality of systems permits him to explain too much. Thus, on the one hand, he states that "no scientific investigations of past behavior can become the basis of predictions of future behavior." On the other hand, in his brief (and to me arbitrary) analysis of history he makes such statements as this: "The tragedy of Germany must be analyzed in terms of a dozen complex historical factors," and he gives various geographical, social, and cultural factors. In this section he proceeds as though he, like the social scientist, sees historical effect proceeding from historical cause. Yet one cannot tax him with inconsistency, since he believes in both freedom and determinism and that the self is both creator and creature. Because he is not specific as to the degree of freedom he believes the self to possess, it is obvious that he need never be at a loss to explain any event, since, if it is not determined, it is the result of man's transcending freedom, and vice versa. This is a comfortable view, but to me not a satisfying one.

Another direction which he takes is the advocacy of a biblical faith. Because it combines a specific historical drama which cannot be understood rationally, with the hope of fulfillment of individual selfhood, this supplies for Niebuhr the most compelling answer. I must confess that it did not seem equally compelling to me.

As a psychologist, I was particularly interested in Niebuhr's view of the self. In his discussion of the dialogue of the self with itself, I found much with which I could agree. In his concept of the self in dialogue with others, he describes both the potentialities and the limiting mysteries of interpersonal relationships, where the "otherness" of the other poses a barrier which must be accepted in some ultimate way. I found that his insights in this respect were in many ways in agreement with my experience. The search of the self for ultimate meaning is also a concept which has much reality for me.

It is in his conception of the basic deficiency of the individual self that I find my experience utterly at variance. He is quite clear that the "original sin" is self-love, pretension, claiming too much, grasping after self-realization. I read such words and try to imagine the experience out of which they have grown. I have dealt with maladjusted and troubled individuals, in the intimate personal relationship of psychotherapy, for more than a quarter of a century. This has not been perhaps a group fully representative of the whole community, but neither has it been unrepresentative. And, if I were to search for the central core of difficulty in people as I have come to know them, it is that in the great majority of cases they despise themselves, regard themselves as worthless and unlovable. To be sure, in some instances this is covered by pretension, and in nearly all of us these feelings are covered by some kind of a façade. But I could not differ more deeply from the notion that self-love is the fundamental and pervasive "sin." Actually it is only in the experience of a relationship in which he is loved (something very close, I believe, to the theologians' agape) that the individual can begin to feel a dawning respect for, acceptance of, and, finally, even a fondness for himself. It is as he can thus begin to sense himself as lovable and worthwhile, in spite of his mistakes, that he can begin to feel love and tenderness for others. It is thus that he can begin to realize himself and to reorganize himself and his behavior to move in the direction of becoming the more socialized self he would like to be. I believe that only if one views individuals on the most superficial or external basis are they seen as being primarily the victims of self-love. When seen from the inside, that is far from being their disease. At least so it seems to me.

So I leave Niebuhr's book feeling that I, too, would like to preserve the self as creator, the self as a free and self-determining being. I wish that I knew how to reconcile this desire with the desire, which I share with other scientists, to find the orderliness which I believe exists in the human psyche. But I have not found the answers in Reinhold Niebuhr's book. I shall hope for some other book, more open to all the complex facts, with perhaps less certainty in it, to inform me more deeply in this perplexing area.

## Discussion by BERNARD M. LOOMER

In Rogers' comments on Niebuhr's *The Self and the Dramas of History* he makes two criticisms of Niebuhr's thought (which I shall list in the reverse order in which they were given). First, Niebuhr believes that man's sin is basically that of self-love or pretension, while Rogers has found in his twenty-five years of psychotherapy that the great majority of his clients "despise themselves, regard themselves as worthless and unlovable." Second, Niebuhr does not really reconcile the dual emphases that man is both free and determined. Rogers wants to harmonize his idea that man is free and self-determined with his desire and concern as a scientist to find the orderliness which he believes exists in the human psyche. Rogers feels that Niebuhr's handling of this tension is unconvincing. I shall deal with each criticism in turn, although quite briefly with the second.

1. On the issue as to what is basically the trouble with man, Niebuhr and Rogers apparently disagree quite flatly. This disagreement is not an easy matter to discuss or adjudicate because it involves great divergencies in total outlooks as well as intellectual concerns. The statement of the issue itself requires some brief mention of the context out of which each man speaks.

To the best of my knowledge, Rogers has no parallel to Niebuhr's doctrine of sin. But from his therapeutic experiences he has derived a conception of man's essential goodness: The more fully a client is able to accept himself because of the therapeutic relationship (which Rogers conceives to be an I-Thou relation and which Buber, incidentally, denies), the more trustworthy he feels his own perceptions and judgments about himself and others to be. He becomes more able to evaluate himself objectively. The greater the degree of the client's self-acceptance, the greater his freedom and self-determination. He becomes more self-initiating and self-sufficient. The more he is open to acknowledge emotionally his strengths and weaknesses, the more freely and willingly he accepts others for what they are. The greater the client's self-acceptance, the more fully is he guided by his finer motives and values.

Niebuhr's doctrine of sin (expounded most fully in his *Nature and Destiny of Man*) emphasizes man's self-love, his tendency to deny God and to make himself the center of his own existence. For Niebuhr, man in his finitude is possessed by anxiety which is the precondition of both his creativity and his refusal to acquiesce to his finiteness. This anxiety is bearable if man trusts God, but man chooses to disobey God and to rebel. This lack of trust and rebellion leads to pride in one or more of its several forms. Pride is self-love. It is man's attempt to transform his contingent form of existence into unconditional significance.

To be sure, Niebuhr takes cognizance of sin as sensuality. But it is important to notice that sensuality is a further consequence of man's refusal to trust God. It is a more obviously degraded stage of his pride. Sensuality is "first another and final form of self-love, secondly an effort to escape self-love by the deification of another and finally as an escape from the futilities of both forms of idolatry by a plunge into unconsciousness" (or nothingness).

To put these points in terms that are perhaps more immediately relevant to the issue at hand, we can say that for Niebuhr (and for much if not most of the history of Christian theology) man sins or contributes to his own downfall because he is strong and not because he is weak. His trouble stems from excess and not deficiency. Basically, man tends to think more rather than less highly of himself than he ought to think. This position is taken partly because man's capacity for greatness is directly related to his propensity to sin.

In the present discussion Rogers seems to be saying that man's tendency is to think less highly of himself than he ought to think, that man's trouble arises from weakness rather than from strength or from deficiency rather than from excess. Only if he is loved sufficiently and with adequate understanding will a man attribute to himself proper worth and status. Since Rogers has no doctrine of sin or its equivalent, I am not clear as to what his answer would be to the question: Why do his clients underevaluate themselves? Because they have not been loved sufficiently? Or have they refused to accept the love that may have been offered to them? If the former, why would no one offer them adequate love? If the latter, why have they rejected love?

Niebuhr's rejoinder would be, in my judgment, that the clients' condition of weakness or deficiency or underevaluation could be characterized in one (or both) of two ways. Either it is temporary, apparent only and ambiguous, in which case it would be an inverted form of pride masquerading as excessive worthlessness, or it is sincere, in which case it is an instance of the strength of pride, or self-love which has turned into weakness.

Therefore the question is: Is self-love the basic evil in man under which we can subsume all other forms? If so, it would appear that Niebuhr (when he stresses pride rather than sensuality, or when he stresses the strength of excess rather than the deficiency of weakness) and Rogers are mainly concerned with two different dimensions or stages of the same fundamental fact or process of man's self-destruction. This difference could be accounted for, in part, by the diversity of their vocations and intellectual preoccupations. Or are self-love and underevaluation totally unrelated phenomena? Perhaps we do not have sufficient evidence to make a responsible judgment, although at the moment I favor the first alternative.

This discussion could be carried to a further stage if we ask the question: When Rogers' clients reach the point in their therapeutic relationship where they do have a sufficiently high evaluation of themselves, do they altogether exemplify Rogers' description of the natural and essential goodness of man or do they exhibit some of the qualities that Niebuhr stresses, remembering that for Niebuhr there is a deep ambiguity in man because of the common rootage and interweaving of good and evil? I am not aware that there are any reliable data on this point and so the question is somewhat hypothetical. Yet a resolution of the two points of view will involve a consideration of this dimension of a client's life. Also, some account must be taken of the more largely social character of human existence before a satisfactory evaluation of these contrasting perspectives can be achieved. Rogers and Niebuhr may each find the other unconvincing because their respective data and outlooks are at the moment not altogether commensurate, although I think it must be granted that Niebuhr's are certainly more inclusive.

2. On the subject of freedom and external determination the issue is much less clear. In the first place I am not sure that Rogers means the same thing by "freedom" or "self-determination" that Niebuhr does. I am inclined to think that the latter's notion of self-transcendence in terms of spirit is not really part of the former's intellectual outlook. Interestingly enough, this idea, which is the primary basis from which Niebuhr criticizes most if not all contemporary schools of psychology, is not dealt with at all by Rogers. This omission on Rogers' part needs to be explained since the idea is decisive for Niebuhr. This notion is part of the key to understanding Niebuhr's criticisms of various forms of rationalism, including rationally intelligible structures of coherence and meaning. It would also apply to Rogers' own conceptions of the good life and the nature of man.

This possible difference in their definitions of freedom accounts in part for their divergence in handling the freedom-determination question. I am not really clear as to what sort of a resolution of this tension Rogers is looking for. Apparently he is searching for a concept of the psyche's orderliness under which the freedom of the self can be subsumed. Possibly the concept of the self's creativity would also be included within the meaning of the self's "orderliness." Does Rogers want to eliminate the tension between order and freedom by systematizing freedom in terms of self-determination? At one point he seems to criticize Niebuhr for not being able to specify "the degree of freedom he believes the self to possess" (although the context of this quotation might lead the reader to think correctly that Rogers meant this remark facetiously).

Niebuhr's view of the relation between historical determination and self-transcendence is such that no resolution of this tension is possible. Both elements are present but inter-related. (In this connection it seems to me that Rogers is incorrect when he states that Niebuhr "wishes to remove both the self and history from the realm of the 'structures of nature.' ") Furthermore the tension is desirable. But this does not mean that Niebuhr is opposed to scientific inquiries. But it does mean that in the last analysis he thinks that a strict science of the self, including its self-transcendence, is not possible. For him, the freedom of the self is indeterminate and therefore cannot be systematized into any rationally structural order. This view has theological presuppositions and implications which are probably not shared by Rogers. The differences between the two men are in large part theological.

## Discussion by WALTER M. HORTON

The editor has asked me to comment on Carl Rogers' review of Reinhold Niebuhr's *The Self and the Dramas of History*. Reading Rogers' judgment, springing as it does from a wealth of clinical experience, gives me a strong impulse to spring into the breach (for breach it is) between these two wise and gifted men, and offer a few words of interpretation.

First, as to the impression of dogmatism and narrow-minded certitude which Rogers got from reading Niebuhr. I have known

Reinhold Niebuhr for a good many years as a fellow member of a small, intimate theological discussion group, and think I can understand the basis of this false impression. "Reinie" does indeed make free use of such terms as "absurd," "erroneous," "inane," in describing false views. His first act in confronting any theological problem is to find two opposing views on the subject, and sharpen them both to the point of absurdity, so that the truth plainly must lie somewhere between them. He does not very precisely identify these views with the actual views of their representatives and, in fact, sometimes gives a biased picture of these, so anxious is he to get a real pair of nutcracking opposites. But listen to him from this point on when he tries to suggest the true alternative to these absurdities, and he becomes very cautious and tentative.

On all ultimate questions, the best the religious thinker can do is to point to a mythical or symbolic solution, of which it can always be said, "We are deceivers and yet true."[2] So great is the peril here of real deception, that Niebuhr frequently whirls on himself in the midst of discussion, and catches himself in the wrong with as much pleasure as if it were some one else. Indeed he *is* "speaking to himself" when he warns against the "pretensions of possessing absolute truth." He is speaking to all and sundry, not just to Roman Catholics, when he develops the paradox of "having and not having the truth" in the second half of his *The Nature and Destiny of Man.* Dogmatism is as hateful to him as to Carl Rogers; the appearance of dogmatism is due to the negative side of his didactical method. On the positive side, even his friends have accused him of being too tentative. No scientist could be more so.

That brings us to Rogers' second point, that Niebuhr gives an antiscientific and therefore profoundly unsatisfactory answer to the problem of freedom and determinism, with which every serious student of human nature has to wrestle. By pointing to the "unpredictable" character of history, rooted in "dramatic choice," Niebuhr seems to imply that empirical science cannot formulate laws about man without falling into the "absurd," and seems to be "telling scientists to stop seeking for orderliness in man's inner nature or in his outer behavior." On this understanding, Rogers finds Niebuhr inconsistent when he enumerates causal factors that help one

[2] *Beyond Tragedy*, New York: Charles Scribner's Sons, 1937.

to comprehend the tragedy of modern German history—*either* inconsistent, or else holding the comfortably loose theory that since freedom and determinism are both there, whatever is "not determined" is "the result of man's transcending freedom." But this is not all that Niebuhr means by the combination of freedom and determinism in human events—not "either one or the other," as if they were wholly disparate factors, but "both together simultaneously." His preference for biblical faith and dialectical thinking in ultimate human problems is not at all inconsistent with an empirical analysis of the same events, pushed as far as it can fruitfully go.

Rogers' principal objection, however, is his third and last, that Niebuhr's doctrine of self-love and pretension as the original sin is contradicted by the findings of psychological counseling experience, which indicate unambiguously that man's basic need is to "begin to feel a dawning respect for, acceptance of, and, finally, even a fondness for himself." It is a "superficial" view of man, says Rogers, that supposes his real disease is self-love instead of *lack* of self-love. This is certainly a terrific conflict of findings, in which two very acute observers—one in the realm of public affairs and the other in the realm of the inner life of persons—appear to belie one another completely. Out of such conflicts, real advances in understanding have sometimes come. Let us see if it may be so in this case.

It will not do to press the title of Niebuhr's *Moral Man and Immoral Society,* and reconcile Rogers' view with Niebuhr's by referring one to the personal life of man, and the other to his social life. The distinction between the personal and social spheres is only a relative one in Niebuhr's thinking; self-love and proud pretension are only more massive and obvious in group life than in personal life. There are plenty of texts concerning self-love and pride in *The Self and the Dramas of History,* the most psychological of all Niebuhr's books, to justify Rogers' interpretation of it.

Nevertheless, there is a further twist in Niebuhr's doctrine of man and sin, not nearly so manifest in this recent abbreviated version as it is in the full-length analysis given in *The Nature and Destiny of Man.* This analysis (surely the definitive statement of Niebuhr's position) starts interestingly enough with a psychological insight borrowed from Kierkegaard—to whom Carl Rogers, from a different angle, has also acknowledged a great debt.[3] The insight is that *anxiety* is "the internal pre-condition of sin . . . the inevitable spiritual state of man." Because of his borderline position, both part of nature as determined and above nature as free, man cannot help but be anxious. This is not sin, but it is a mighty *temptation* to sin. Self-love and pride are not the only forms of sin; they are attempts to overcome anxiety through trying to make one's self more secure than any finite creature can be. An opposite form of sin, also listed by Niebuhr, is *sensuality,* which tries to escape from the anxiety of selfhood by trying, like Walt Whitman, to go and be like the animals who are "not forever moaning about their sins." Beneath both these escape-reactions is a fundamental attitude of *unbelief*—unwillingness to trust God and accept his forgiving, empowering grace, which can overcome the threat of anxiety. Thus it is not strictly true to say that, for Niebuhr, self-love and pretension are the very root of sin. Beneath these and other prevalent forms of sin are anxiety and lack of faith in God—which, most observers agree, is intimately related to lack of faith in the human Other and in the Self. Is this doctrine so remote as it first seemed from Carl Rogers' emphasis upon the basic need of normal self-love and an "acceptance" rooted in agape?

Let us not be too hasty in our eagerness to reconcile these two antagonists. Their approach to the study of human nature and their major emphasis in describing it remain opposed. Carl Rogers takes such an "accepting" and "permissive" attitude toward his counselees that it appears to him as though their nature were fundamentally wholesome, needing only to be released from shackling external bonds in order to heal and save itself by its own internal powers. This at least leans in the direction of Pelagian self-salvation. Reinhold Niebuhr lays such stress upon the essential helplessness of man, and his utter dependence upon divine grace, fears complacency so like the very Devil, that he can cry, "Cursed be the man that putteth his trust in man!" Could any view be more opposed to Pelagian optimism than this new Augustinian pessimism? Yet because Niebuhr actually defines God's grace in terms that overlap with

[3] See Carl R. Rogers' Nellie Heldt Lectures, "Becoming a Person" (Oberlin, 1954), on Kierkegaard's doctrine of *choosing to be oneself* as the great antidote to despair.

Rogerian "acceptance," and because both have deep compassion upon man's anxiety as the deepest source of his distress, there is room for increased agreement if they should continue to converse. Why be discouraged by the first frustrated encounter?

## Discussion by HANS HOFMANN

I have been asked to comment upon Reinhold Niebuhr's *The Self and the Dramas of History* in the light of the remarks made by Carl R. Rogers. It is sometimes hard for an outsider like Rogers, not totally familiar with either the background or the present-day development in the theological and religious thinking, to appreciate Reinhold Niebuhr's stand and contribution. The undebatable and surely still most actual merit of Niebuhr's writing lies in his constant reminding that unwarranted and thus harmful optimism about the nature of man is just as unrealistic and hence fruitless as it would be to disregard the complexity of the human predicament and to deflate man to a mere sum total of deterministic mechanism and the consequent predictability of his development. Niebuhr is rightly sensitive to the danger that such a theological or so-called scientific understanding of man will lull us into being irresponsibly unaware of the creative and unguarded against the destructive abilities of human nature, which never conform totally with our philosophical presuppositions or experimentally gained premature conclusions.

He is, therefore, very keen to discern sharply the diverse factors which constitute the human self-appreciation and its paradoxical impact on the human participation in history. He sees a permanent and inevitable tension between human creativity and human enslavement to environmental conditions. These polar elements in the nature of the human self-awareness Niebuhr is unable to reconcile, but he believes them to be immensely essential, so much so that he dwells on this at every opportunity—even with the danger of falsifying the true picture or of making mistaken accusations. This may account for the embarrassing fact that as much as he lauds the Christian faith for fitting his own premises, he does not always tell us exactly what he means by Christian faith, nor does he give us sufficient impression that he is really intimately familiar with the secular aspects of the understanding of man to be in a position to pass his usually harsh judgments upon them. This creates certain problems of which we may briefly mention some.

We should never forget that in spite of Reinhold Niebuhr's ever-growing sensitivity to God's reality and activity through man in this world, which has provoked his interest in a more sweeping than precise understanding of history, he never really changed his primary if not exclusive interest in the nature and destiny of man. The book under discussion sharpens the foregoing thesis as none of his previous works had ever done.

It is not without significance that Niebuhr credits Martin Buber at the outset of his own book. Very much like Buber, Niebuhr would like to posit the human self as a unique agency in order to have it act and react in its environmental setting. But this is neither theologically nor scientifically proper or useful.

Theologically, the human self is constituted and kept alive by its experiencing itself as a unique and concrete life-expression of God's self-realization in this world. Not that God and man are thereby identified or indiscernibly merged. Nevertheless, whenever the human self is theoretically conceived as either apart from this God-man relationship or prior to it, then the Christian faith claims that we really speak of either an illusory or distorted self-awareness which, by postulating its independence, actually destroys it and, in turn, has the Promethean destructive influence to which Niebuhr is so eager to refer. The true selfhood of man lies in our grateful and joyful acknowledgment that through God's sovereign dwelling in us we are set free to build our own images—be they of ourself, the world, or of God.

Original sin is a theological term for that peculiar but constant temptation of man to establish his selfhood in competition with his true nature as it is given by God and as it can be fulfilled within its own appropriate limitations. Knowing this, Niebuhr is, at least, guilty of not making it expressly clear, which is evident in his utterly deficient understanding of the Holy Spirit.

From the same mistaken concept of the self stems his inability to differentiate clearly between sin as being exclusively the separation between God and man and its secondary symptoms in man's behavior. Only the latter can be phenomenologically investigated and subjected to any moral or ethical evaluation.

Self-love, if one should even continue to use this highly ambiguous

and misleading term, is not sin—original or otherwise. Nor is it a
mere bad habit of man. Niebuhr and other theologians could greatly
profit from listening patiently to psychopathologists who make clear
to us that undue self-concern is the symptom for a far more profound lack of self-realization and self-confidence. After we have
studied how this originates from not being appropriately or sufficiently loved, then we may be ready to reflect upon the theological
rootage of such a phenomenon.

When we formulate our theological or philosophical insights and
conclusions in scientific terms, then we run the risk of clashing with
the experimental scientists who may tell us that their findings contradict our conclusions. In turn, they should not be tempted to exceed phenomenological results and trespass with their own inadequate conclusions into spheres where the explanation of either
ultimate cause or future result is beyond the reach of their experimental means.

Basically, the controversy between the theologian, Niebuhr, and
the scientist, Rogers, arises where on the part of the scientist the
most fitting endeavor, to seek "for orderliness in man's inner nature or in his outer behavior," turns into wishful thinking that
knowledge and the proper use of it will in itself eliminate man's
need for a source and explanation of his life which is beyond himself. On the other hand, where the theologian is all too hasty to
prove the identity between theological concepts and truth, he is
tempted to blindly override better evidence instead of taking the
burden of rethinking his own premises.

Without question, there is an orderliness in the human psyche,
as much as it is constantly endangered by chaotic interference if not
destruction. It would be utterly obsolete even to discuss this were
it not for the fact that unlike stones and animals, human beings are
able to interfere with their own or others' psychic structure. The
fundamental reason for so doing may lie in a depth of which the
theologian is meant to speak. Its expression with its psychological
and environmental results is to be examined entirely objectively
by the scientist whose own philosophical presuppositions should be
recognized in order not to color unduly the evaluation of his own
findings.

One might simply state the paradox of man's being at once creature and creator as most indicative that where man's being creature relates to his real Creator, then the avenue is open for his creative enjoyment and the application of his gifts without abusing or distorting them to achieve the impossible, namely, to posit himself as autonomous, unrelated creator. The latter robs him of the freedom to discover and accept orderliness where it can be found since it may point to the humbling experience that any such orderliness is not authored by us, nor is it to be exploited by us irresponsibly for our own desires. True human freedom is inseparably linked to genuine and thus self-confident humility, which usually is least available where one is under the compulsion to prove himself and his own ideas.

Pastoral psychology can learn from Reinhold Niebuhr to be sensitive to the complexity of human nature and man's place in history, precisely since it is the place where God's wisdom is always above our thoughts but wants to reveal itself wherever we are open to the possibility of being enlightened and delighted by it. I cannot see at all why such a freedom should not allow us to be very unbiased students of secular understandings of man without falling prey either to their unconfessed philosophical premises or to sharing an equally unwarranted optimism or pessimism about man. The experience of those who do not derive their practical observations from preconceived theoretical notions, but conversely, realize the value of intellectual reflections and hypotheses on the basis of their concrete findings, has led them to seek a structured understanding of their insights. None the less, they are open to the challenge to abandon outworn premises and to restructure their understanding in the light of better evidence. Like the incarnate God, proved to be the true God, since man came truly alive through him; so the quiet and unobtrusive truth surprises us always where we expect and like it least, we, who are too much enamored of our own insights.

## Concluding Comment by CARL R. ROGERS

I find myself much informed by the wise and thoughtful comments of Walter M. Horton and Bernard M. Loomer. I am sure they are correct when they suggest that if I had a closer acquaintance with

Reinhold Niebuhr and with his other works, I would understand this book in a different way. They have helped me toward this understanding. I even found it interesting to learn that I am seen as a Pelagian. It is useful to know the labels for one's heresies.

I found myself less responsive to, and more puzzled by, Hans Hofmann's comments. I felt that in his world the scientist searches for the truth in the scientific area, and the theologian *has* the truth in the theological area. This must indeed be a comfortable world in which to live, but unfortunately for me, it is not the world I live in. Mine does not contain this built-in division, and I can see why he views me as an "outsider."

As to the major points at issue, I find three on which it might be helpful to present my own views. Horton, Loomer, and Hofmann agree that in his other and major writings Niebuhr sees an inevitable, permanent, irresolvable tension between the freedom and creativity of the individual on the one hand, and necessity, determinism, enslavement to environmental conditions, on the other. I trust they are correct in this understanding of Niebuhr's thinking. The book under review seemed to me to try to resolve this tension in ways which, as I pointed out, were unsatisfying to me.

If this *is* Niebuhr's view, then we are closer than I thought in our conception of this issue. I would only change the adjectives. I would say that the freedom of man, experienced so vividly in psychotherapy, and the determined nature of man's behavior, evident so clearly in psychological research, exist today in a currently almost unnoticed, but certainly unresolved tension. I do not know if the contradiction is inevitable, or whether it is permanent. I tried to hold a place for both these elements of truth in my symposium (or was it a debate?) with B. F. Skinner, when I spoke of

the great paradox of behavioral science. Behavior, when it is examined scientifically is surely best understood as determined by prior causation. This is one great fact of science. But responsible personal choice, which is the most essential element of being a person, which is the core experience in psychotherapy, which exists prior to any scientific endeavor, is an equally prominent fact in our lives. To deny the experience of responsible choice is, to me, as restricted a view as to deny the possibility of a behavioral science. That these two important elements of our experience appear to be in contradiction has perhaps the same significance as the contradiction between the wave theory and the corpuscular theory of light, both of which can be shown to be true, even though incompatible. We cannot profitably deny our subjective life, any more than we can deny the objective description of that life.[4]

I do not know the resolution of this paradox. Contrary to Loomer's perception of my position, I hold that it is the subjective choice which is prior, and that "we can choose to use the behavioral sciences in ways which will free, not control; which will bring about constructive variability, not conformity; which will develop creativity, not contentment; which will facilitate each person in his self-directed process of becoming; which will aid individuals, groups, and even the concept of science to become self-transcending in freshly adaptive ways of meeting life and its problems."[5] I point out that a deterministic behavioral science can lead in these directions if it clearly recognizes its fundamental basis in personal, existential choice, and if it places its emphasis upon the process of becoming, not upon the achievement of end states.

To take up another point, Loomer quite soundly raises the question as to why clients undervalue themselves. He will not be fully satisfied with my answer because it is not an absolute or theological answer. I can only report my thinking as far as my experience has carried me. The initial estrangement of the individual from himself —the experience which causes him to distrust and devalue himself, appears to follow this pattern. At some point the infant, to retain the love of his parent, takes over (introjects) the value placed on his experience by his parent, and deserts or distrusts his own organismic valuing of experience. This comes about because the love of his parent is conditional—"I will love you only if you place the same value [good or bad] on your experience that I do." As this distrusting of one's own valuing process is repeated countless times, the individual comes to distrust and scorn himself as a guide to life. All his criteria for attaching values to experience come confusedly from others. His feelings, which are the best index of his own valuing process, are denied to awareness, and he is now a man divided, estranged from self, or, to use the term I would be more likely to use, psychologically maladjusted. As one partial index to the ac-

[4] Carl R. Rogers & B. F. Skinner, "Some Issues concerning the Control of Human Behavior," *Science*, 1956, *124*, 1057-1066.
[5] *Ibid.*

curacy of this formulation, it appears clear that the more unconditional the love which the person has received as infant and child,
the more secure he is in trusting his own experiencing as a guide by
which to live, and the more creative is his adjustment. I am not sure
that this highly abbreviated statement of my views will do more than
create confusion, but readers may pursue the issue further in more
extended writings if they wish.[6]

Let me bring in one further aspect of my thinking. It disturbs
me to be thought of as an optimist. My whole professional experience has been with the dark and often sordid side of life, and I know,
better than most, the incredibly destructive behavior of which man
is capable. Yet that same professional experience has forced upon me
the realization that man, when you know him deeply, in his worst
and most troubled states, is not evil or demonic. I tried to express
this in a recent article.

The basic nature of the human being, when functioning freely, is constructive and trustworthy. For me this is an inescapable conclusion from a
quarter-century of experience in psychotherapy. When we are able to free
the individual from defensiveness, so that he is open to the wide range of
his own needs, as well as the wide range of environmental and social demands, his reactions may be trusted to be positive, forward-moving, constructive. We do not need to ask who will socialize him, for one of his own
deepest needs is for affiliation and communication with others. As he becomes more fully himself, he will become more realistically socialized. We
do not need to ask who will control his aggressive impulses; for as he becomes more open to all of his impulses, his need to be liked by others and
his tendency to give affection will be as strong as his impulses to strike out
or to seize for himself. He will be aggressive in situations in which aggression is realistically appropriate, but there will be no runaway need for
aggression. His total behavior, in these and other areas, as he moves toward
being open to all his experience, will be more balanced and realistic, behavior which is appropriate to the survival and enhancement of a highly
social animal.

I have little sympathy with the rather prevalent concept that man is
basically irrational, and that his impulses, if not controlled, will lead to
destruction of others and self. Man's behavior is exquisitely rational, moving with subtle and ordered complexity toward the goals his organism is en-
deavoring to achieve. The tragedy for most of us is that our defenses keep
us from being aware of this rationality, so that consciously we are moving in

[6] Carl R. Rogers, *Client-centered Therapy* (New York: Houghton-Mifflin, 1951),
chap. 11.

one direction, while organismically we are moving in another. But in our person who is living the process of the good life, there would be a decreasing number of such barriers, and he would be increasingly a participant in the rationality of his organism. The only control of impulses which would exist, or which would prove necessary, is the natural and internal balancing of one need against another, and the discovery of behaviors which follow the vector most closely approximating the satisfaction of all needs. The experience of extreme satisfaction of one need (for aggression, or sex, etc.) in such a way as to do violence to the satisfaction of other needs (for companionship, tender relationships, etc.) —an experience very common in the defensively organized person—would be greatly decreased. He would participate in the vastly complex self-regulatory activities of his organism—the psychological as well as physiological thermostatic controls—in such a fashion as to live in increasing harmony with himself and with others.[7]

It will be clear, I hope, that I have not tried to argue with Niebuhr or with those who have commented on my views of his work. I have simply tried to set forth my own tentative views on three issues which seem crucial to this whole discussion. The first is the issue of freedom and determinism, which phrases itself anew in every era, but with an urgency which never dims. The second is the issue as to the origin of man's difficulties—whether it is an original, inherent, "sin," or whether its source lies in man's human environment. The third is the question as to the basic characteristics of man. It is my hope that the reader will, from reading Niebuhr's book and the various comments which have flowed from it, find himself impelled to formulate his own thoughts on these issues.

[7] Carl R. Rogers, "A Therapist's View of the Good Life," *The Humanist*, 1957, No. 5.

# PART TWO

*Good and Evil in Man*

## CHAPTER 6

## *ROOTED AND GROUNDED IN LOVE*

HOWARD L. PARSONS

THE affirmation that men are by nature good and that love is the law of human life is an old affirmation. The Hindu and Chinese sages voiced it. And since the writers of Genesis first said that "God saw everything that he had made, and, behold, it was good," and "The Lord God said, it is not good that man should be alone," these thoughts of the goodness and unity of life run like a theme through the Bible and Western culture generally.

But just as shortly thereafter in the Genesis story the Devil enters to disrupt man's primal goodness and unity, so thinkers have proclaimed the darkness of evil and of destruction in the world. Today the affirmation of the Enlightenment—Goethe's "Howsoe'er it be, life is good," and the "fraternity" of the French Revolution—has been challenged by the denouncers of man and the prophets of doom: exponents of existentialism, neo-orthodoxy, and fascism. It is easy now as it always has been to point to the actual doings of men and declare: "Behold, brother is at the throat of brother; man is a wolf to man, and life is a war of all against each." Indeed, it does seem that the human ideals of goodness and unity are fantastic, heavenly dreams, masquerading as natural and achieved facts.

Recently, science has been telling us that these ideals are not a snare and a delusion, but are rooted in the most *real* of facts, ever present and universal. Perfectibility and universal benevolence, to use eighteenth-century terms, are grounded in the structure of human life itself. Progress and brotherhood, growth and integration —these, it develops, are not religious myths and tender-minded vagaries, but are abiding, pervasive, solid facts of our personal and social existence.

Recent books like Fromm's *Man For Himself,* Miller's *The Community of Man,* Overstreet's *The Mature Mind,* Montagu's *On Being Human,* Whyte's *The Next Development in Man,* Morris' *The Open Self,* and Wieman's *The Source of Human Good* have forcefully and scientifically brought to our attention the facts of human potentiality for good, and human unitedness. But these books are only the outflowering of a long, modern growth, initiated even before Kropotkin's *Mutual Aid* in 1902, which stated the case for co-operation in biological and evolutionary terms. Evidence now is literally pouring in from the biologists and social scientists asserting that men are not basically degraded or inherently hostile to one another but, insofar as they live, and live abundantly, insofar as they are distinctively human, they develop creatively and are members one of another.

This tradition of ideas affirming the creative oneness of mankind first appeared with clarity and vividness in the Hebrew culture, where the notion became eventually universalized from a tribal concept of brotherhood. It emerged in the Pythagorean philosophy, whence Plato transmitted it to the Stoics, who interpreted his concepts about human beings in broad, moral terms. Christianity, with roots in Hebraism, reacquired the ideal via the Greco-Roman culture. Then Humanism and the Enlightenment gave it the added depth of man's new-found rationality, and Romanticism enriched it with the fertile concepts of biology. The contemporary evidence, impelled by both the Enlightenment and Romanticism, simply extends these accumulated insights into the realm of the personal and interpersonal.

The new books, therefore, can seem striking only to one who is not familiar with this growing tradition. By the same token, the attacks on the ideas of human goodness and brotherhood are as old as the tradition, and are simply variations on an old theme—the pessimism that enters Hebrew literature at the time of the individualistic Exile, and today reappears as men find themselves frustrated, divided, and lonely.

At first glance it may seem that all pessimistic philosophies have been antinaturalistic, otherworldly philosophies. Such is not entirely the case—Schopenhauer and Sartre are exceptions. Nor, on the other hand, is it true that all supernaturalists oppose the notions of man's creativity and brotherhood—Jesus and Royce are exceptions. But there is probably a positive correlation between the notions of man's goodness and brotherhood, and the theory and method of naturalism. (The concept of "nature" has of course undergone many transformations in meaning.) Men once thought, and many still think, that mind and personality and their creative activity, along with the love of man for man, are mysteries passing man's natural understanding. For this reason Plato located them in the non-natural. But Locke's *Essay concerning Human Understanding* (1691) and Hume's *Treatise of Human Nature* (1739)—whose very titles bespeak their significance—are, as first attempts to treat human nature empirically, proofs of Plato's mistake. Contemporary studies, like Pearse and Crocker's *The Peckham Experiment, A Study in the Living Structure of Society* (1943), have carried the inquiry from the mainly introspective methods of those philosophers to careful observation, experiment, and control of human beings *in vivo*— that is, in everyday social relations. The experiment at Peckham, like the Menninger Clinic and many another such project, is the co-operative work of men and women in all the human sciences. The very undertaking of such projects implies not only that man is a part of nature and can be studied, but also that no important scientific study occurs unless there is unity among the scientists.

At this point the antinaturalists raise an objection. If brotherhood is "natural," then why is the life of man but a walking shadow in a vale of tears? "In the darkness with a great bundle of grief the people march." Not brotherhood, but conflict, hate, and war. Not goodness in the soul of man, but evil. These are the dominant "natural" facts: distrust, fear, and enmity, not faith, and hope, and love. Hence whatsoever is good and virtuous in man cannot be natural (since "nature" is so evil), but must be sought beyond, outside the natural man.

So runs the continental divide between Sartre, Niebuhr, Eliot, and Hitler on the one side, and Dewey, Wieman, Neruda, and Nehru on the other. The natural man is either good or bad, altruistic or egoistic, creative or destructive. Man is either at home here, or an alien; his environment is either a help or a hindrance, it either can be controlled by man for his enjoyment, or stands over against him as an intractable enemy. Whether natural man is viewed as good or evil depends partly on how nature in the large is thought of.

Two other important corollaries follow. The first is theological. God, for the naturalists, is a helpful, beneficent companion, while for the antinaturalists God is a wrathful, merciless judge, sometimes even a kind of Caliban's sadistic deity. It appears that as less is imputed to man, life, and nature, more is imputed to a *deus ex natura* to balance things, to supply the values that nature lacks, or to overcome the evils by which she is beset. The fact that naturalists claim to discover God in nature does not necessarily mitigate the power and goodness of God; further, the concept of God is less apt to be a purely psychological compensation if it refers to something observable in nature.

Similarly, naturalists tend to be democrats, believing that people potentially good can govern, educate, adjust, and help "save" themselves; whereas the antinaturalists tend to be authoritarians, holding that citizens, students, the maladjusted, and the lost are incapable of self-direction, and require arbitrary authorities not so much to make them better as to keep them from getting worse. The latter are conservatives, not wanting to exchange the precarious and hard-won goods of history today for the dubious experiments of a stupid and sinful populace tomorrow. The naturalists, by contrast, are forward-looking and believe in change, transformation, and growth, trusting to what the Quakers call the "seed" of the spirit in every man. From their ranks come most of the radicals and reformers.

This conflict is an old one. It is symbolized in the differences between men like Arius and Athanasius, Pelagius and Augustine, Abelard and Anselm, Erasmus and Luther, Locke and Hobbes, Paine and Burke, Mill and Newman, Wieman and Niebuhr. The pessimists have contended that (1) man is depraved, and (2) values, which reside beyond this depraved world, cannot be determined by man's natural inquiry but must be determined by some non-natural method such as the Bible, revelation, special intuition, or an élite whose power is beyond question. The good life has thus come to be both interpreted and administered by the chosen few—chosen by the grace of hereditary power, political intrigue, luck, unique opportunity, and the like. But in practice it has turned out to be very natural forces operating which have determined the values of a given culture, rather than the Bible or revelation.

With the rise of the biological and social sciences these authoritarian claims with regard to values received, paradoxically, added weight. Darwin, Freud, Frazer, and their immediate successors showed that values are *relative* to the biological organism in its particular cultural environment. But for the popular mind this conclusion simply reinforced the belief that the "absolute" is beyond history. Nietzsche's "God is dead," and Marx's "I despise all the gods" express the academic reaction against supernaturalistic absolutism. Yet it was in the same period that new, naturalistic value-systems took their rise: the various socialisms including the "scientific socialism" of Marx and Engels, and the nonscientific absolutisms of protofascists like Carlyle and Gobineau.

This relativism in theory of value reflected and sanctioned the *laissez-faire* chaos of the nineteenth century. In the same way that the weekdays were divided off from Sunday for the Victorians, so the hard facts of business and science were divided off from the ineffable religious values of life and personality. The doctrine of economic relativism not only bolstered exploitive business practices; it also satisfied the churches, whose ministers could go unquestioned in preaching, without responsibility to fact, the divinely revealed absolutes of the Bible as over against the less fortunate, though still immoral, Chinese and Polynesians. Where a minister dared apply these absolutes to the relativities of business practice, he was told as was Mr. Gruffydd (the minister in *How Green Was My Valley*) when he suggested to the exploited Welsh miners that they form a union: "Are you coming outside your position in life? Your business is spiritual."

But relativism in the social sciences (and hence in the science of value) has slowly given way, first to agnosticism regarding values, and now, to cautious, tentative formulations looking toward a genuine body of scientific knowledge about universal value. (The term "absolute" need not mean anything more than what, according to men's best natural knowledge here and now, is the most important value for human living on this planet.) As an illustration of this change of attitude, while Freud and his associates tended to think of personality in mechanical and negative terms, the second generation of psychoanalysts, notably Sullivan, Fromm, and Horney, viewed personality as possessed with essentially positive, dynamically creative and constructive powers. As Sullivan put it: "People strive however blindly toward mental health."

It is now possible for those who believe in the unity and goodness of man to answer the pessimists in scientific terms. In times past they were forced to appeal to the "image of God," the "divine spark," the "inner light," "God-given rights," "natural rights," the "vital force," and so on. But today they need do no more than cite the studies of the Yale Clinic of Child Development for evidence to support their view that people possess a tremendous capacity for good—for creative growth in human relations. The ancient question, Is man good or bad? is no longer a matter for unresolved dispute between men of varying temperamental biases, vested interests, emotional concerns, political creeds, religious sects, and the like. It has been passed over to the scientists for determination. The pessimists have virtually lost the battle of whether man can be studied by naturalistic tools of inquiry. The second question—whether values are open to human study—is being answered in the affirmative. The scientists are looking on what man *can* make of man, and are calling it good.

But they do not thereby deny that man can and does under certain circumstances *become* evil. Some scientists, such as Freud, have gone so far as to despair that men in the mass will ever achieve a common life of peaceful and productive brotherhood. Even in the most advanced countries of the world they are able to point to world wars, recurrent economic depressions, and widespread neuroses as evidences of man's failure. Undoubtedly, for the mass of men, over one billion of whom today lack the bare minimum of physical necessities, life is and has been throughout the ages "solitary, poor, hasty, brutish, and short." In their appeals to the supernatural the pessimists capitalize upon this misery of mankind which persists with such tragic stubbornness. But while man's inhumanity to man, his lovelessness and loneliness, are facts writ large in human history, they are not necessary components of man's nature. They are what happens to man when his human nature is misdirected and deformed. They are not inborn but are acquired, and they are acquired at the expense of his *human* nature.

What is that human nature? What is it that makes us distinctively human? In a phrase, it is our unique capacities for growth. These capacities are manifest in the facts of human interaction—in the fact that a dependent, highly sensitive and responsive, unspecialized organism is born into a co-operative unit, the family, and in the fact that for survival co-operative interaction is necessary. The results of the interaction between baby and family are truly profound. Given even a minimum of care and attention, the skill of communication begins to emerge in the human infant, affording him a powerful tool for relating himself in progressively satisfying ways to his environment, particularly his environment of other persons. He thereby learns intelligence and love, for he learns to solve problems and to co-operate with others.

Language is the main tool by which he grows. By it he feels what others feel, guides his experiences in the satisfaction of needs, controls himself and others, plans and chooses, and apprehends the perspectives of the far-distant Plato and the contemporary L'il Abner. To be truly human, to have mind and personality, is to be united in ties of sympathy and understanding to others, for we are indeed "members one of another." The baby does not merely conform to the world, but is transformed according to the creation of its mind in its active relations with the social world. This creative process is not entirely of man's doing or in his control—in this sense it is "nonhuman" but still quite natural, open to observation and human assistance.

It is this process which transforms the raw, unsocialized, unhumanized baby into the unique integrate called personality; and personality is, so to speak, a knot of diverse social strands, creatively united. This creative activity makes us human. It makes our natures. Therefore any other characteristics of human beings—such as original sin, anxiety, pride, pugnacity, power, sex, etc.—although widespread and even universal, and although claimed as the ultimate in man's nature—must by this description be secondary and derivative. Such characteristics are deviations from the human norm, do not define man's nature and destiny, and indeed could not exist save for the prior creation of the personality. Thus, as Augustine said, evil is a privation of the good; it depends on the good, for apart from the healthy, integrated structures of the good there could be no neuroses or indeed psychoses.

That we love one another is the law of human life. The works of

Cooley, Mead, Follett, Dewey, to mention only a few, amply support this fact. Jesus made it plain in a less discursive way, by speaking penetrating parables about human relations. The claims that love is not the law of our beings usually fail to consider such evidence, or give undue weight to the established facts of evil. Pessimists tend to consider only one life, or a few (think of the suicidal), rather than the generic character of all human life; they confuse the accidental with the fundamental, because the fundamental, being, like oxygen, ever present, is not apt to be noticed. They may admit that a light shines in the darkness. But like Niebuhr they are so depressed by the drag of evil, usually identified with "nature" or, as in Niebuhr's case, with man's selfish abuse of his idealizing capacity, that they are forced to say that the kingdom of God is a light that never was, on land or sea.

Consequently, they argue, men ought to be restrained, religiously as well as politically, by certain authorities until such time as they will be ruled by love—a time that is not a time, because it is not in history. But considering the great poverty and ignorance of the centuries it is not surprising that such theories of human depravity should have prevailed. As poverty and ignorance have been relieved, optimism has increased. The Greeks, although enlightened, lamented the fateful force of destiny; but Bacon, two thousand years later, could take a sanguine view of man's control of nature by obedience to her laws. After all, it has been less than a century since Lister and Pasteur first established empirically the germ theory of disease; and we should not expect too rapid a progress in the pathology of personalities and cultures.

Our natures are so constructed and normally so develop, that our deepest need is for love and growth. When we love and are loved, then we may grow in wisdom and stature; and as we grow we are better able to love. ("That ye being rooted and grounded in love, may be able to comprehend with all saints what is the breadth, and length, and depth, and height.") The process described by H. N. Wieman, which includes both love and growth, is "creative interaction"—rightfully called God. It issues in richer and finer forms of integration in personality and interpersonal relations. Each human being possesses capacities for achieving creative relations with his environment, relations of progressively deepening and widening mutuality in thought, feeling, and action. The disorders of mind and body and society are not innate in man's nature. They are disorders precisely because there existed some prior order to be disturbed. They are, as Virchow would say, normal responses of normal organisms to abnormal environments.

It is idle to argue that the source of evil lies within the newborn infant. Of course there are occasional constitutional defects. (Mall says that of one hundred human pregnancies, about one [.06] produces a monster at term.) But if disease, physical, mental, and social, is a normal response to an abnormal environment, a method of accommodating to an unfavorable environment—then the source of psychic evil is rather in the human environment into which the baby moves and which is unfit to sustain it in healthy development.

But parents who provide the formative environment for children fail to provide the creative environment not because they are born evil but rather because, as children themselves, their potentially creative resources have been diverted to defending themselves against a hostile environment. Their consequent inmaturity, with these infantile defenses now become habitual, visits its iniquity upon the children unto the third and fourth generation. Such evil is the function of a *normal* organism, with great capacities for sensitivity and responsiveness. Simpler or less sensitive organisms respond to an unfavorable environment with simple, automatic mechanisms.

Even in our disordered moments we are all, in Sullivan's happy phrase, "much more simply human than otherwise." Understood in their origins our aggressions and withdrawals are no more mysterious than chills and fever. These disorders were once (and in some regions still are) thought to be the work of the Devil or of some other supernatural power. The origins of psychic disorders are crucial interpersonal relations, whether infantile or adult. Further, human disorder is always set within the larger context or social order, and derives meaning from that social order—just as dreams, which appear so disorderly, display an underlying order explainable by reference to the normal social order of personality and culture.

As Horney puts it, neurosis is the attempt of the personality to cope with the conflicts that arise in its interpersonal relations. There seems to be a sort of moral or social sense ("awareness" is perhaps a better word) native to the individual, although conditioned by his

particular culture; and illness seems to occur when this delicate
needle of orientation is damaged and the personality loses its way.

Much physical disease and virtually all psychic illness are the
outcomes of failures in social relations. One-third of a nation (not
to mention more than one-half of a world) is ill-fed, ill-clothed, and
ill-housed because the other two-thirds do not love them sufficiently
to so arrange the economic and political order as to get them fed,
clothed, and housed. One out of ten people in this country suffer
severe mental illness because their fellow human beings in family,
neighborhood, school, and church have failed to provide those relations of trust and love, of security and freedom, necessary to healthy
development. They have supplied rather mistrust and hostility, insecurity and constriction. Under such conditions, as Kunkel says, a
person must either commit suicide or go psychotic. The will to grow
cannot be repeatedly thwarted without some kind of rebellion; and
since people have different constitutions and dispositions, they will
rebel in different ways—some by rapid changes in mood, some by
aggression, some by withdrawal.

By contrast, the creative man is he who has not lost the capacity
to yearn with his whole being for richer unities with his environment. He thereby grows "from glory unto glory." He does not rejoice in injustice, but rejoices in the truth. In him the drive for
integrity is dominant. He is his brother's keeper; and he may say:
"Every man's death diminishes me, for I am involved in mankind."

For we are bound by ties not merely to our families and friends,
but to the society of mankind. Where does our brotherhood begin,
where does our responsibility cease? When the bell tolls for one it
tolls for all. Of every soul broken by mental illness we may say:
"There but for the grace of God go I." Yet part of me does go there.
All that we are, all that we may hope to be, we owe to our relations
to others. The debt of goodness which we owe to others because
of their doings and sufferings is at best felt only dimly, and discharged only partially. It is apparent in our sense of duty, which
moves a man to lay down his life for his friend. "Freely give, as you
have freely received."

But more: personalities are functions of bodies; and bodies need
food, clothes, and houses for their health; and the accessibility of
food and clothes and houses depends on jobs and prices and wages;

and these in turn depend on the economic and political systems in which people live. How can a man say: "This for Sunday, and this for weekdays. This for religion, and this for politics"? Life is one. A man cannot love God and hate his brother any more than he can pay lip service to peace and support senators who abet war in international relations. Precisely because life is one and is interpenetrated with the law of love, no man can serve two masters.

But if a society is split into warring factions, then a man, its child and microcosm, will also be split. A house divided against itself cannot stand, nor can a personality. Every man is born with the divine light of integrity; it is the law of his various members to grow, "forgetting those things which are behind, and reaching forth unto those things which are before." It is his need to be whole—to be reborn progressively into a new man. But how may he be whole if his society is not whole? The man and the group interlock. If there be conflict, segregation, isolation in one, they will reflect themselves in the other.

Since each affects all, as all each, none can enjoy health and growth unless all do; none can rise if but one falls. Our destinies are indivisible. The hunger and the sorrow that prevail are evils not merely for particular men; they are the deaths of all. A world dismembered cannot long stand. Better it is that a member perish, than that the whole die in the hellfire of chaos. The healing of individuals needs the healing of the nations. And the healing of the nations can begin only when the total fabric of our common lives is transformed strand by strand, throughout family and neighborhood, school and church, factory and farm, office and senate, into a seamless web—a unified pattern that will serve the more abundant life of love and growth for all.

Only then will the seed sprout, the light shine, the promise rise to fulfillment. Only then will men achieve what by their natures they can become. Only then, although for centuries we have seen as in a glass darkly, only then will we see our true selves face to face. Fear and hate, which perfect love casts out, will die away. What was lost will be found, and what was hid will be revealed. Men will then live together in brotherhood, neither will they learn war any more.

# CHAPTER 7

## A CREDIBLE DOCTRINE OF MAN[1]

### WILLARD L. SPERRY

HOWARD L. PARSONS' paper, "Rooted and Grounded in Love," was bound to start a discussion. Perhaps he intended just that. It is, at the moment, the theological fashion to think badly of human nature. One must admit that there is, in the history of these last years, much warrant for thinking thus. An English essayist has recently said that the religious question is no longer whether we can believe in God, but whether and to what degree we can continue to believe in man.

Parsons cites Kropotkin's *Mutual Aid* as a warrant for his thesis that it is the nature of living creatures to co-operate with one another. He then goes on to say that evidence is now pouring in from biologists and sociologists to confirm this fact. He is still somewhat in advance of the facts if he assumes that the case for co-operation vs. competition has been universally decided in favor of the former. It should be pointed out that this mutual aid in the animal kingdom seems to operate for the "in-group" of a single species. It does not extend to the "out-group" of other species. Homo sapiens is presumably a single species, but for practical purposes he is divided into in-groups on political, racial, social, economic, and religious bases.

Parsons is quite right in adding that the Quakers trust the "seed" of the spirit in every man. The mystics have always rested their case upon confidence in the *Fünklein*—the divine spark—in our hu-

[1] This chapter by the late Dean Willard L. Sperry is a discussion of the preceding chapter by Howard L. Parsons, "Rooted and Grounded in Love" and the critical comments which this article evoked upon publication. *Ed.*

manity. John 1:5, according to the King James translation, says that the darkness has not comprehended this spark of light. A more accurate translation should read, "the darkness has not been able to put it out." Classical Christian mysticism is, therefore, on Parsons' side, and most of us think that the mystics were more nearly right than wrong. But it must be added at once that this mysticism is not to be identified with modern naturalism.

In general, Parsons identifies himself with the now rather outmoded and unfashionable liberalism which was the order of the day from the mid-eighteenth century until the onset of World War I. In view of the events which have intervened in these later years, that liberalism seems, in retrospect, a little too good to be true. Lord Bryce, the greatest of the champions of modern democracy, said in lectures delivered at Yale in 1909 that after one hundred and fifty years of experimental democracy there was "a painful contrast between that which the theory of democracy requires and that which the practice of democracy reveals." Man had not measured up to the vote of confidence which the founding fathers of our democracy had vested in him; he had not turned out as good a person as the dogma presupposed. There is no doubt that our conventional liberalism, whether in politics or in theology, had overbid its hand. Even those of us who continue to call ourselves liberal, because we feel that this position has permanent values which cannot be destroyed by tragic happenings in history, and that the position is worth holding against a better time, feel that our doctrinal overconfidence in man needs sober reconsideration and perhaps a more realistic restatement.

At the same time we are aware of a similar element of overstatement in the theological reaction of those who fall back, rather than fall forward, upon neo-orthodoxy. There would seem to be in religious circles a kind of pathological glee in confessing our inherently sinful nature. Contemporary acts of penitence have an almost masochistic quality. The revival of the ancient idea of our innate sinfulness still seems to lack concrete moral content. R. J. Campbell in his *New Theology* said many years ago that we get down on our knees on Sunday and confess that we are miserable sinners, but that if someone actually accuses us on Monday of being sinners, we ask him to particularize and then probably sue him for slander. Leslie

Stephen said much the same thing in a comment on Jonathan Edwards' statement that every little child born into the world is more hateful to God than the most loathsome viper that crawls on the ground: "Nevertheless Edwards seems to have had a very happy time of it in the midst of a brood of eleven little vipers of his own begetting." Much of our modern neo-orthodox celebration of our sinful natures seems to me to reveal the same paradox. It should be added, however, that if the case is appealed from the theologian to the anthropologist, the sociologist and, in particular, to the psychologist, a stubborn moral malaise seems to persist. Thus one of our Harvard anthropologists has said that while scientists no longer believe in "sin," they have to recognize in most human beings a baffling "guilt feeling" which is something more than a matter of social maladjustment. The accepted modern term is little more than a new name for an old and deep awareness of a profound unhappiness.

I wonder: is Parsons right in seeming to suggest that there is any uniform vindication of the love of man for man, running through the Bible? Such a theory is undoubtedly proposed as an ideal, but biblical practice often falls far short of it. Many of the most tender psalms are punctuated by the most unloving passages. The author of Psalm 139 says that there are those whom he hates with a perfect hatred. So, again, the exile by the waters of Babylon concludes his lovely lines with a celebration of the happiness of those who dash the little ones of Babylon against the stones. I have never been able to feel that such passages are the voice of a purely dispassionate and holy anger, and if they are vicariously spoken in God's behalf then the God who is invoked is all that the conception of a loving God would seem to require. So, again, the Hebrew prophets give vent to moods of vengefulness and hatred which are only human, all too human. The "yelp of the beast" as Tennyson calls it, can be heard in a disquietingly large number of Bible passages. The truth is that "biblical theology" is far from being the uniform and consistent system which its advocates seem to assume that it is.

I find myself by tradition and temperament in sympathy with much that Parsons has said. If what he says is not yet fully true, it ought ideally to be true. But with the mystics I should have to fall back upon a realm at least other-than-natural, in the common usage of the term, to account for the divine, slumbering spark of life in man. I doubt if the case for love can be made on a purely naturalistic basis, which excludes all reference to what is commonly called the supernatural. F. W. H. Myers was once asked, "If you could ask the Sphinx one question and only one, what would that question be?" He said, "If I could ask the Sphinx one question and only one, and hope for an answer, I think the question would be this, 'Is the universe friendly?' " Failure to ask that question, due to a parochial and provincial religious concern for man-as-man, leads to studied agnosticism in such matters and has always seemed to me to fall short of that which any adequate theory of religion requires. Men may eventually succeed in loving one another, but the question still remains whether this virtue is a lonely racial achievement without warrant or counterpart in the environing universe. Christianity believes that we love God and neighbor because God first loved us.

Protestant theology needs nothing so much today as agreement upon a credible doctrine of man. The hope of arriving at any such doctrine may rest upon the outcome of the clash between orthodoxy, old and new, and our conventional liberalism. They may have to fight it out between them. Meanwhile, there is no doubt that this issue gives zest to life in a seminary study or classroom. Whether or not the layman understands what is at stake, or indeed cares theoretically for the outcome, he will continue to beget his little vipers or his little saints, as the case may be. His practical problem is whether human nature is running true to form, or not, when it is employed in devising and dropping bigger and better bombs. If he is basically a person who loves his fellows how did he get, corporately, so far off the track? If he is running true to his form as a sinner, is there any "power not himself which makes for righteousness" that can save him from himself?

Alfred North Whitehead used to speak of the "vice of oversimplification." All those who live a reflective life are liable to that vice, since the mind always seeks some unified account of things. In moments when we seem to be in danger of oversimplifying this problem of the true nature of man it does no harm to revert to Pascal's account of human nature, merely for the sake of realizing how complex the problem is and how contradictory the facts are. Thus, in his *Thoughts* on "The Greatness and Littleness of Man," Pascal says,

In measure as men possess the light, the more they discern both the great-ness and littleness of man. In a word man knows he is little. He is then little because he is so; but he is truly great because he knows it. . . . What chimera then is man! how strange and monstrous! a chaos, a contradiction, a prodigy. Judge of all things, yet a weak earthworm; depository of truth, yet a cesspool of uncertainty and error; the glory and offscouring of the Universe. . . . Know then, proud man, how great a paradox thou art to thy-self.

Pascal's paradoxes are baffling; they do not seem to make sense. But they are curiously like our own self-consciousness, and at least they escape the vice of oversimplification.

# CHAPTER 8

# THE NATURE OF MAN[1]

## CARL R. ROGERS

MY VIEWS of man's most basic characteristics have been formed by my experience in psychotherapy. They include certain observations as to what man is *not*, as well as some description of what, in my experience, he *is*. Let me state these very briefly and then endeavor to clarify my meanings.

I do not discover man to be well characterized in his basic nature by such terms as fundamentally hostile, antisocial, destructive, evil.

I do not discover man to be, in his basic nature, completely without a nature, a *tabula rasa* on which *anything* may be written, nor malleable putty which can be shaped into *any* form.

I do not discover man to be essentially a perfect being, sadly warped and corrupted by society.

In my experience I have discovered man to have characteristics which seem inherent in his species, and the terms which have at different times seemed to me descriptive of these characteristics are such terms as positive, forward-moving, constructive, realistic, trustworthy.

Let me see if I can take the discussion of these points of view into a fresh area where perhaps we have somewhat fewer preconceived biases. Suppose we turn to the animal world and ask ourselves what is the basic nature of the lion, of the sheep, of the dog, or of the mouse. To say that any one of these is basically hostile or antisocial

[1] This statement by Carl R. Rogers, published originally in the *Journal of Counseling Psychology*, Fall, 1957, represents a reply to an article by Professor Donald E. Walker of San Diego State College on "Carl Rogers and the Nature of Man," which appeared in the Summer, 1956, issue of the same journal, in which Walker stresses the similarity of the philosophy of Carl R. Rogers to Rousseau and its dissimilarity to the philosophy of Sigmund Freud. *Ed.*

or carnal seems to be ridiculous. To say that we view their nature as neutral means either that it is neutral in terms of some unspecified set of values, or that their natures are all alike, all putty waiting to receive a shape. This view seems to me equally ridiculous. I maintain that each has a basic nature, a common set of attributes generally characteristic of the species. Thus, the sheep is by far the most gregarious or group-minded, the mouse the most generally timorous. No amount of training—therapeutic or otherwise—will make a lion out of the mouse, or vice versa, even though a wide degree of change is possible. There is a basic substratum of species characteristics which we will do well to accept.

We might take a closer look at some of those characteristics. Since the lion has the most pronounced reputation for being a "ravening beast," let us choose him. What are the characteristics of his common nature, his basic nature? He kills an antelope when he is hungry, but he does not go on a wild rampage of killing. He eats his fill after the killing, but there are no obese lions on the veldt. He is helpless and dependent in his puppyhood, but he does not cling to the dependent relationship. He becomes increasingly independent and autonomous. In the infant state he is completely selfish and self-centered, but as he matures he shows, in addition to such impulses, a reasonable degree of co-operativeness in the hunt. The lioness feeds, cares for, protects, and seems to enjoy her young. Lions satisfy their sexual needs, but this does not mean they go on wild and lustful orgies. His various tendencies and urges come to a continually changing balance in himself, and in that sense he is very satisfactorily self-controlled and self-regulated. He is in basic ways a constructive, a trustworthy member of the species *Felis leo*. His fundamental tendencies are in the direction of development, differentiation, independence, self-responsibility, co-operation, maturity. In general the expression of his basic nature makes for the continuation and enhancement of himself and his species.

With the appropriate variations, the same sort of statements could be made about the dog, the sheep, the mouse. To be sure each behaves in ways which from some specific point of view are destructive. We wince to see the lion kill the antelope; we are annoyed when the sheep eats our garden; we complain when the mouse eats the cheese we were saving for our picnic; I regard the dog as destructive when he bites me, a stranger; but surely none of these behaviors justifies us in thinking of any of these animals as basically evil. If I endeavored to explain to you that if the "lionness" of the lion or the "sheepness" of the sheep were to be released, these animals would then be impelled by insatiable lusts, uncontrollable aggressions, wild and excessive sexual behaviors, and tendencies of innate destructiveness, you would quite properly laugh at me. Obviously, such a view is pure nonsense.

I would like now to consider again the nature of man in the light of this discussion of the nature of animals. I have come to know men most deeply in a relationship which is characterized by all that I can give of safety, absence of threat, and complete freedom to be and to choose. In such a relationship men express all kinds of bitter and murderous feelings, abnormal impulses, bizarre and antisocial desires. But as they live in such a relationship, expressing and being more of themselves, I find that man, like the lion, has a nature. My experience is that he is a basically trustworthy member of the human species, whose deepest characteristics tend toward development, differentiation, co-operative relationships; whose life tends fundamentally to move from dependence to independence; whose impulses tend naturally to harmonize into a complex and changing pattern of self-regulation; whose total character is such as to tend to preserve and enhance himself and his species, and perhaps to move it toward its further evolution. In my experience, to discover that an individual is truly and deeply a unique member of the human species is not a discovery to excite horror. Rather, I am inclined to believe that fully to be a human being is to enter into the complex process of being one of the most widely sensitive, responsive, creative, and adaptive creatures on this planet.

So when a Freudian such as Karl Menninger tells me (as he has, in a discussion of this issue) that he perceives man as "innately evil," or more precisely, "innately destructive," I can only shake my head in wonderment. It leads me to all kinds of perplexing questions. How could it be that Menninger and I, working with such a similar purpose in such intimate relationships with individuals in distress, experience people so differently? Perhaps these deep differences do not matter if the therapist really cares for his patient or client. But how can the analyst feel a positive caring for his patient, if his own innate tendency is to destroy? And even if his own destructive tendencies were properly inhibited and controlled by *his* analyst, who controlled the destructiveness of *that* analyst? And so on ad infinitum.

It will be clear that my experience provides no evidence for believing that if the deepest elements in man's nature were released we would have an uncontrolled and destructive id unleashed in the world. To me this makes as little sense as to say that the "lionness" of the lion would be an evil thing. I respect the men who hold such views, but I find no evidence in my experience to support them. I stand by a statement made in an earlier paper, "A Therapist's View of the Good Life":

> I have little sympathy with the rather prevalent concept that man is basically irrational, and that his impulses, if not controlled, will lead to destruction of others and self. Man's behavior is exquisitely rational, moving with subtle and ordered complexity toward the goals his organism is endeavoring to achieve. The tragedy for most of us is that our defenses keep us from being aware of this rationality, so that consciously we are moving in one direction, while organismically we are moving in another. But in our person who is living the process of the good life there would be a decreasing number of such barriers, and he would be increasingly a participant in the rationality of his organism. The only control of impulses which would exist or which would prove necessary is the natural and internal balancing of one need against another, and the discovery of behaviors which follow the vector most closely approximating the satisfaction of all needs. The experience of extreme satisfaction of one need (for aggression, or sex, etc.) in such a way as to do violence to the satisfaction of other needs (for companionship, tender relationships, etc.)—an experience very common in the defensively organized person—would be greatly decreased. He would participate in the vastly complex self-regulatory activities of his organism—the psychological as well as physiological thermostatic controls—in such a fashion as to live in increasing harmony with himself and with others.[2]

I have puzzled as to the reasons for the wide discrepancy between the Freudian view of man's nature and that which has seemed justified by experience in client-centered therapy. I have two hypotheses which I should like to present for consideration, though they may seem shocking to devoted followers of psychoanalysis.

First, it appears to me that Freud was understandably very much excited by his discovery—a tremendous discovery for his time—that beneath a conventional or "good" exterior, man harbored all kinds

[2] *The Humanist*, No. 5, 1957.

of aggressive and sexual feelings and impulses which he had success-fully hidden from himself as well as from others. This discovery was shocking to the culture of that period and hence both his critics and Freud himself focused on the "evil" feelings in man which lay be-neath the surface. This continued to be the focus even though Freud's own experience with his patients must have shown him that once these "evil" feelings were known, accepted, and understood by the individual, he could be trusted to be a normally self-controlled, socialized person. In the furor of the controversy over psychoanalysis this latter point was overlooked, and Freud settled for what is, in my estimation, a too-superficial view of human nature. It was of course a much more deeply informed view than that held by his contempo-raries, but it was not so profound a concept as his own experience would have justified.

My second hypothesis would explain why Freud did not assimilate this deeper meaning which he might have perceived in the therapy he carried on. It has been my experience that although clients can, to some degree, independently discover some of their denied or re-pressed feelings, they cannot on their own achieve full emotional acceptance of these feelings. It is only in a caring relationship that these "awful" feelings are first fully accepted by the therapist and can then be accepted by the client. Freud in his self-analysis was de-prived of this warmly acceptant relationship. Hence, although he might come to know and to some extent to understand the hidden and denied aspects of himself, I question whether he could ever come to accept them fully, to embrace them as a meaningful, acceptable, and constructive part of himself. More likely he continued to per-ceive them as unacceptable aspects of himself—enemies, whom knowing he could control—rather than as impulses which, when ex-isting freely in balance with his other impulses, were constructive. At any rate I regard this as a hypothesis worthy of consideration. It does not, I admit, explain why his followers have continued to accept his view.

In closing I would like to agree with Walker that the view the therapist holds of human nature does have consequences in his ther-apy. Hence I believe it is important for each therapist to abstract for himself from his own experience those trends or tendencies which seem most deeply characteristic of the human being. I have indicated that for myself man appears to be an awesomely complex creature who can go very terribly awry, but whose *deepest* tendencies make for his own enhancement and that of other members of his species. I find that he can be trusted to move in this constructive direction when he lives, even briefly, in a nonthreatening climate where he is free to choose any direction.

# CHAPTER 9

## MODERN PSYCHOLOGY
## AND MORAL VALUES

NOEL MAILLOUX

I AM going to talk about the struggle of a conscience trying to assert itself in the growing man, and to describe the way it functions in the mature man. But before I do that I would like to clear away some misconceptions about modern psychology and moral values.

Being born in a so-called age of science, modern psychology was confronted with a distorted picture of moral values—distorted by minds confused by decades of materialistic thinking. It was then impossible for modern psychology to approach the study of good and evil as affecting human behavior without being biased by current prejudices. However, it is most comforting to observe how these prejudices are crumbling one after the other as more adequate and precise knowledge about the motivation of conduct is accumulated.

It has now become possible, on a strictly empirical basis, to straighten out those distortions which still prevail and which still disturb the peace of those who are sincerely convinced that Christian belief can be reconciled with scientific conclusions.

Undoubtedly empirical science has recently made a brilliant contribution to the understanding of how a moral conscience is born in the individual and how the individual progressively acquires genuine moral values. Because of this new understanding, psychology has been able to liberate itself from the fetters of biologicophysical frames of reference, which did not apply in this specific realm, and which hampered for far too long the correct understanding of mature moral behavior. Let me here mention just a few of these which are now being confined to their proper sphere of application.

First, the principle of determinism. Usually this was formulated in

97

mechanistic terms—it was the theory that everything one does is determined by forces which are independent of the will. But it has been modified by contemporary psychologists, to the point of embracing self-determination, that is, free will. It has finally been understood that the alternative to psychic determinism is not freedom but its opposite, namely indeterminacy, chaos, and unpredictability in human behavior. Now it is widely recognized that when it is affirmed that human acts are determined, this means precisely, not that these acts have a necessary cause, but that they necessarily have a cause which may well be a deliberate, free, autonomous decision.

Another distortion which can now be straightened out is that moral laws can be formulated in the same way as physical laws. We know now that this is not so. Even if the curve of normal distribution, let us say, offers a reasonably satisfactory frame for arriving at a physical law, it is no sufficient basis for the establishment of moral law. Statistical frequencies can no more be regarded as normative principles of conduct than statistical correlations can replace a dynamic or causal interpretation of it. There will be less confusion in the modern approach to the study of values when it becomes quite clear that what men generally do is not a valid criterion to determine what they should do or what it would be most reasonable for them to do. Then, also, scientists will not continue to encourage parents to rear their children in conformity with transient social standards entirely devoid of compelling obligation, and to be satisfied with this so-called adaptation or adjustment to reality as a substitute for moral virtues.

Finally, we were confronted with the amazing assumption that the categories of right and wrong were to be replaced by the categories of rational and irrational. This led again to the old confusion between "being normal" and "being moral." A few centuries ago it was all too common for people to regard insanity as a sign of diabolical depravity. In the same way, in our period of enlightenment, scientific authorities did not hesitate to proclaim that right and honest behavior as well as human happiness derived immediately from mental equilibrium and emotional maturity.

To understand the proper functioning of moral conscience, instead of relying on the centuries-old experience of spiritual life and sanctity they unhesitatingly resorted to the naïve use of the newly elaborated models of psychopathology. From then on, the asceticism of the virtuous man, the remorse of the regretful sinner, and the mystical love of the saint were regarded as disguised manifestations of grossly pathological conditions. The ascetic was a masochist; the remorse of the sinner was nothing but delusional guilt feelings, and the saint suffered from misplaced and distorted eroticism. Finally, religious dogmas were equated with the magical superstitions of the obsessive-compulsive neurotic. Of course, such speculations have nothing to do with science. Finally, in recent times, several scientists have restricted the use of psychopathological frames of reference to the interpretation of pathological phenomena. They have stressed the reality of genuine moral values and the highly integrated functioning of a fully developed moral conscience as distinct from the distorted and rigid claims of an infantile superego.

These considerations lead us to deal with what is the deepest conflict in the moral conscience. You are well aware that in the moral sphere maturity implies the capacity to recognize the Good as absolute value, and to see in it the sufficient and principal motivation of conduct. Man can show himself to be reasonable only in the measure that he achieves in himself the triumph of the rational over the irrational, and is capable of basing his conduct on judgments of value truly independent yet sustained by this absolute principle. Hence there arises in him a state of continuous conflict. He is pulled by primitive fixations back to the state of the infantile conscience—this so-called superego. The imperative demands of this imaginary conscience in the unconscious are ever seeking to re-establish their dominance in conduct. Indeed, in the normal individual, rational conscience but slowly arrives at affirming itself, and at purifying the moral judgment so as to liberate it from the concrete, subjective, and selfish considerations which controlled it in childhood.

In this typically human conflict between the infantile and the mature, the reason of the normal individual triumphs only by virtue of lucidity and determination. But the conscience of the neurotic allows itself to be overcome by fantasies in the pursuit of infantile aims. For the sake of clarity let us get back to the child who is just beginning to learn to be master of his own acts. He is beginning to learn to deliberate—to choose—without as yet being able to base his conduct on an idea of good or evil which still remains beyond the grasp of his imagination.

First of all it is evident that good and evil for the child bear the aspect of pleasure or pain, and he esteems as good whatever gives him satisfaction, as evil whatever causes him suffering. His educators, aware of this state of mind, attach reward to good conduct, punishment to bad. Later the child has to learn that certain actions pleasant in themselves must be avoided, whereas others disagreeable in nature must be done. Take the case of the youngster who persists in sucking his thumb, or who is careless about habits of normal hygiene. In these cases recourse is had to praise or to blame in order to overcome resistance and to aid the child in this new phase of self-conquest. Finally a time comes when his conduct can no longer be the object of our constant vigilance. At this point we induce him to act in accordance with our demands by emphasizing the possibility of his losing our affection or of keeping it.

It is but natural that these primitive motivations, which gave to our emotional life its first orientations and dominated for so long our behavior, by no means lose their power when the notion of the Good in itself arises in conscience and renders it autonomous. At this moment we are at the threshold of a new stage, the most difficult of all, which leads us to the full development of moral maturity, of a virtuous life. Yet, paradoxical though it may seem, the criteria of value of our infantile conscience frequently continue to exercise sufficient attraction to arrest our progress or even cause us to retrace our steps. Moreover, if in spite of everything we persevere in our forward march, we may be haunted by an excruciating sense of inferiority in which one must finally recognize the feeling of guilt peculiar to the infantile conscience. Think of the terrible crisis which must normally and inevitably be encountered by all those who devote themselves to scientific, artistic, social, or moral pursuits.

As is well known, it is precisely at the moment when these men of "values" turn to the end to be realized, in a spirit of greatest disinterestedness, that discouragement attacks them, and the temptation to doubt their own capacity paralyzes their creative effort. Their intense and assiduous meditation imposes on them many sacrifices. Their career, far from immediately exciting the admiration and love of those around them, often subjects them to a certain contempt and isolation. At this point the infantile conscience which still survives in them makes itself heard by disapproving a conduct too far removed from the norms which it upholds. It is only by the exercise of great firmness and strength that the rational adult conscience succeeds in pointing out the path to be followed. It is with no little difficulty that it succeeds in dominating the primitive feeling of guilt, if it does not succumb to its urgings.

It is little wonder, then, that for the average man, who in many respects remains a child, gain, human respect, and fear of abandonment by friends, should continue to appear as the determining motivations in conduct. At the critical time of temptation, the rational conscience, ever hesitant and weak, all too easily capitulates to the infantile conscience. The individual has recourse to a petty compromise, and becomes the prey of remorse to escape the feeling of inferiority.

In the case of the neurotic, the possibility of envisaging such a compromise does not even exist. The conflict in which he finds himself implies but two alternatives: the toleration of his inferiority or the escape from it by self-destruction. In fact, incapable of self-satisfaction, of maintaining his self-respect, of establishing a genuine love relationship with others, he feels himself to be utterly worthless, without value, and sees no other solution to his situation than self-destruction. By enlightening us upon this issue, psychopathology has rendered one of the greatest services we would have expected from it. The moralist can now with greater clarity understand the fearful and insidious obstacle which the individual has to overcome in his upward path. He can use this penetrating intuition to formulate more precise directives for the education of human personality.

These few illustrations of the functioning and characteristics of the neurotic conscience also enable us the better to understand the deformations of the religious attitude of the neurotic. It is not our intention here to make a study of these peculiarities. It is enough to say that the neurotic is often a believer who endeavors to be religious according to his capacity. Unfortunately, in the exercise of his religion he encounters what seem insurmountable obstacles, which inevitably lead him to an impasse or to discouragement. His religiosity becomes the unconscious vehicle of his infantile longings and a source of uncontrollable anxiety. Against this he mobilizes his habitual mechanisms of defense, denial of reality, compensation, rationalization, etc. But all this is too widely known to be insisted upon. It is more to the point to retrace the origin of these deviations

and to show how they all derive from the ever-stronger interference
of the infantile conscience with the functioning of the rational
conscience.

The first characteristic of the rational conscience is that it is a
faithful witness to conduct. It maintains an adequate contact with
reality, and all the actions which it dictates are, we may say, but the
response to its demands. From this fact the motivation of these acts
possesses an objectivity that cannot be ignored. Not so with the infantile or neurotic conscience. Dominated by a strong primitive
sensualism, it attains to God as to all other realities, under the veil of
an imagery extremely unprecise and subject to the arbitrariness of
instinctual influences. Thus we can understand the obsessions and
the exalted "mysticism" of certain neurotics as well as the myths and
magic rites of uncivilized peoples. Unfortunately, certain thinkers
have been so naïve as to believe that true religion is reducible to
these primitive and delirious fantasies. In my opinion, it is as far
removed from them as a musical symphony is from the clatter and
noise of the street, as a perfect work of art is from a vulgar rigma-
role, or as inspired poetry is from an incoherent reverie.

In the second place, judgments of conscience appear to us as imperative, commanding a particular form of action. In other words,
conscience commands obedience. Here again a profound difference
separates the rational from the neurotic conscience. Like the infantile conscience, the neurotic conscience continues to feel itself
dependent and heteronomous. But the rational conscience chooses
with deliberation; it is independent, autonomous. In face of the demands of the Creator, of the demands of the natural and of the
positive law, the only alternatives for the neurotic conscience are
passivity or revolt. On the contrary, the rational conscience discovers
a relation of justice, and freely assumes all the obligations deriving
therefrom. Acts external and internal, corporal gestures and intimate sentiments of the soul are ordained by this virtue of justice,
with a view to rendering complete homage to him who is recognized
as the Supreme Excellence.

Finally every deliberate action merits the approval or disapproval
of conscience, which performs, as it were, the function of a judge.
From conscience we derive the immense satisfaction of being able to
love ourselves rightly, the reason being that we know ourselves to be

better after submitting voluntarily to the Deity our poverty as creatures, and after serving duly him whom we reverence. On the other hand, if we fail, conscience arouses in us a reasonable feeling of guilt, remorse. But far from crushing us, this sorrowful regret for error committed contains already in itself the desire for resurrection and for aspiration to a love more intense and more stable. Remorse prepares the way for hope. Such is not the case with the neurotic conscience. Here we can experience only the narcissistic and illusory satisfaction of being able to love ourselves, because, blind to our indigence as creatures, we exalt ourselves to the point of equating our human selves with the Creator. When, however, this narcissistic identification fails, we inevitably feel our personality attacked by an irrational feeling of guilt leading to a complete breakdown. The feeling of guilt experienced as an irremediable inferiority, paralyzes every effort at resurgence and leads to the dread and rage of despair.

It will be clear that we cannot be charged with not entertaining for science a due respect. Indeed, in our opinion, neglect even of the smallest scientific discovery would be tantamount to sinning against the light. Yet even when he has explored the domain of psychology to the best of his ability, the priest who is endowed with a profound faith and some experience of human unrest, will be acutely aware that he has need of an added illumination if he is to understand those who suffer. Moreover, he cannot ignore the supernatural dynamism of grace, which intervenes unconsciously to lead us to actions which neither the motivations of irrational unconscious, nor those of deliberate reason are sufficient to explain. The priest will be grateful to psychology for what he can learn from it. Nevertheless, since as a matter of fact a certain aspect of life transcends the range of psychological techniques, and being unable to remain satisfied with an exclusively naturalistic interpretation, he will look to theology for light on the nature of moral and religious conflicts.

We know indeed from the experience of the ages, that the pressure of grace in hours of purification is infinitely more to be reckoned with than the most violent pressure of temporal reality. The supernatural world has demands, exigencies, more arduous, more imperious than the natural. Beholding it, even the individual who has attained the limit of human perfection and the level of greatest personal maturity, begins to fear. The average man is afraid to be free: the superior personality, also, is afraid—afraid to be free as God wills him to be free, that is to say, afraid to go beyond to surpass his human liberty, so as to will what God wills, to will the good and the end that God wills he should pursue. At this level the individual is inevitably caught in a terrifying inner conflict, in which it is the divine intention that he is humanly aided. Here a knowledge of dynamic psychology will be useful. The same mechanisms of defense will operate here as elsewhere. Nevertheless if dynamic psychology be separated from the data of empirical theology it will afford a purely *material* understanding of the phenomena. One will have an illusion, and only an illusion, of solving the problems.

Just as the psychologist learns to efface himself before the human reason he has helped to liberate, so the spiritual leader learns to efface himself before the spirit whose ways he has prepared. To both one can recommend a passivity respectful to the inner forces of organization. On the one hand, the data on which they labor are the same. Yet beyond a certain limit their respective contributions appear complementary, one to the other.

# CHAPTER 10

## PASTORAL PSYCHOLOGY
## AND CHRISTIAN ETHICS

### SEWARD HILTNER

THE general thesis of this chapter is that pastoral psychology contributes to our understanding of, in this instance, Christian ethics—
and on the other side that study of our operations as Christian
ethical leaders deepens, corrects, or illuminates our pastoral psychology.

What is usually referred to as Christian ethics is the great body of
knowledge and conviction built up over the centuries, more or less
systematic. That is, it has become customary to think of Christian
ethics as a content, whether it is related to operations or not. If so
related, then it is usually considered to be "applied," that is, its content has been discovered somewhere else than through our operations
and activities.

This usual view of Christian ethics seems to me partially mistaken.
To be sure, there would be no Christian ethics without the Christian
tradition; neither would there be Christian pastoral care without the
Christian tradition. But a conception of Christian ethics which considers its operations only in terms of application, and not in a polar
two-way relationship between tradition and operation, seems to me
inadequate. I can only touch on this complex question here; but so
much is necessary to understand what will follow.

If pastoral psychology (or anything else, even another aspect of
the Christian tradition than the ethical) is to contribute to our understanding of Christian ethics, then Christian ethics must be so
conceived initially that such a contribution is not ruled out of account in principle. And if Christian ethics is to correct, deepen, or

illuminate our pastoral psychology, then it cannot be so conceived initially as to make no contact with the content of pastoral psychology. Since not a little of the current writing on Christian ethics does both these things, my warning seems justified even if it cannot be adequately supported by extended argument here.

I will first present a pastoral contact in which ethical principles are rather obviously involved. After some general analysis of this contact, I shall explore what it has to teach us in reference to several important current questions in Christian ethics. Pastoral psychology will of course be my principal instrument in making the case analysis.

## Charles

Charles is a young man of twenty-five, of the middle-class type often described as "clean-cut." About a year ago he moved to the middle-sized city in which Pastor Berg's church is located. Charles is a minor business executive who, so far as the pastor knows, is getting along well in his work. Soon after arriving in the city, Charles began attending worship regularly in the church, and very soon became well known and liked throughout the congregation. What the pastor describes as his "pleasing appearance and manner and sincere attitude" soon brought many requests for him to assume various responsibilities within the church and its organizations, but Charles was very hesitant about all of these and has accepted hardly any of them. In casual talks with him, Pastor Berg discovered that Charles had been active in church back home all his life, had come from a very stable and generally conservative family of middle-class status, and that the value of attending church regularly had been emphasized throughout his youth. In such casual chats, the pastor had noted, Charles made frequent references to his father and mother, and referred with approval to their ideals and principles of living.

Following the Sunday morning service of worship, Charles approached the pastor, said there were some things he had been thinking about, and asked if he might make an appointment to discuss them. When the date was kept, the following took place:

CHARLES: I don't really know how to tell you about this, but I've been thinking about it quite a bit, and felt that I ought to talk it over with someone.

PASTOR BERG: Well, Charles, if I can help in any way, I'll be glad to do it.

CHARLES: It's really kind of a long story. I suppose if I were home I would talk to my father about it. It doesn't amount to so much, I guess, but it's kind of got me down. I thought if I talked it through with someone I might get things straightened out a little better in my own mind.

PASTOR: It often does help to talk things through with someone else.

CHARLES: Well, a couple of months ago, I met a girl at a party given for the office staff and their friends. I didn't take the girl to the party: I came alone. She was with another fellow. I felt a strong attraction for her right from the start.

PASTOR: Tell me about her, Charles.

CHARLES: We did a good deal of talking that night. I'm not much of a dancer, and she said she didn't like to dance very much either. We spent most of the evening talking. I guess the guy that brought her did not like it so much. But she was really very interesting. We talked about all sorts of things. She told me that she had finished college and had taught school and now she had a good job as a secretary. Before she left with the guy who brought her, she asked me if I didn't want to see her again. I guess she knew I did, but I told her so. She gave me her 'phone number, and asked me to call her.

PASTOR: Did you call her?

CHARLES: You bet I did. Although I often feel as if I would have been smarter to have let it drop right there.

PASTOR: I gather that things haven't gone so smoothly from that time on?

CHARLES: No. Oh, they've gone smoothly all right. That's the trouble. Or at least in a way they've gone smoothly. As far as she's concerned, things are rosy right now.

PASTOR: Tell me, then, why you think it would have been smarter to have dropped the matter.

CHARLES: Well, it's the way I feel about it. Or rather, it's the way I feel about the things she likes to do. I didn't used to drink at all. We never did at home. Oh, Dad had a glass of beer once in a while on a hot summer evening, but when we were kids, we didn't even know about that. Well, June doesn't seem to think that an evening is complete unless we stop for five or six drinks before going home. And she doesn't let it stop at that. When I take her home, she always asks me to come up to her apartment, even the first night I took her out.

PASTOR: You feel that you would rather have things go along on a more gradual basis?

CHARLES: That doesn't give quite the right meaning. I want a girl I can respect and think highly of, not one who acts like anything's all right any time.

PASTOR: Just what is your problem with June, then?

CHARLES: Well, the thing is this. I don't really believe I respect her, and doubt if she is the kind of person I could get along with over a long period of time. I came to this conclusion a week ago, and decided the thing to do was not to see her any more. The only trouble is, I miss her terribly. I think about her all the time. I'm afraid I'm not going to hold out very long. If I don't call her, she will probably get in touch with me. She has tried to call me a couple of times already, but I was away from my desk. If she does get in touch with me, I know I'll be back in the same old grind.

PASTOR: On the one hand, then, you feel that she is not the kind of girl you should think seriously about; but, on the other hand, you miss her very much if you don't see her?

CHARLES: I guess I feel upset whether I see her or not. Even when I was seeing her every night, I didn't feel very good about it.

PASTOR: You mean there is something about your relationship with June that disturbs you, whether you are seeing her regularly or not?

CHARLES: (Nods head, looks a bit puzzled).

PASTOR: Tell me what it is.

CHARLES: Well, I don't know exactly. I guess she is really not the type of girl for me. I don't think our moral principles coincide. I doubt if she could ever get along with my family, for example. She doesn't think going to church makes any difference. That's one point on which we couldn't get along.

PASTOR: You don't think the kind of life she leads would be compatible with yours?

CHARLES: No, I'm sure it wouldn't.

PASTOR: Why, then, do you think you feel so strong an attraction toward her?

CHARLES: That's the funny part of it. Now that I've had the chance to think it through a little more, I really don't have such a strong feeling for her. I suppose it amounts pretty much to the fact that I have done little dating since I got to the big city. I think I was probably thrown by the fact that she is a very attractive girl physically, and has always acted like she enjoyed herself so much when she has been with me.

PASTOR: But you never felt that things were quite right between you?

CHARLES: No, I never did. In my rather lonesome state, her physical attractiveness and apparent happiness when we were together were enough to make me pretty eager to see her. I think I see now, though, that she doesn't add up to the kind of girl I want. She doesn't have the things that are necessary for a lasting relationship. We don't think the same things are important. Our homes and early training haven't been the same.

PASTOR: I think I understand what you mean, Charles, and, from what you have told me, I agree with you. But don't you think that social relationships of some sort are important?

CHARLES: That's part of the reason I was so attracted to June. I was pretty lonely. I guess the thing for me to do is to begin to date a girl who has a background similar to mine.

PASTOR: Yes, I think that would be an important step for you to take. But don't think that the next girl, necessarily, will be the right one, even if her background is more similar to yours. Sometimes it takes quite a while for the right girl to come along.

We might consider this contact simply from the point of view of pastoral counseling, in what degree the pastor gave Charles the help he needed at this time. If we did, there are some fairly obvious critical remarks which would be made. For example, the pastor is preoccupied with content at the expense of the underlying feelings Charles expresses. The pastor is openly coercive at points. The pastor wants action, is much less concerned with clarification. And there are others. As counseling, the pastor's work is not very effective.

But the contact is also, and in many ways primarily, an attempted bit of moral education, or of ethical guidance. I propose to analyze it from this point of view; and then to see what light our ethical analysis may shed not only upon the pastoral counseling here but also on pastoral psychology in general.

### The Nature of Moral Problems

What is the real moral or ethical problem in Charles's life? In moving toward an answer, we may first examine what Pastor Berg felt it to be. He wrote: "His problem arose at the point where he realized that essential disharmony existed between his ethical standards, acquired earlier primarily through the influence of home and church, and those which June had in her life." This statement accords well with the inferences we may draw from the contact report itself concerning the pastor's view of the ethical problem. We might spell it out a little more, as it seemed to appear in Pastor Berg's mind.

Here is a young man, Pastor Berg seemed to feel, who was blessed with a fine home background. Through his Christian parents, he acquired a loyalty and devotion both to the church and to Christian moral standards. He has always lived a Christian moral life. But he is human, and is not above the lusts of the flesh. Accordingly, when he met a girl with a lot of sex appeal, whose moral standards were different from his own, he was swept off his feet by the strong attractiveness. But fortunately his ethical standards were too high to let him get deeply involved with such a girl. He finally saw that she would not do for him, and made a decision. Essentially, what he wanted Pastor Berg to do was help confirm his decision so it would stick. The moral problem is not, of course, that he has some interest in sex. That is thoroughly human and important. But he should have it for the kind of girl who sees life as he does, and has the same kind of standards he has. Maybe he can make some moral growth through this experience, for he is likely to be swept off his feet a good deal less if he meets another girl like June.

Our first question, is, then: Is this the real moral problem? To which my reply is: No. Not only is the real moral problem different from what Pastor Berg believes it to be; but his conception of the moral problem is likely to lead away from a truly moral or ethical solution of the problem. In the sections which follow, we shall be moving toward what seems to me a better understanding both of Charles's real moral problem and the road toward its solution.

## Vitality and Personality

In moving toward an understanding of the real moral problem, let us first imagine what would happen if the moral problem as Pastor Berg seemed to conceive it were answered on the terms he would seem to consider desirable. In that case, Charles would at once give up his association with June, would meet other girls socially whose standards were like his own, and would eventually marry one of them. But at the same time, there is a good deal of evidence to suggest that Charles, and eventually his wife also, would approach life in a pallid or anemic manner. They would attend church, but not assume responsibility in connection with its activities. They would be conventionally good people, but not good for very much. From experience with many actual marriages of this kind, we can predict that they would get along fine in a routine kind of way so long as they continued to take everything for granted and still find that they agreed. Their genuine concern with anything beyond themselves might be slight and passive, such as attending church but never being disturbed by religion; nevertheless, they would be upstanding citizens not consciously unhappy.

But let us suppose that the things each takes for granted are only 95 per cent the same rather than 100 per cent. Suppose that one has slightly different assumptions about neatness than the other, or that one is shocked by certain aspects of sex which seem all right to the other. The dissenter may be shocked, but he or she will be silent. Because their union has rested upon unstated shared assumptions, they have no machinery, and indeed no attitudes, for dealing with unshared assumptions. In effect, this means that they get along only if they have the same degree, kind, and content of repressions. At best, this makes life flat. At worst, it produces explosions which are a complete mystery to all the friends who considered them the most devoted couple they knew.

These comments are not, of course, a diatribe against the notion that it is rather a good idea to marry someone with whom one can share some assumptions. The real point is that it makes an immense difference what kind of assumptions one wishes to have shared. In the case of Charles and his hypothetical wife, these assumptions have one general characteristic—that the drives or the vitalities of life must be kept under pretty rigid control, in fact, that they be largely repressed. The girl of high standards is the girl who is not free and easy. She is not only the girl unattracted by alcohol and kisses, but the one who demonstrates little spontaneity about anything. She is deliberate, controlled, legalistic, rigid, and repressed.

Whatever her deficiencies, June is none of these things. Instead of being like a car whose engine purrs so slowly and quietly that it can hardly be heard, June drives with the exhaust open all the time. She may be free and easy about alcohol and kisses, but she is apparently spontaneous about things in general. What she appeals to in Charles is not only his sex impulses, as he believes. It is much broader than that—the vitalities of his life as a whole, the inward creative urges, which do not want to see life as a flat and mediocre affair that crawls along with its foot always on the brake.

Consciously, Charles understands nothing of this. He believes that June attracts him sexually, and that's all. While slightly disturbing, the conviction that he has lost his head a bit owing to June's sex appeal is not basically threatening to Charles. This is something from the outside, something external, something for which he need feel no responsibility so long as he does not succumb to the temptation. He need not feel ashamed for feeling sexually attracted to June.

But if June appeals to him, as we have suggested, in a much more fundamental and comprehensive way than sex in the narrow sense, the situation is different. If June is a kind of symbol crying out to him to release his powers, his creative energies, his inner potentialities, and his spontaneity, then the whole current balance of his life is under threat. June symbolizes to him a life whose tone is spontaneous fulfillment rather than deliberating restraint, creative expression rather than watchful control, carefree confidence in his own powers rather than persistent suspicion of them. And this is not a mere matter of suggesting to him that he ought to be like this rather than as he is. The appeal indicates that there is something like this already present in him though unrecognized. Its nature is deeper, more pervasive, and more important than sex, although to be sure sex is included in it.

If the nature of the appeal which June makes is as I have suggested, rather than what Charles and Pastor Berg believe it to be, then it becomes fairly clear that their conception of the moral problem and the moral answer must be replaced. If the moral problem is merely bringing some refractory sex impulses into line, then we would see Charles as a whole and integrated person who is moral insofar as he refuses to yield to an outside invasion which appeals to his lower nature. But if the situation is different, then the moral problem is whether integration can be achieved, whether Charles's creative energies can be assimilated into his total personality and used for deeper fulfillment instead of remaining in the psychic storage bin, whether the energy of his own inner potentialities can be harnessed to serve his personhood or instead be shoved back as too dangerous to play with, whether what we have rather vaguely called his "vitalities" can be recognized and assimilated into his picture of his life or instead be relinquished with a consequent loss in wholeness.

To avoid any possible misunderstanding, it can be said plainly that the resolution of the moral problem, understood in this way, will not come through the pastor's urging Charles to give vent to his impulses. In not a few people like Charles, who have lived similarly unintegrated lives based on repression, flatness, and conformity, there has come at some point a swinging of the pendulum toward the side of rebellion, compulsive expression of impulses, in such forms as sexual license. But such a course, far from being a solution to the problem, in some ways makes it worse. The basic pattern has not changed. One is as far as ever, and sometimes farther, from integrating his creative impulses with social responsibility. He has merely changed the form of his disintegration.

The basic moral problem in Charles is integrity or its lack. If he merely sits on the lid, he is precisely like the man of one talent who hid it in the ground. If he merely takes off the lid explosively, he would be like the one-talent man who spent it immediately, carelessly, and to no one's benefit. What is needed is cultivation of the talents, not sitting on them or throwing them away. But it is no answer to deny that they exist, that one has no responsibility for them because their very existence is pushed out of awareness.

## Fulfillment and Control

Let us suppose that Pastor Berg had had our view of the moral problem in Charles rather than that which he had in fact. In that event, he would have been especially alert to anything Charles was expressing which indicated a yearning to come to terms with the creative energies of life. Anything of this kind (and there are several indications that Charles would have made some steps in this direction if properly understood) would have been picked up sensitively by the pastor in the conviction that the more squarely Charles faced the inner facts the more likely was the solution to be an integrated and therefore ultimately moral one. On the face of it, Charles feels a bit guilty because he does not have his sex impulses under perfect control. This guilt is, however, merely symptomatic. It diverts attention from the real guilt Charles dimly senses, that his trying to approach life by hiding his talent is immoral. If counseling in such a case were successful, Charles would eventually dig through to confront this real guilt, would then begin to assimilate symbolically those aspects of himself previously denied, and would be on the road to integrated selfhood and the capacity for truly moral action.

There would be, we know from many other similar situations, a gradual and uneven movement away from the general tone of rigid control toward that of responsible fulfillment. Far from being prey to June or others like June, he would be able to distinguish the Junes as persons from the Junes as symbols. Not only would his resulting behavior be more responsible in relation to himself, but in relation to the Junes as well. Because not compelled to regard them as symbols, he could see them as persons and act accordingly, even if that action should be to have as little to do with them as possible. If he now sees no more of June, he will feel that he achieved a victory by control; but he will always have the haunting sense that there was something which eluded him in the experience. This will make him resolve more firmly than ever to clamp down, to yield to no temptations. But a tone toward life in which one concentrates on the temptations to which he plans not to yield can hardly be called one of fulfillment and creative endeavor. One may be good, but it is a goodness of conformity, of anemic control, and of permanently divided selfhood, with consequent loss in genuine social as well as personal responsibility. It is, now as always, the road to legalism.


## Character and Act

As the situation actually is, Charles fears that he will break down and see June again. In effect, he seeks Pastor Berg's reinforcement to his resolution not to see her. From the point of view which we have been developing, he will be morally damned if he does and if he doesn't see June—for in either event he will be failing to follow through on the growth in character which the June experience has potentially brought to his attention as necessary. His belief, and for the most part that of the pastor, is that the morality lies in the act. Our position is that the act is meaningless either way except as an expression of character. He feels that he will win a moral victory if he can prevent himself from seeing June. Our position is that he will yield to a moral defeat so long as he considers the problem to be only one of seeing or not seeing June, that the nature of the act is less important than the character which does the acting.

We may concede to Charles, and to Pastor Berg, that the consequences of one kind of act may be more immediately and painfully negative than of the other. If Charles should rush off and marry June, in panic over how bad he would feel if he had sex relations with her while unmarried, there would be plainer pain than if he succeeds in his resolve not to see June again at the price of a few things like insomnia. The difficulty in this kind of commonsense reasoning is that it tends to become exclusive, to deny that there is anything else to be considered. It is not wrong, but it is far from being the whole story. It invites a moral legalism; and when this becomes too repressive, invites a rebellious antinomianism to break it up. The cycle may go on and on, centering around acts; while all the time the real moral problem, involving character, is never viewed at all. Morality is a function of character. If act is seen in the context of character, then it too can be considered morally, that is, does this act lead toward genuine moral growth on the part of this person and others involved? But if isolated from character, and from the meaning of the act to the person, it cannot, strictly speaking, be in the moral realm at all.

## Freedom and Responsibility

The argument has already made it plain that Charles is unfree, under compulsion—that either seeing June or not seeing June will be done under a compulsion. His decision, whatever its content, will not represent the integrated coherence of a total personality, but of one part winning a dubious victory over another part and thus making more certain the continued enmity among the parts.

If Charles should be helped, however, by the pastor or in other ways, to assimilate (symbolically) in himself those forces whose existence and power he now denies, he would become capable of a decision in relation to June, other Junes, or many other things, which would represent much more of him as a total being than is now possible. Relatively speaking, he would be free whereas he is now compelled. This seems to require no further argumentation.

The ethical question then becomes: Would his growing freedom be at the expense of responsibility? In principle, I believe the answer to this is plain—that increasing freedom, if genuine, is automatically accompanied by increasing responsibility or capacity for responsibility. If Charles becomes more genuinely free to see and feel what June means to him, then he is more free to take her or leave her, as a total person, as she really is. It would seem not beyond the bounds of possibility that June is quite a girl; and so it is not impossible that Charles might become more deeply attracted to her even than before. But if this occurs in freedom, then it means that June is actually the kind of person, down underneath, who does not threaten Charles's most basic positive standards about life. But if Charles continued and deepened the relationship on this basis, in freedom, it would also be in increasing responsibility. Similarly, if June were shallow, and had been principally a symbol to him, Charles would make a free decision to break off, and this too would be responsible. If Charles continued under compulsion—either seeing June or concentrating on not seeing her—he would by the same token continue irresponsible.

This is not to say that everything going under the names of freedom and responsibility would be in similar accord. If Charles began to engage in promiscuous sex relationships, with June or other girls, and this were referred to as "freedom," compared to previous "control," it would hardly be what we mean by freedom. Or if Charles should become depressed fearing that he had hurt June irretrievably by leading her on and then dropping her, it might be spoken of as his sense of "responsibility," but it would hardly be what we have called responsibility. Properly understood, freedom and responsibility do go hand in hand.

## Moral Principles and Casuistry

We have certainly not explored all the ethical implications of Charles's situation, and are far indeed from having presented a total point of view on Christian ethics. Indeed, we have been able to say little or nothing about the distinctive principles of Christian ethics, which certainly exist and are important. Our concern has been to suggest that pastoral psychology makes basic, and not merely peripheral, contributions to our understanding of ethics including Christian ethics; and that an adequate understanding of ethics makes a contribution to our knowledge of pastoral psychology. Pastoral psychology is of course not the sole contributor to our understanding of Christian ethics.

Within these limits, however, I hope that I have demonstrated a vital and basic relationship. This type of discussion, in which casuistry is used to explore moral principle and moral principle is examined to aid casuistry, has been very little used in recent Christian ethics, to the impoverishment both of casuistry and of our understanding of moral principle. As the Anglican Kenneth Kirk has wisely pointed out, the misuse of casuistry two hundred years ago resulted in the creation of a Christian ethics which contented itself too often with a statement of general moral principles. Kirk calls for a casuistry as well as a statement of principles, but he tends to suggest that the relationship should be one way—from moral principle to cases or actual situations. My contention would be that the relationship must be two way—that an examination of actual situations informs and corrects our understanding of moral prin-

ciples, just as our understanding of moral principle helps our understanding of actual situations.

My conviction is that there can be no genuine ethics without a
casuistry, a theory of dialectical relationship between actual concrete situation and general principle. We have done much better
with this in recent years on the ethics of larger social questions; but
we are only at the beginning of doing it in regard to ethics in a
broader sense. For proof, we may ask how many pastors might have
agreed with Pastor Berg's conception of Charles's moral problem
and its solution. The number, I suspect, is less than it would have
been a few years ago; but it still seems likely to be alarmingly high.

Thus far, the neo-orthodox trends in theology seem to have helped
us very little at this point. They would tend to warn Charles against
believing, no matter how successful his basic transformation, that
he must still confront the limitations inherent in his human finitude,
that he may win a victory over sensuality but if he does not take
heed he will fall with a greater sin, pride. This would all seem
quite true, and relevant, provided Charles gets to the point where
we have said we want him to be. But in that case, he has something
to stand on, a new security which has emerged along with his new
freedom and responsibility, which makes it possible for him to hear
the good news of sin and heed it. He will be tempted to overlook
it, minimize it, deny it; and here our pessimistic prophets are real-
ists indeed, and correctly so. But what do we learn about how Charles
may reach this point? So far as I can see, little or nothing. God's
judgment, to be sure, would be on a Charles gaining increasing
psychic freedom just as it is on Charles now under compulsion. But
there is quite a difference between the two Charleses. In the concern to expose the smugness of all moralistic striving, it is hardly
helpful to speak as if there were no true moral difference between
Charles-compelled and Charles-free. I believe the new and deeper insights of our theology can become deeper and more relevant if they
take our point into account.

## Conclusion

Approaching the relation of pastoral psychology to Christian
ethics through the study of a single pastoral contact, we have at-

tempted to show how our knowledge of pastoral psychology, or lack of such knowledge, basically affects our understanding of the ethical problem in the actual situation. Conversely, we have attempted to indicate that our understanding of the true ethical problem, and therefore of what must be accomplished before it can be considered solved in any sense, enriches our understanding of pastoral psychology. If pastoral psychology were a morally neutral affair, it might be much less of a required subject than it actually is.

We have seen that the capacity for truly moral action depends upon the degree of integration which a person has, and that the most obvious enemies of moral action are compulsion, unfreedom, irresponsibility—all of which are tied up together. In the case we had on view, what stands against integrity of personality is unassimilated creative energies. In another case, it might be something quite different in content which is excluded from the recognized personality although actually present. The nature of the content is not the point. It is rather that any real aspect of one's personality or experience which is not assimilated symbolically into one's selfhood by so much destroys the base upon which truly moral conduct may build. Such conduct is as responsible as it is free, because it flows from the character of integrity. As Erich Fromm ably says, there are no virtuous or vicious acts apart from virtuous or vicious characters.

Morals and ethics are, to be sure, even when of this kind, not enough. But if the parable of the talents has any meaning at all, they are not without some basic significance.

# PART THREE

*Man's Problems and Potentialities*

# CHAPTER 11

## EMOTIONAL MATURITY

### FRANZ ALEXANDER, M.D.

*According to the teachings of modern dynamic psychology, emotional maturity is characterized by ability to become interested in things and persons; to appreciate things for their own sake, to give love to other persons. In other words, capacity for altruism is one fundamental characteristic of emotional maturity. This fact supplies the biological foundation of Christian morality.*

THE expression, "maturity," refers to a significant phase in the growth of a living organism. Maturity is achieved when individual growth is completed and the organism is ripe for propagation. The concept of maturity is used also in psychology and psychiatry. In this field it designates that phase of personality development which corresponds to biological and psychological maturation. We call a person psychologically mature after he has reached a certain level of intelligence and emotional outlook. If the development of a person is undisturbed, biological and psychological maturation progress more or less parallel with each other. Usually, however, biological maturation proceeds ahead of emotional maturation.

Each phase of biological development is characterized by certain well-defined psychological attitudes. Biologically, the newborn infant is completely dependent upon the mother and accordingly his emotional attitude is characterized by this dependence. He seeks gratification for his needs from the mother; his security is based on being cared for, and loved by, the mother. Gradually, the first signs of independence appear. The child learns to use his biological equipment, he learns to focus with his eyes, to masticate food, to co-ordinate the innervations of his skeletal muscles, he learns how to grab objects and to walk. He learns to exercise conscious control over his excremental functions and to communicate his needs by speech.

All these functions at first are mastered separately. The eyes learn how to focus, the hands how to grab, the legs how to walk; but finally all these functions become co-ordinated with each other and the child is able to spot objects in environment, approach them, and take hold of them. The greatest step towards independence is accomplished by the development of the functions of intelligence which allow a high degree of independent orientation in the surrounding world. The most important phase of development begins with the maturation of the sex glands during puberty. By now the growing organism has acquired all functions, to which finally the faculty of propagation is added.

There follows a period called adolescence, which in many respects is in sharp contrast with maturity although it introduces maturity. We speak of adolescent attitudes often when we want to emphasize that they are juvenile and immature. We refer to adolescent boastfulness, insecurity, awkwardness, instability, etc. Although biologically the adolescent organism reaches the end of its growth and is in possession of all its potential faculties, psychologically it can be sharply differentiated from maturity. In this age the parallelism between biological and psychological development does not prevail. Biological growth by now is a full phase ahead of psychological maturation.

In order to define maturity, it is helpful to point out in detail the striking differences between adolescent and mature emotional attitudes. The mentality of the adolescent can best be understood if we consider this phasic difference between the faster biological and the slower psychological maturation. Adolescence is as if the biological functions of mature sexuality were foisted upon an organism which emotionally is not fully prepared for it.

The outstanding features of adolescence are insecurity and awkwardness which often makes a comical effect. Here is a young man or woman, biologically full-grown but in many respects emotionally still a child. One has the impression that they do not know what to do with themselves in their newly acquired status. Their insecurity manifests itself in self-consciousness, both about their body and about their personality. They do not know what to do with their hands and feet, there is a lack of spontaneity in their movements and speech and a constant effort to overcome their own feeling of awkwardness. A full-grown body is entrusted to an inexperienced mind.

Another conspicuous feature of adolescence is an excessive competitiveness. The adolescent feels as if he were constantly in a test situation. He must prove to himself that he is already a man or a woman. *Noblesse oblige!* Bodily they are full-grown men and women, and this obliges them to behave as full-grown men and women. The only way to do this is by measuring up to others, both adults and contemporaries. Adolescent assertiveness, bragging, intensive competitiveness are the natural manifestation of this state of mind. The inexorable law of growth imposes upon them the obligation to perform according to their age and faculties. Lack of experience, the novelty of this new state, is what creates the feeling of inadequacy which the adolescent tries to overcome by competing with others.

The understanding of adolescence gives us the clue to the essence of the mature state of mind. This consists in overcoming the insecurity and in being able to take oneself for granted. The period of competition during adolescence gives the person opportunity to prove himself to others and to one's own self. Moreover, this steady competition affords a continuous practice of one's full-grown capacities. During the period of adolescence the young person gradually grows emotionally into the advanced mature status which biologically he had already reached several years ago. The self-confident attitude of the mature person is based on taking himself and his capacities for granted. This is in sharp relief to the insecurity of the infant and of the adolescent. As a consequence of this inner security the mature adult's interest no longer centers around the self. It can now be turned outward toward the environment.

Maturity can be best understood from the so-called vector concept of life. Life can be viewed as a relationship between three vectors: the intake of energy in the form of the nutritive substances and oxygen; their partial retention for use in growth; and the expenditure of energy to maintain existence, its loss in waste, heat, and in propagation. As long as the organism grows, intake and retention outweigh expenditure. Propagation may be understood as growth beyond the limits of the individual biological unit, and follows the pattern of the propagation in monocellular organisms.

The process of growth has a natural limit when the cell reaches maturity. Thereafter reproduction occurs through the division of the cell. When a biological unit reaches a certain size, addition of substance and energy becomes impossible because its capacity to organize living matter has reached its limit. Individual growth then stops and propagation serves as a means of releasing surplus energy.

All energy which is not needed to maintain life can be considered as surplus energy. This is the source of all sexual activity; it is also the source of all productive and creative work. This surplus of energy shows itself in the mature person in generosity, the result of the strength and overflow which the individual can no longer use for further growth and which therefore can be spent productively and creatively. The mature person is no longer primarily a receiver. He receives but he also gives. His giving is not primarily subordinated to his expectation of return. It is giving for its own sake.

Giving and producing, as Dr. Leon Saul correctly emphasizes in his book on maturity, are not felt by the mature person as an obligation and duty; he gives, produces, and spends his energies with pleasure in the service of aims which lie outside his own person. Just as for the growing child, receiving love and help are the main sources of pleasure, for the mature person pleasure consists primarily in spending his energies productively for the sake of other persons and for outside aims. This generous outward directed attitude is what in ethics is called altruism. In the light of this view, altruism, the basis of Christian morality, has a biological foundation; it is a natural, healthy expression of the state of surplus characteristic for maturity.

You may have the impression that I am speaking of something unreal, of a blueprint instead of reality. But we must realize that things in nature never correspond to abstract ideals. The platonic ideal of maturity in its pure and complete form is never found in nature and is only approached by human beings to a greater or lesser degree. Every adult carries in himself certain emotional remnants of childhood. Even the most perfect machine does not fulfill the ideal conditions of Carnot's famous heat machine, which exists only on paper—an apparatus which works with the theoretically calculated maximum effectiveness in converting heat into useful mechanical energy. There is always attrition; a part of heat energy is lost for productive uses. The same is true for the living organism, which essentially is a complicated thermodynamic machine.

Whenever life becomes difficult, beyond the individual's capacity to deal with its pressing problems, there is a tendency to regress towards less mature attitudes, in which a person could still rely on the help of parents and teachers. In our heart, deep down, we all regret being expelled from the garden of Eden by eating from the tree of knowledge—which symbolizes maturity. In critical life situations, most persons become insecure and may seek help even before they have exhausted all their own resources. Many occupations require so much responsibility that a person's ability is taxed beyond his inner means. I could not use a better example than the occupation of the nurse. The nurse's function toward the patient in many respects resembles the maternal role because it is so onesided in relation to giving and receiving. Like the child, the patient demands help and attention and gives little in return.

It must be realized that there is a proportion between receiving and giving which has limits for each individual and which cannot be transgressed without ill results. As soon as a person begins to feel that his work becomes a source of displeasure for him, this is the sign that the balance between giving and receiving is disturbed. The load must be reduced to such an extent that the work becomes again a source of pleasure. It is therefore highly important that the occupational and the private life should be in a healthy compensatory relationship to each other. Many occupations in which a person assumes leadership and must take care of the dependent needs of others, involve an unusual amount of responsibility. Even the most mature person has his own dependent needs, requires occasional help and advice from others. In occupations which require a great deal of expenditure of emotional energy there is a danger of what might be called living beyond one's emotional means. Harmonious human relationship in marriage and friendships are most suitable to fill these emotional deficits and restore the balance between emotional receiving and giving. Vacations and recreational activities are of similar significance. And finally, one cannot overemphasize the importance of nature's own great and universal device for restoring spent energy: sufficient amount of sleep.

This leads us to another important characteristic of emotional maturity, to the faculty of appraising realistically one's own limitations. The mature person is able to face not only the facts in the outside world but also the facts concerning his own self. He adjusts his work, his ambitions, and efforts to these facts and seeks his gratification within the limits set by external conditions and by his own personality. This faculty to adjust one's needs to the existing and continuously changing external and internal conditions we call adaptability. It enables the person to meet in a flexible manner changes in the environment and changes in himself which are involved in the process of growth and decline through aging. This is the function of the central governing portion of the personality, the ego.

This flexible adaptive behavior stands in sharp contrast with automatic responses, for example, blind obedience to existing standards. The child's ego is not capable of sizing up each single situation on its own merits. As we say, he has not yet acquired a sufficient amount of discriminatory judgment. Lacking those faculties on which flexible adaptation is based, experience and precise reasoning, the child's behavior is regulated by parental supervision and guidance. He cannot yet use his own mind and must, by obeying them, borrow from the experience and knowledge of the adults.

Mature behavior, however, is characterized by flexible adaptation to a given situation. The patterns learned in the past do not fit every new emergency. If the world and the individual were both stable, fixed automatic patterns would be sufficient to ensure harmonious adaptation to given conditions. Adaptation is much simpler therefore when conditions remain unchanged. The same is true for adults who live under extremely stable conditions. They do not need flexible adaptation to a changing environment. The typical Parisian or Viennese is a fish out of water elsewhere. These fine representatives of their native culture do not even attempt to change their way of life when they emigrate but create little Parises and Viennas abroad. A similar example is the tragedy of the older generation in a rapidly changing world. Superb representatives of their own age, they become disgruntled and neurotic when a rapid social change forces them to live in a new era.

This problem did not arise during relatively static periods like the feudal period in Europe. In such times conditions and customs remained the same from generation to generation and the place of each individual in society was rigidly determined. The same patterns of behavior descended from parents to children for centuries. Sociologists correctly emphasize rapid social change as the most conspicuous feature of our present industrial era. Not only do two subsequent generations live under different conditions, but an individual during his own lifetime has to readjust himself repeatedly to rapidly changing material and ideological conditions. As a youngster he lived in a world of rugged individualism, in his twenties he was taught the blessings of political paternalism only to face in his mature years a renaissance of individual initiative.

From this it is obvious that the first requirement of industrial civilization is a highly flexible and adaptable personality. As we have seen, the instrument of flexible adaptation is the conscious ego. The comfort of living according to well-tested traditions is not enjoyed by man in the modern era. Habitual behavior patterns do not require conscious deliberation but become routine. Men living in a period of rapid change must develop the faculty of rapid adjustment. They must therefore be more aware of themselves and of their needs than was necessary for their predecessors.

We have characterized the mature person as one who is able to use those energies not needed for survival in a productive, creative fashion by expending them for the sake of others. We have seen also that this generous productive state of mind requires security. Only that person who is not involved in his own internal conflicts, who is not handicapped by anxiety and confusion about his own problems, is able to turn his interest outward.

In order to obtain such internal peace of mind, the person must be able to adjust his internal needs in a flexible way to changing external and internal conditions. In order to have surplus energy which can be spent productively, the ego has to accomplish his adaptive functions in a smooth and economical way. Finally, we have seen that the complexities of modern life make the adaptive functions of the ego more and more difficult. The inevitable conclusion is that to reach emotional maturity in this present era becomes more difficult than it was in those periods in which life was simpler and regulated by well-tested traditions.

In its struggle for self-preservation, humanity develops in each period of history the knowledge and skills it needs for survival. One of the crucial problems of our industrial era has been to create sanitary living conditions for people in large cities. An understanding of contagious diseases became a question of life or death, and bacteriology and physical hygiene arose to meet the problem of congested areas. Dynamic psychiatry plays a similar role in respect to the psychological difficulties arising from rapid cultural change. The aim of psychoanalysis is to increase the effectiveness of the conscious ego by replacing automatic adaptations and repressions with conscious control and flexible adjustments to the changing conditions of modern life. It helps a person to approach more closely the ideal of a self-reliant mature state of mind. This requires facing facts not only outside but within ourselves. The Greek maxim, "Know thyself," may once have been a luxury; today it is a necessity. Man can adjust himself to his changing environment only by knowing himself, his desires, impulses, motives, and needs. He must become wiser, more judicious and more self-reliant; in one word, more mature. Otherwise, he will become confused and frightened and regress to the ways of dependent childhood and thus become the prey of power-seeking minorities who will induce him to believe that his security lies in doing what he is told.

# CHAPTER 12

## THE ATTAINMENT OF MATURITY

ELLIOTT DUNLAP SMITH

IN OUR increasingly crowded and interrelated society, no aspect of maturity is more important than the maturity of an individual in his relations to those about him. Such maturity consists largely of his capacity to work and live with others, thinking self-reliantly and being truly himself, and at the same time letting others think for themselves and be themselves—that is, of his capacity to combine full integrity with outgoing considerateness.

The integrity and considerateness of which maturity in human relations consists are not abstract and static. They are concrete and dynamic qualities. They can never be completely attained. Nor can they be precisely defined. Since they arise out of human relationships, they vary in meaning with these relationships. And yet in all circumstances the essence of the integrity and the considerateness which give rise to social maturity is unchanging.

In order to understand this unchanging essence it is helpful to examine the requirements of maturity as they change under the stress of a major transition, such as occurs when an individual goes from the shelter of college or graduate school into the unsheltered world outside. In a college a student lives in a segregated environment. His colleagues are there for a common purpose, are of about the same age, and have been carefully screened before admission to ensure conformity to common standards of intellect and character. In college a student works under the direction of teachers whose primary task is to help him learn. Even when he does "independent work," he does it under his teachers' guidance. And when the work is done, his teachers' comments and grades let him know the extent to which he is doing "the right thing" and where to try to improve.

Moreover, much of what a student does in college is essentially "role playing." Although he may do assignments that are called "work" and solve problems that are called "real," no bridges fall, no sales are lost, and no one is injured or misled because of his errors. Although he often ardently discusses intellectual, moral, religious, political, or other serious matters in classes and in "bull sessions," if he stops to think he knows that he is usually just trying his wings, not making critical decisions. In all these ways, although he has long been physically mature, his life in college contains much of the quality of infancy. To live and work with others, standing on one's own feet and letting them stand on theirs, is under these conditions a relatively agreeable and friendly attainment.

## Maturity and Adulthood

When, however, a student leaves college or graduate school, he finds himself in an unsegregated, adult world where disagreement is more likely and more serious. There are no teachers to watch over his development and bolster his confidence. The problems he must deal with are real. His decisions look to action and his mistakes are costly. Standing on his own feet in making decisions and in speaking out no longer has the carefree abandon of the college "bull session." Often it is a hard and lonely task. It is especially hard when it relates to significant questions on which people differ. It is even harder when he isn't sure of his decisions or even sure that he is qualified to make the decisions he is faced with. It is harder still when his decisions affect the welfare of others. It is hardest and loneliest of all when his superiors, his closest friends, the people he looks up to, the great majority of his colleagues, or the public, think he is wrong, and yet if he is going to amount to anything, he must stand on his own feet no matter how hard and lonely it may be to do so.

Moreover, it is when one is on the verge of doing something significant or creative that he is most likely to find himself standing alone and least likely to feel unquestionably sure that he is right. The more one grows in stature, the more difficult maintaining integrity becomes and the more courage it requires. As an individual moves from college into the adult world outside, integrity in human relations takes on a new and sterner meaning.

The meaning of considerateness also changes. With the greater differences in background and character of one's associates, considerateness of the position, problems and values of others must be much more searching and sympathetic. The fact that people are no longer "role playing" but are making serious decisions which may lead to benefit or harm, and the fact that these decisions may affect friendships, public respect, and personal or business opportunity intensifies differences and often adds emotional content to them, thus making it more difficult to differ understandingly and pleasantly. To have true considerateness under these difficult conditions, a person must accept difference and even welcome it. He must explore difference and profit from it. He must get results by working *with* others, and not by working over them or under them or against them. To combine considerateness with integrity, he must do this without letting the desire to please and to be liked distort his judgments or prevent his standing up for them.

The shift from student to adult life and its influence upon the problem of maturity are especially illuminating in the student's relation to his family. When a student leaves school and goes to college, he is removed from his family, is usually largely "on his own," and has few occasions of difference between himself and his family. Hence the problem of maintaining his integrity and considerateness is an easy one.

Because college is a sheltered community, because the faculty is there to guide him, because his college problems are so different from his home problems, a college student is very much in the position of a grandchild allowed to visit grandparents whom his parents trust to take care of him. When the student leaves college and returns home, however, he finds that he had not really left the family control, but had merely been given a leave of absence from it. He and his parents are again living together in the same difficult, real world with which his parents have struggled so long. His problems—what job to take and how to go about it, how to spend his leisure, whom to marry, what his religious faith is and how to express it—are the same problems which his parents are facing and have faced. The old relationships of home thus reassert themselves, but now the former student is an adult leading his own life and no longer a dependent child. He finds that he now differs with much that he formerly accepted, especially as to what he, as an individual, should think and do; and yet the old family love and habits of thinking for him make both his family and him unhappy if he differs from them on important, and often even on quite unimportant, matters. He thus finds that the problem of living maturely with his family has profoundly changed, for he cannot live in continuous agreement with them without losing his integrity and yet it is extremely difficult to differ from them without being disagreeable.

### Maturity and Marriage

When he marries and really leaves home, the areas of difference and the difficulty of dealing with difference, instead of decreasing, increase. There are now two families, not one, to adjust to. Both are deeply concerned with the new family which he and his wife are trying to establish. When children come, they bring new problems with which both his parents and his parents-in-law have deep associations and long experience, and thus feel qualified to participate in. Even in his relations with his wife and children, the very love and intimacy which play such a vital part in the extent to which he and they in this closest of all relationships can truly understand each other, can share joy and sorrow, and can give help to each other, may easily become a source of intensifying conflict, of giving pain and of strengthening domination. The marriage intimacy can lead to enduring happiness only if it can somehow combine integrity with complete freedom. Husband and wife must each feel responsible to be wholly himself or herself and yet completely to let the other be so. They must each accept difference with the other as something that is right and that, like friction, can either lead to devastating heat or be made into a major source of progress. They must each imbue intimacy with high integrity and sensitive considerateness in spite of great temptation to assume that agreement is so essential as to justify every effort to attain it. And in all these respects the integrity and the considerateness which permeate the intimate marriage relationship must be of the heart as well as of the head.

In every relationship, to work or to live well in close association with others requires faith—faith that one is being told the full truth and faith that one's opinions are being given genuine consideration.

Without this faith one can neither put one's heart into the relationship nor act with confident understanding. Integrity and considerateness must thus be both given and received. Supine conformity and forceful domination, in themselves and in the distrust which they engender, are destructive of life's most important relationships and values. Nor are they rendered any less destructive because they are collective instead of individual, or because the domination results from disregarding, instead of overpowering, the point of view of others. Human relations can be mature and ennobling only when all who are involved in them are both fully and honestly themselves, and accord responsive, freedom-giving consideration to what others feel and think.

Although a school, college, or graduate school may do much to prepare one to attain adult maturity, such maturity can be attained only in the unsheltered, often painful, world outside. It must arise out of adult experience, and must grow and change as life's problems change. Although the shift from college to the adult maturity is an especially vivid and difficult transition, similar transitions must be faced again and again until, decision by decision and act by act, one gradually builds habits of thought and feeling which in the form of self-discipline become deep aspects of one's character. In making these decisions and acting upon them, there are three important distinctions which, if made, clarify the problems of maturity and release mature behavior from complicating stress.

### Function and Responsibility

The first of these distinctions is between discriminating responsibility for doing one's own function—for carrying out the particular obligations and opportunities it is one's duty to fulfill—and undiscriminating responsibility for doing good. This distinction arises out of the fact that people living or working together in organizations, in communities, in families and with friends, gradually but inevitably establish relationships one to another. Often these relationships are informal. Often they are inconspicuous and even unrecognized. Since, even when they are formal, they are changing, growing things, the most important aspects of which arise largely unconsciously out of the interplay of personalities and action, their character is not easily determined. At any one time one can know their true character only by thoughtfully puzzling out from little incidents of give and take just what at the time the relationship actually is and what is essential to its functioning.

No matter how clearly defined or how unexpressed these relationships are, they have great influence upon the way each person can helpfully do his part. For in large measure they determine the area of responsibility of each person and set boundaries between officious intermeddling and permissible action or influence. Take, for example, the ever-changing relationships between parents and children. At the start a baby's relationship to his parents is one of complete dependence. They are responsible for meeting all his needs and it is right for them to make every decision for him. But when he develops into childhood and acquires the ability to decide and do many things for himself, and thus to make mistakes, much of what was formerly right for his parents to do or decide for him becomes wrong. Their responsibility has become as much one of refraining from helping their child or deciding for him in some respects as it is to help him and guide him in other respects. Only if the parents see that a new relationship has now arisen and that as a result the areas have changed where it is wise or unwise, right or wrong, for them to feel responsible for him, to seek to influence him or to be disturbed if he differs from them, will they give him a chance to develop as he should. Again and again, as the child grows into manhood his relationship to his parents, and hence his parents' responsibility for him and their function in regard to him thus change. Unless at each such stage the parents think out what this change is, the child's development and his relationship with his parents are both bound to suffer.

Similarly, the relationships which arise in one's work, in one's church, and in one's community define function and thereby affect the problem of what is mature integrity and considerateness. Whatever the relationship, if one goes beyond doing one's function, one is likely to intermeddle, blunder, and do harm. He is also likely to impair the relationship itself and its future power to bring happiness and good. For every problem in human affairs is a double problem. On the one hand it is a problem of getting something accomplished—the misdemeanor of a child corrected, a contract made, an argument or a law suit won. On the other hand it is a problem of establishing, altering, or maintaining relationships. Both problems are always important. Both should be carefully explored, recognizing that one's duty or even one's right to help others or to decide for them extends only to one's function in the particular relationship, and that this function can only be discovered by examining the relationship with care.

In doing this, however, one must be as concerned with what his full function is as with what it is not, and must take care that the temptation to escape involvement does not reduce his sympathetic insight in seeing the possibilities of being of help to others. The question, "Who, then, was neighbor unto this man?" is as vital today as ever; but its answer is not a simple one. It involves sympathetic wisdom in recognizing both the limitations and the obligations of a truly helpful sense of duty. In thus determining what it is one's duty to do and one's duty not to do, an awareness of the nature and importance of relationships, and of their effect upon function, clarifies and simplifies the problem of living or working maturely with others.

## Aims and Goals

The second distinction which helps guide the growth of maturity is that between aims and goals—between the directions in which one seeks to progress and specific points of attainment. This distinction is most readily recognized in sports. Any person with whom one cares to play not only has as his goal the winning of the match, but has also a deeper aim—to play fairly and well. The goals of the two sides are directly opposite, but their aims are common. Only one side can attain its goal, but both can pursue, although never fully attain, their aims. The harder such an opponent plays to attain his goal, the more fun he gets and the more fun it is to play with him. Whether he wins or loses, the friendly relationship between him and his opponent will be strengthened; for his intensity in seeking his goal is guided by a compelling aim of fair play—of integrity and considerateness in sport. He can lose without ill temper or distress, for the goal is temporary and confined to the particular game, while the aim is enduring and is not dependent on winning.

The distinction between goals and aims is further illustrated by the problem of overcoming fear of failure. Almost all conscientious or ambitious young people, such as students entering college or young graduates entering upon the practice of their professions, set themselves goals—to make an honor society or an editorship, or to win a particular appointment, recognition, or promotion—and then they eat their hearts out for fear of not reaching them. If they fail to reach their goals, they are desolated. Even if they attain them, they are faced with the dilemma of either setting new goals and again eating their hearts out in fear, or of complacently settling down as young people with a future behind them. With conscientious or insecure people, this dilemma occurs again and again throughout life and is hard to resolve so as to give inner peace unless the subordination of goals to aims is kept clear. Then one can realize that since aims are directions of aspiration and not specific ends to be attained, if his aims are good and his dedication to them is sincere, in the most important sense he can neither succeed or fail. This was especially well stated by Oliver Wendell Holmes, one of America's greatest jurists, when, in talking in retrospect to his campmates in the Civil War, he said, "To our great good fortune, in our youth our hearts were touched with fire. It was given us to learn at the outset that life was a profound and passionate thing. . . . While we were permitted to scorn nothing but indifference . . . we have learned that the one and only success which it is ours to command is to bring to our work a mighty heart." This is as true in peace as in war, and it is true in business, in politics, in the church, in the community and in the family.

Goals are thus expedient things which one sets for oneself primarily to make clearer the immediate steps by which to pursue aims. They are individual, and what is the best goal for one person may not be the best for another. Hence integrity is not sacrificed by seeking to adjust one's own goals to the goals of others, and it is important to agree on goals only if the relationship requires joint action. Here lies the virtue and the charm of mature discussion, whether it is formalized in committees, conferences or boards, or informal in family, working or social contacts. The most fundamental aims are usually common in substance if not in expression. These common aims are kept vital and agreement brought about, not by the negative process of cutting out areas of difference, but by the constructive one of utilizing the initial differences in goals and the reasons envisioned for them to point the way to new and better goals not thought of before.

People who are truly mature can thus work happily and well together in spite of differences in goals. But with aims, it is another matter. It is of critical importance to associate with people and to work with people whose fundamental aims one shares. If one cannot admire the aims of those with whom he works or associates, he is little likely to gain satisfaction or happiness, or to achieve significant results from working or living with them. Keeping in mind the distinction between goals and aims thus points the way in which integrity and considerateness, instead of militating against one another, can be unified and made mutually contributory.

### Clarity and Depth

The third distinction which contributes to the attaining of maturity arises from the fact that the deepest relationships, aims and values which guide individuals in living and working maturely together, unlike the principles of physics, cannot be reduced to a single formulation which exactly expresses them once for all. Often they can best be understood without words from the daily acts and lives of people. Yet clarity is so appealing to the mind that even in subtle, inexpressible matters such as these one is likely to value it above a deep, implicit or artistically communicated understanding that lies nearer to truth. In the field of subtle human affairs, such depth of understanding is as hard and as important to achieve as is precision in objectively commensurable fields. In both fields it is vital to struggle to attain the closest possible realization of truth; but in many aspects of human relations depth of understanding is primary, and often such depth is incompatible with precise clarity of formulation.

Recognition of this distinction between depth of understanding and clarity of articulation is important in organized as well as informal human relationships. It has, for example, played an important part in enabling our common law, in spite of social disorders, wars and even revolutions, to remain over many centuries both a source of social order and a safeguard of individual liberty. For our common law is not formulated in rigid, explicit rules which in regulating precisely would regulate rigidly and often wrongly. Its essence is never formulated but lies in the understanding achieved through the contemplation of countless previous decisions—an understanding far more profound and flexible and therefore more capable of adaptation to human circumstances than exactness and finality of formulation would permit. The failure to recognize the fact that a single explicit agreement as to the formulation of religious faith was not essential to a true community of faith and worship led to the religious wars and persecutions of the past, and prevented the great interdenominational and even interfaith religious fellowship which plays so vital a part in religious progress today.

Although in human problems of every sort it is important to explore the character of the relationships involved, thinking out as clearly as possible both the essence of one's aims and the relation to them of his goals, to seek to reach too explicit agreement on the statement of fundamental aims, values, and relationships may create unhappy and unnecessary differences even where fundamental agreement really exists. On the one hand, undue insistence on articulateness in formulation may destroy much of the inner substance and integrity of human relationships and values, and may even profane them. For in human relationships integrity consists in loyalty to inner truth, not to formulated statements. On the other hand untimely or overexacting insistence on formulation may constitute a lack of considerateness. For considerateness involves respect for the inner values of others and concern lest their values be distorted or profaned by being forced into the rigid molds of exact words, or lest others may be driven into precise agreement before they are able to accept it without humiliation or fear of domination.

## Integrity and Considerateness under Stress

All these three distinctions are hard to bear actively in mind at times of tension when maturity in dealing with others is most difficult and most important to maintain. At times of difference with others, it is not easy to remember the value of exploring the relationship between oneself and others, and one's part—his function—in it; and to remember also that his chance to do good is almost wholly confined to doing his own function well. In struggling to attain specific goals, it is not easy for one to remember that their significance is independent of his success or failure in attaining them, but lies in the extent to which for the time being they clarify his aims and sustain his dedication to these aims. At times of tension it is not easy to realize that if actions show common impelling aims and a common dedication to them, it may be unnecessary and even undesirable to try to reduce either the aims or the relationships to too specific or binding agreement.

But if one can bear these illusive concepts in mind, they will not only help him solve his problems of working and living maturely with others but will help him make the solving of each problem contribute to the development of greater maturity: a maturity consisting of a profound integrity which never lets him be deflected from his aims, combined with a heartfelt considerateness which causes him to welcome difference, study it and seek to learn from it; a maturity which adds dignity and significance both to his own life and to the lives of those with whom he works and lives; but also a maturity the attainment of which will be a never-ending struggle calling for the best that is in him.

To develop social maturity then, one must unite integrity with considerateness. To have mature integrity in human relations, one must have the inner courage to think clearly and fearlessly for himself, to hold valiantly to what he thinks, and to do both no matter how widely or bitterly he is opposed. Only then is one able to be wholly himself and to live up to the best that is in him. To be maturely considerate in human relations, one must be truly and feelingly concerned with what others think and feel, translating this concern into understanding conduct; and he must do so not merely in relaxed relationships or where there is general agreement, but also when he differs with others, and when the difference is both deep and deeply felt. If one can combine such integrity and such considerateness, his maturity will enable him to bring to his aims "a mighty heart" while contributing to the opportunity of others to be freely and fully themselves.

# CHAPTER 13

## THEOLOGY AND THE
## UNDERSTANDING OF CHILDREN

### RANDOLPH CRUMP MILLER

THEOLOGY provides insights for the understanding of children, and theology provides the basis for the integration of children's personality in their religious growth. Theology has been a missing ingredient in Christian education, either due to irrelevance of the theology taught or to the unsound basis of the theology accepted. Before we can get at either the understanding of children or the relevance of theology for children, we need to rethink our theological positions in terms of the goals of Christian maturity.

Theology is simply the truth about God in relation to man. By this, I mean that theology is concerned with truth, with concepts which reflect the meaning of actual events. The truths of theology are interpretations of the acts of God in the cosmos, in history, and in human experience. The basic source of theology is the Bible, which contains a record of the acts of God centering in the focal point of history which is the Incarnation. When we say "God was in Christ reconciling the world to himself," we are interpreting a series of historical events (which quite obviously happened) in terms of the truth about God in relation to man.

But theology also tells about man, who is a creature of God. In telling us that God is the Creator and that man is the creature of a particular kind of God who revealed himself in history, we are saying that human history reveals also the nature of man. Man is not only what science says he is; he is also what theology says he is.

The heart of theology, then, lies in the idea of *relationship*. We are not concerned simply with abstract truths about God. God in the abstract is not "a very present help in time of trouble." We are not concerned with man in himself, for while man in himself is a concrete person, it provides no framework for understanding what man is. Man as an element in a scientific cosmos may provide an interesting function for the observation of scientists, and their findings are of great significance for theology; but theology begins at a different point, and asks, "What is man *in relation* to God?" By this, we get away from both abstract ideas and scientific concepts, no matter how helpful both may be in providing an answer to the problem. When we turn to the *relationship*, we want to know what a living person is in relation to a living God who is in our midst. Thus theology becomes dynamic and relevant.

Much theology is static and irrelevant. It was not meant to be. The theological implications of the Bible are always dynamic and relevant, answering the question of what God and man are in the relationship established by the work of Christ. But the Bible and the councils and modern theology have not always been treated in terms of such relevance. As a result, Christian educators have either turned to a static theology or away from theology altogether; and in neither case has there been increased understanding of the nature of children or adequate relating of theology to the development of children into mature Christians.

The task of developing a relevant theology is not an easy one. Just recently, a questionnaire was sent to members of a congregation, and the answers revealed a startling ignorance of theology in the abstract. Further analysis showed that the congregation had not been thinking in terms of the questions asked. And if the questions did not seem relevant, certainly the answers would not prove satisfying. Theology is relevant when it answers questions which are basic to existence, when it tells who the person is, what life means, where he is going and why. The Christian faith does this, but such faith has to be expressed in theological terms where the relevance is hidden or distorted.

The most significant contribution of theology to the understanding of children lies in the doctrine of man. Theology gives us insights into the nature and destiny of man which are not part of either the data or the interpretation of the scientific view of man. It begins with the assertion that every man is the creature of God. It says that man becomes a child of God through the special blessings of baptism. It says that a man grows in grace through participation in the life and fellowship of the church. It says that man's destiny is to live in harmony with God and to achieve eternal life now, and that after death there will be a resurrection.

The Christian view of man, with its dual citizenship in this world and in the kingdom of God, provides an ultimate environment of dynamic peace which passes man's understanding and a present environment which is full of conflict, tension, and strife. The "abundant life" which is promised, is to be achieved through "peril, toil, and pain." Man is truly a climber of the steep ascent of heaven.

Man, who is the loved creature of God and who lives in an environment of strife and achievement, reflects the same tensions within himself. He wants to be a child of God, and yet he wants to follow his own decisions at the same time. He wants to be "naughty but nice," a saint and a sinner. Yet when he is a sinner, he knows he should be a saint; and when he is a saint, he is dissatisfied because there are no sins to give momentary pleasure. This mixture of urges is described quite adequately by psychologists and psychiatrists, and they are helpful in getting below the surface symptoms to the basic diagnosis. Yet the theological factor is overlooked, and the true depth of man's nature is provided by theology.

The church, at its best, has always seen its theology centered in the cross. Man is so disobedient, so selfish, so profoundly traitorous to the nature which God implanted, that he crucifies the best that God can do in sending his own Son. Here, not in psychoanalysis, but in history, is the revelation of the truth about God in relation to man, which also tells us a basic truth about man. Thus man is capable of crucifying the best man that God has made, but man is also capable of being the Christ. One historic incident reveals in its full depths the glory and misery of man.

But Christian theology never stops with analysis. It turns to the cure immediately. It is the reconciliation which comes in Christ which is the heart of the matter. God has acted so that man will be saved if he turns in faith to the Father. It is the relationship of faith and grace which is the heart of Christian nurture. Christian maturity comes as man comes into the fullness of faith.

Now all of this is part of the story of the relationship of theology to the understanding of children. The hopes and fears, ideals and images, virtues and sins, of children as well as adults, need to be understood within the context of the Christian doctrine of man.

Developmental psychology has shown us that many actions are normal for children and abnormal for adults. So children pass through "stages," while adults have sins. There is just enough truth in this to make us unaware of the dangers of this assumption. Little children have a certain degree of freedom, and when they choose against what they know to be right they are not going through an amoral stage; they are being disobedient to the highest they know. For example, there are certain stages when children tell lies, and the motivation is not against telling the truth but is the product of imagination; there are other stages when children deliberately tell untruths when they know better, and when the motivation is to get out of an unpleasant situation.

It takes a combination of developmental psychology and theology properly to evaluate such situations. The capacity for sin is present in the small child, which is what the doctrine of original sin is trying to say, but the doctrine of "intention" as found in the Gospels also makes it clear that we must distinguish between evil acts which are willed and those which are due to immaturity.

A noncritical theology makes the mistake of treating little children as adults, and therefore makes no place for childish behavior patterns. This was the weakness of the New England theology which treated all children as guilty of original and actual sin at every point in their development. This led in some cases to a guilt complex concerning acts which were not motivated by sinful desires or intended as disobedience to the laws of God.

A sound theology will recognize the fact that children are sinners and that they need the grace of God and the resources of the church as much as do adults; but it will also recognize that sin is a relative term, depending upon the maturity of one's relationship with the living God and understanding of God's laws as relevant to him. God does not demand the same thing for each person, for there are diversities of vocations and varieties in the ways we serve him. So it is that God does not expect children to act like little adults, but as faithful children. The psychology of childhood behavior and the study of the religious readiness of children become tools for an adequate theological understanding of childhood.

This leads to another theological insight which is shared by modern progressive educators for different reasons. Theology tells us that each child is of ultimate value in the sight of God, and is to be treated as such. Modern idealism talks of respect for personality, which leads to the same results but for the wrong reason. The only reason for treating persons as ends rather than as means is that God has created them as ends in themselves. Any other reason will break down in certain situations, while the theological basis is permanent. The reason Jesus said, "Let the little children come unto me," is that little children are persons, not things—creatures of a loving, heavenly Father.

The little child is to be treated as a child of God and as a sinner at the same time. He has the same value as an adult and in his childish freedom the same responsibilities. Yet he is to be treated as a child and not as a little adult. He is expected to grow up and to put away childish things. He is not to think like a child any longer, but after he becomes mature he is still to be capable of childlike faith in God.

The church has underscored this understanding of children in the sacrament of baptism. Those communions which postpone baptism until the years of discretion are saying that the child comes to the place where he is developed enough to make his own choice. The communions which practice infant baptism say that the church, through the parents and godparents, will provide the faith that makes baptism an introduction to Christian nurture and the life of fellowship in the church. In each case, the child is recognized as being a child of God and as capable of sin. The doctrine of spiritual regeneration is simply a recognition of the tendency to sin and the need for constant spiritual renewal or rebirth. Where baptism is postponed to adult years, a service of "dedication" is becoming popular to meet the needs of God's grace as surrounding the little child from the beginning; and where baptism is of infants, there is a service of confirmation or its equivalent to meet the needs of responsible choice in adolescence. These services provide in the worship of the church a theological understanding of childhood which stands the tests of modern experience.

So far, we have dealt with theology as it provides insights for adults who seek a profounder understanding of children. But theology is relevant to children at a far different level. In the religious growth of the child, truth about God in relation to man is an experience of childhood. Therefore, theology contributes to the self-understanding of the child and to his understanding of the world. If the living God is to be a reality in the experience of the child, he needs to have an understanding of what it is all about within the limits of his capacities. It is in this sense that I have written elsewhere of *The Clue to Christian Education*.[1] Theology stands in the background behind all the experiences of faith and grace, which are the gift of God to the little child as well as to the mature Christian. It is partly a matter of vocabulary, of providing an area of discourse and communication so that the child can comprehend within limits who he is, where he came from, what his world and the people in it are like, and where he is going.

He finds the reality of God, first of all, in his experience of his parents. His parents are God and the church to him. When he is loved by his parents, who meet his needs by providing security in this midst of his development and background for his independence when he needs it, he is having the gifts of God mediated to him through the ministry of his parents. At the youngest ages, this may not be verbalized at all, for it is the reality of the atmosphere, attitudes, and experiences which are vital and dynamic. But an embryonic theology, in terms of the relationship of God to himself, is present in these earliest experiences. The whole study of Christian parenthood is being revised in terms of these theological insights, which are as old as the Hebrew family and as new as modern child psychology. Once theology makes clear that God is neither an absentee landlord nor an abstract idea, then the spirit of the living God will come alive. Theology is basic, even though it is the experience of faith and grace that saves.

Theology becomes relevant at every point in the child's development. He keeps asking the same basic theological questions over and over again, and frequently his teachers fail him. They fail for several reasons: chiefly because they have failed to formulate a dynamic theological outlook for themselves, often because they use a static

[1] New York: Charles Scribner's Sons, 1950.

theological vocabulary which has lost its meaning even for adults, and more often because they have no idea at all of how to interpret what they do believe in terms of childhood experiences and vocabulary.

It is difficult to work out the doctrine of redemption with a six-year-old. Yet reconciliation is a constant element in his experience. There is rebellion followed by forgiveness. This is symbolized by the child striking his mother. Reuel Howe points out that from a psychological point of view, the child thereby wills his mother's death, although his existence depends on her. There is a momentary sense of complete desolation and loneliness expressed either by striking or speaking, followed by the agony of separation. The child cannot will the rebirth of his parent by reform, offering self-punishment, or providing a scapegoat. The parent comes to life by taking the initiative, by showing love and forgiveness, by becoming reconciled to the child. This is the fundamental meaning of death and resurrection in all of life, existing on the level of very young children. The theological aspects are obvious, although it is difficult to put them in a child's language. The point is that experiences of profound theological significance are relevant to the child.

Theology is significant for the integration of the child's personality. If it is true that our basic beliefs determine our action, then it is important that the child have the right beliefs. But these beliefs are not to be verbalized expressions in language which has no meaning; they are to be meaningful expressions which reflect life experiences. They are to be beliefs based upon the facts of life. Insofar as theology is true, it is an interpretation of experience; it is factual. According to the religious readiness and intellectual capacity of the child, his experiences are to be interpreted to him in terms of facts which he can recognize. His developing system of beliefs becomes the structure of his personality, and the process of integration is determined by the actual divine Person to whom he gives his allegiance. His faith in God opens the doors to God's grace, and it is the power of God's grace which is the source of his integration.

Therefore, Christian education must always be concerned with facts. Facts are experienced in the relationship between man and his environment; between man and other men; between man and God. Knowledge of facts may be given by tradition and history, or they may come from immediate experience. Both history and contemporary experience are necessary to check one's knowledge of facts. But as the church has a revelation (which is an interpretation of actual events) given to it in Scripture, history, and experience, so it has a responsibility to pass on that revelation in the context of present-day culture.

Also, Christian education must be concerned with character. The developing personality is understood in terms of increased loyalty, increased poise and stability, and increased integration. And because this growing loyalty is given to a living God and not simply to a static idea of God, Christian character develops. Character education and Christian faith are thus indissolubly intertwined.

This means that Christian education involves evangelism, becoming almost identical with evangelism in its goals. For the end of Christian education and Christian evangelism is to draw men to Jesus Christ within the fellowship of the church. The theology which acts as background for the faith and grace in the foreground guides men into greater and sounder loyalty. But this development of Christian character cannot be guaranteed by processes either of education or of evangelism. The response of children and adults to the gospel of Jesus Christ is in the last analysis a personal decision that rests in the mystery of God himself.

The theology which leads to our understanding of children and to their understanding of the world in which they live, is the product and the property of the Christian Church. There is no way to understand the theology of Christian faith except from the inside. The outsider simply lacks the data by which to judge the Church's theology. Furthermore, only the fellowship of the worshiping congregation can supply the channels of integration, for this Christian integration is never simply a private relation between God and a man. It is always a covenant between God and the fellowship of men. Biblical religion has always insisted that this is so.

The expression of the fruits of Christian education always implies full membership in the church. It is the worshipping society which is truly the recipient of God's grace. It is no accident that the sacraments of baptism and the Lord's Supper are central to Christian living. Just as baptism is truly an initiatory rite of regeneration, so the Holy Communion is fully the symbolic expression of Christian fellowship in the presence of the living Christ.

Theology has much to say about the nature of the church and **its** sacraments, for the church is thought of as the body of Christ, of which all baptized people are members. It is within this "congregation of faithful people," where one hears the word of God and takes part in the sacraments, that the covenant relationship between God and man is most fully expressed. The little child finds his developing purpose in life as he partakes in the experiences of worship and fellowship within the church. It is integration within a social context, and with a transcendent reference. The child, who comes to know himself as a sinner and as a child of God, knows he is a forgiven sinner when he partakes of the church's worship. The child who has found security in the love of his parents in the home, grows into the same sense of security in the presence of his heavenly Father in the church.

Theology, we have said, is truth about God in relation to man. God and man are living persons, and it is the relation between them which is basic. Our understanding of children is enriched when we see them first of all from the point of view of this interpersonal relationship; their understanding of themselves is deepened when they know themselves as children of God; and we and they find the relationship itself made more manifest in the fellowship of the church. In this context, the truths of theology and the facts of existence are brought together in the presence of God as shared by the worshiping congregation.

# CHAPTER 14

## THE HUMAN SITUATION: A FEMININE VIEWPOINT

### VALERIE SAIVING GOLDSTEIN

I AM a student of theology; I am also a woman. Perhaps it strikes you as curious that I put these two assertions beside each other, as if to imply that one's sexual identity has some bearing on his theological views. I myself would have rejected such an idea when I first began my theological studies. But now, thirteen years later, I am no longer as certain as I once was that, when theologians speak of "man," they are using the word in its generic sense. It is, after all, a well-known fact that theology has been written almost exclusively by men. This alone should put us on guard, especially since contemporary theologians constantly remind us that one of man's strongest temptations is to identify his own limited perspective with universal truth.

I propose to criticize, from the viewpoint of feminine experience, the estimate of the human situation made by certain contemporary theologians. Although the views I shall outline receive their most uncompromising expression in the writings of Anders Nygren and Reinhold Niebuhr, I believe that they represent a widespread tendency in contemporary theology to describe man's predicament as rising from his separateness and the anxiety occasioned by it and to identify sin with self-assertion and love with selflessness.

The human condition, according to many contemporary theologians, is universally characterized by anxiety, for, while man is a creature, subject to the limitations of all finite existence, he is different from other creatures because he is free. Although his freedom is qualified by his participation in the natural order, he is not simply bound by inherited instinct to a repetitious living-out of the life-

151

pattern common to all members of the species. Instead, he can stand apart from the world and survey it, envision multiple possibilities and make choices, elaborate his own private ends and imagine larger harmonies, destroy given natural structures and create new ones in their place. This freedom of man, which is the source of his historical and cultural creativity, is also the source of his temptation to sin. For man's freedom, which from another point of view can be called his individuality and his essential loneliness, brings with it a pervasive fear for the survival of the self and its values. Sin is the self's attempt to overcome that anxiety by magnifying its own power, righteousness, or knowledge. Man knows that he is merely a part of the whole, but he tries to convince himself and others that he *is* the whole. He tries, in fact, to become the whole. Sin is the unjustified concern of the self for its own power and prestige; it is the imperialistic drive to close the gap between the individual, separate self and others by reducing those others to the status of mere objects which can then be treated as appendages of the self and manipulated accordingly. Sin is not an occasional, isolated act but pervades everything man does, even those acts which he performs for the most pure and "unselfish" motives. For the human creature has a marvelous capacity for blinding himself to the fact that, no matter how altruistic his goals may be, he always inserts his own limited individual goals into his attempts to achieve them.

Love is the precise opposite of sin. It is the true norm of human existence and the one real solution to the fundamental predicament in which man stands. Love, according to these theologians, is completely self-giving, taking no thought for its own interests but seeking only the good of the other. Love makes no value judgments concerning the other's worth; it demands neither merit in the other nor recompense for itself but gives itself freely, fully, and without calculation. Love is unconditional forgiveness; concerning the one to whom it is given, it beareth all things, believeth all things, hopeth all things, endureth all things. Love is personal; it is the concrete relatedness of an *I* to a *Thou*, in which the *I* casts aside all its particularities, all its self-affirmations, everything which separates it from the *Thou*, and becomes wholly receptive to the other.

It is important, I think, to emphasize that the foregoing analysis of the human situation and the definitions of love and sin which accompany it are mutually dependent concepts. The kind of love described is normative and redemptive precisely insofar as it answers to man's deepest need. If human nature and the human situation are not as described by the theologians in question, then the assertion that self-giving love is the law of man's being is irrelevant and may even be untrue. To the extent that contemporary theology has, in whole or in part, described the human condition inaccurately, to that same extent is its doctrine of love in question.

It is my contention that there are significant differences between masculine and feminine experience and that feminine experience reveals in a more emphatic fashion certain aspects of the human situation which are present but less obvious in the experience of men. Contemporary theological doctrines of love have, I believe, been constructed primarily upon the basis of masculine experience and thus view the human condition from the male standpoint. Consequently, these doctrines do not provide an adequate interpretation of the situation of women—nor, for that matter, of men, especially in view of certain fundamental changes now taking place in our own society.

But can we speak meaningfully about feminine experience as something fundamentally different from masculine experience? Is there such a thing as an underlying feminine character structure which always and everywhere differs from the basic character structure of the male? Are not all distinctions between the sexes, except the purely biological ones, relative to a given culture? Are we not all, men and women alike, members of a single species?

Of course it would be ridiculous to deny that there is a structure of experience common to both men and women, so that we may legitimately speak of the "human situation" without reference to sexual identity. The only question is whether we have described the human situation correctly by taking account of the experiences of both sexes. We know, too, that we can no longer make any hard-and-fast distinctions between the *potentialities* of men and women as such. The twentieth century has witnessed the shattering of too many of our traditional conceptions of sexual differences for us any longer to ignore the tremendous plasticity of human nature. But perhaps the most telling evidence of all that every distinction between the sexes above the physiological level is purely arbitrary comes from the descriptions given by cultural anthropologists of many primitive societies whose ideas about the behavior appropriate to each sex are widely different from, and in many instances contradictory to, those held in our own tradition.

And yet, curiously enough, it is the anthropologists themselves who have begun in recent years to question the assumption that the characters of men and women are essentially alike in all respects. It is even more startling to note that among them are two women of unquestioned professional competence.

It was Ruth Benedict—who in *Patterns of Culture* stressed the relativity of the character ideals held by various societies and the inability of science to account for their diversity on a biological basis —who also wrote these words: "To me it seems a very terrible thing to be a woman." And again: "Nature lays a compelling and very distressing hand upon woman, and she struggles in vain who tries to deny it or escape it—life loves the little irony of proving it upon the very woman who has denied it; she can only hope for success by working according to Nature's conception of her make-up—not against them."[1]

Margaret Mead's concern with the problem of sex differentiation has been expressed in much of her research and writing. In 1935 she published *Sex and Temperament in Three Primitive Societies*,[2] in which she came to the conclusion that there are no natural—that is to say, innate—differences between the character traits of men and women. Rather, the way any particular society defines masculinity and femininity is by a purely arbitrary assignment to one or the other sex of qualities to which members of either sex could be trained with equal ease.

Fourteen years later Margaret Mead published *Male and Female,* in which she returned to the problem, but this time from a slightly different perspective:

In every known society, mankind has elaborated the biological division of labour into forms often very remotely related to the original biological differences that provided the original clues. . . . Sometimes one quality has been assigned to one sex, sometimes to the other. . . . Whether we deal with small matters or with large, with the frivolities of ornament and cosmetics

[1] Quoted by Clyde Kluckhohn in a review of Margaret Mead, *An Anthropologist at Work: Writings of Ruth Benedict* (Boston: Houghton Mifflin Co., 1959), *New York Times Book Review,* May 31, 1959.

[2] New York: William Morrow and Company, 1935.

or the sanctities of man's place in the universe, we find this great variety of ways, often flatly contradictory one to the other, in which the roles of the two sexes have been patterned.

But we always find the patterning. We know of no culture that has said, articulately, that there is no difference between men and women except in the way they contribute to the creation of the next generation; that otherwise in all respects they are simply human beings with varying gifts, no one of which can be exclusively assigned to either sex. . . .

So . . . we are faced with a most bewildering and confusing array of apparently contradictory evidence about sex differences. We may well ask: Are they important? Do real differences exist, in addition to the obvious anatomical and physical ones—but just as biologically based—that may be masked by the learnings appropriate to any given society, but which will nevertheless be there? Will such differences run through all of men's and all of women's behaviour?[3]

Miss Mead answers this question in the affirmative, not because she has found new evidence which contradicts the evidence presented in her earlier book, but because she has put the question in a different way. Instead of asking the question most of us ask: "Are character differences between the sexes the result of heredity or environment, of biology or culture?" she asks, rather, whether there may not be certain basic similarities in the ways in which men and women in *every* culture have experienced what it means to be a man or to be a woman. Cultures may and do superimpose upon the fundamental meanings of sex membership other ideas which are irrelevant or contradictory to the basic structure of sexuality. Nevertheless, if such regularities do exist, then we may find that, underneath the specific additions which each culture has imposed, there remains a substratum or core of masculine and feminine orientations which, if too drastically contradicted by the superstructure, may threaten the very existence of the society and its members.

In my description of a few of these biocultural differences between masculine and feminine experience, I shall draw heavily upon Margaret Mead's[4] analysis because I personally find it most illuminating. Nevertheless, I wish to make it clear that I am not attempting to

[3] Margaret Mead, *Male and Female* (New York: New American Library, 1959, by arrangement with William Morrow and Company [originally published in 1949]) , pp.16-17.

[4] Every reader who is familiar with *Male and Female* will recognize the extent of my indebtedness to Miss Mead in the discussion which follows. Only the impossibility, as it seemed to me, of disentangling her insights from my own observations and convictions has prevented me from documenting this debt more fully.

summarize her thought, which is far too complex to present fully here, nor (since even anthropologists are not in agreement in these matters) do I present her as an authority. Primarily, what I shall say is based upon my own experience and observation as it has been clarified and substantiated by Miss Mead and by a number of other writers, including Helene Deutsch,[5] Erich Fromm,[6] and Theodor Reik[7] (psychoanalysts), Talcott Parsons[8] (sociologist), and Ashley Montagu[9] (anthropologist).

What, then, are the distinctions between the experiences of men and the experiences of women as they occur in any human society, and in what way do these contribute to the formation of differences between the masculine and the feminine character and orientation?

We must begin with the central fact about sexual differences: that in every society it is women—and only women—who bear children. Further, in every society the person closest to the infant and young child is a woman. This fact, based on the physiology of lactation, remains true even in our own culture, in which the formula has so largely replaced the mother's breast.

The close relationship between mother and infant plays the first and perhaps the most important role in the formation of masculine and feminine character, for it means that the person with whom the child originally identifies himself is a woman. Both male and female children must learn to overcome this initial identification by differentiating themselves from the mother. But the kind and degree of differentiation required of the boy are strikingly different from what is required of the girl. The little girl learns that, although she must grow up (become a separate person), she will grow up to be a woman, like her mother, and have babies of her own; she will, in a broad sense, merely take her mother's place. She learns, too, that she will attain womanhood quite naturally—merely by the maturation

---

[5] Helene Deutsch, *Psychology of Women* (New York: Grune and Stratton, 1944), Vols. I and II.

[6] Erich Fromm, "Sex and Character," in Ruth Nanda Anshen (ed.), *The Family: Its Function and Destiny* (New York: Harper & Brothers, 1949), chap. xix.

[7] Theodor Reik, *Of Love and Lust* (New York: Grove Press, 1957, by arrangement with Farrar, Straus and Cudahy [originally published in 1949]).

[8] Talcott Parsons, "The Social Structure of the Family," in Anshen (ed.), *op. cit.*, pp. 186-88.

[9] Ashley Montagu, *The Natural Superiority of Women* (New York: The Macmillan Company, 1953).

of her body. In fact, she already is a woman, if in miniature, and must therefore be protected against the premature exploitation of her femininity. And so the emphasis for the girl is upon the fact that she *is* a female and that all she needs to do to realize her full femininity is to wait.

The boy's process of differentiation from his mother is much more complex and difficult. He learns not only that he must grow up but that he must grow up to be a man; that men are different from women, since they do not have babies; and that he must therefore become quite a different sort of creature from his mother. Instead of imitating her, he must relinquish completely his original identification with her. He also finds that, while he is not and never will be a woman, neither is he yet a man. It will be many years before he can perform sexually as a man, and therefore he does not need to be guarded, like his sister, against sexual activity before he is ready for it. He is thus permitted far greater freedom than the girl. But this freedom has its drawbacks for him, since along with it goes a certain set of standards which he must meet before he will be judged to have achieved manhood. He must learn this or that skill, acquire this or that trait or ability, pass this or that test of endurance, courage, strength, or accomplishment. He must *prove* himself to be a man. True, he has certain advantages over the girl, particularly in the fact that he has visible organs which demonstrate his sex. But, on the whole, the process of self-differentiation plays a stronger and more anxiety-provoking role in the boy's maturation than is normally the case for the girl. Growing up is not merely a natural process of bodily maturation; it is, instead, a challenge which he must meet, a proof he must furnish by means of performance, achievement, and activity directed toward the external world. And even so his reward for achieving manhood is not easily grasped in imagination. It is quite obvious to a child what motherhood is; it is not nearly so obvious what it means to be a father.

This early divergence between masculine and feminine sexual development is repeated, reinforced, and elaborated in later stages of the individual's life. For instance, the girl's history as a female will be punctuated and authenticated by a series of definite, natural, and irreversible bodily occurrences: first menstruation, defloration, childbirth, menopause. Each of these events, to be sure, occasions anxiety

for the woman and thus might seem to be the female equivalent of
the constant anxiety regarding his maleness which besets the man.
Yet these physiological events which mark the woman's life have a
reassuring aspect, too, for each of them is concrete, unmistakable
proof of her femaleness. The boy's history will provide no such dramatic, once-for-all physical signals of his masculinity.

Even more significant are the differences between male and female
roles in the various aspects of adult sexuality. The processes of im-
pregnation, pregnancy, childbirth, and lactation have a certain
passivity about them; they are things which *happen* to a woman
more than things that she *does*. The sexual act itself, for example,
has for her this basically passive quality. The woman, of course, *may*
take an active role, but it is not necessary for her to do so, either to
satisfy the man or to fulfill her reproductive function. In fact, she
may be quite without desire or may even have strong feelings of re-
vulsion, and yet she may, for any number of reasons, submit to the
man—sometimes with sufficient grace so that he is completely unaware of her feelings. In the extreme case—rape—the passive structure of female sexuality unquestionably appears. The case is quite
otherwise for the male, whose *active* desire and *active* performance
in the sexual act are absolutely required for its completion. And
here again the demand for performance is coupled with an inevitable
anxiety; in order to prove his maleness, he *must* succeed in what he
has undertaken—and it is possible for him to fail.

Considered in terms of its reproductive consequences, the sexual
act has greatly different meanings for men and women. The male's
part in the creation of a child seems indirect and is completed very
quickly, while a woman's participation is direct, immediate, and
prolonged. It is true that we now know as scientific fact what some
primitive peoples have only suspected and others denied: that the
man's role in reproduction is essential and that his genetic contribution is equal to the woman's. Yet the birth of a child is never an absolute guaranty to a man of his maleness, as it is to a woman of her
femaleness. For, while there can be no doubt as to who is the mother
of the child, "paternity remains, with all our modern biological
knowledge, as inferential as it ever was, and considerably less ascer-
tainable than it has seemed to be in some periods of history."[10]

[10] Mead, *Male and Female*, p. 125.

There is a sense, too, in which woman's biological creativity appears to present a challenge to a man; he perhaps feels his inability to bear children as a deficiency for which he must compensate by other kinds of creativity.[11]

The man's sense of his own masculinity, then, is throughout characterized by uncertainty, challenge, and the feeling that he must again and again prove himself a man. It also calls for a kind of objective achievement and a greater degree of self-differentiation and self-development than are required of the woman *as* woman. In a sense, masculinity is an endless process of *becoming*, while in femininity the emphasis is on *being*. Another way of putting the distinction is that woman is more closely bound to nature than is man. This has advantages and disadvantages for her as a human being. The advantages lie in her greater degree of natural security and the lesser degree of anxiety to which she is subject, both of which make

[11] The suggestion that men feel inferior to women because they cannot give birth to children, which sounds fantastic to most men (and women) in our own culture, is nevertheless supported by an impressive amount of anthropological and psychoanalytical evidence. See, for example, Bruno Bettelheim's *Symbolic Wounds* (Glencoe: The Free Press, 1954), which came to my attention after the original publication of the present essay. Dr. Bettelheim interprets various aspects of the male initiation rites of primitive peoples (nearly all of which include a ritual or myth in which it is asserted that the adolescent boy is reborn by the agency of *men*) as motivated by the need of the male "to alleviate fear and envy of the mother and of women in general [because of their childbearing capacity], and to reassert the relative power and importance of men as compared with women" (p. 87). Dr. Bettelheim stresses, however, the *positive* or *constructive* quality of such rites; they are "efforts at self-realization; through them man seeks to express and then free himself of his anxieties about his own sex and his wishes for experiences, organs and functions which are available only to persons of the other sex" (p. 264). That the historical and cultural creativity of man in more advanced stages of civilization (which is analogous in some ways, perhaps, to the initiation ceremonies of preliterate societies) ought also to be seen as positive acts, as truly creative rather than merely compensatory, has been brilliantly stated by Dr. Norman Kelman in his valuable paper, "Social and Psychoanalytic Reflections on the Father" (*American Scholar*, Vol. 29, No. 3, Summer, 1960):

"If we start with the notion that the father wishes to be as intimate with gestation as the mother, and cannot, one might evoke the theory that makes his explorations of the intellect, of art, of music, a sublimation. This interpretation derives from the tendency to psychologize away all of man's aspirations. But, considering that his awayness from gestation is simply his own condition, the wish to become intimate will be realized with his own resources. His intellectual, artistic, manual explorations become not sublimations, but rather his ways to enter into the mysteries of human relations. Needless to say, this does not exhaust the meaning of man's intellectual explorations."

it easier, all other things being equal, for her to enter into loving relationships in which self-concern is at a minimum. Yet if it is true, as Niebuhr says, that man stands at the juncture of nature and spirit, then woman's closeness to nature is a measure of the distance she must travel to reach spirit. That she, too, is a free human being is proved by the fact that she can reject the feminine role; but, having chosen it, she has chosen a kind of bondage which is not involved in a man's acceptance of his sexual identity.

For masculinity can with good reason be defined as the distance between spirit and nature. Because of his less direct and immediate role in the reproductive process, including nurture during the long period of human infancy, man is, in his greater freedom, necessarily subject to a kind of anxiety—and, consequently, to a kind of creative drive—which is experienced more rarely and less intensely by most women.

I have drawn the distinctions between masculine and feminine experience in the sharpest possible terms in order to clarify the divergence between them. But it is important to remind ourselves of the countless changes which have been rung on these basic themes in human societies. Every culture, we have said, superimposes upon the necessities of sexual roles a whole structure of masculine and feminine character traits. Many of these addenda are only tenuously related to the foundation on which they rest, and they may even be completely contradictory to that foundation. When this phenomenon is carried to its extreme, so that women, for example, are educated by their society to despise the functions of childbearing and nurture, then the society is in grave danger of bringing about its own destruction. Similarly, where procreation is valued so highly that men attempt to participate directly in the processes of pregnancy, birth, and the rearing of children to the exclusion of other kinds of creative activity, the social fabric again becomes dangerously weak. Both types of society have been discovered among preliterate peoples,[12] and, as we shall see, our own society has not escaped the tendency to overvalue the traits characteristic to one or the other sex.

The truth is, of course, that there is no impassable gulf between the ways in which men and women may look at themselves and at

---

[12] See, among others, Mead, *ibid., passim.*

their world. Just as sexuality is not the whole of human existence, so the individual's sense of his own identity is not derived solely from his sexual role. Human beings of both sexes have certain basic experiences in common from earliest infancy—hunger and satiety, constriction and freedom, defenselessness and power, resentment and love. Men and women can and do learn from each other, too; women can be aggressive and ambitious, and men can be fatherly. Neither sex is exempt from anxiety, and both experience the temptations of passivity. Yet the individual's sense of being male or female, which plays such an important part in the young child's struggle for self-definition, can never be finally separated from his total orientation to life; in those cases—which are the majority—in which adult men and women accept and are able to actualize their respective sexual roles, the characterological tendencies based on sex membership are reinforced and strengthened. This is surely the reason why, although there have been women philosophers, musicians, and murderers, there have been no female Platos, Bachs, or Hitlers. It is also the reason why even those men who enjoy being fathers most fully can scarcely be imagined as finding complete self-fulfillment in fatherhood. "A woman, as Madame de Staël remarked, either has children or writes books."[13] As for men, Margaret Mead has observed:

In every known human society the male's need for achievement can be recognized. Men may cook, or weave or dress dolls or hunt hummingbirds, but if such activities are appropriate occupations of men, then the whole society, men and women alike, votes them as important. When the same occupations are performed by women, they are regarded as less important. In a great number of human societies men's sureness of their sex role is tied up with their right, or ability, to practise some activity that women are not allowed to practise. Their maleness, in fact, has to be underwritten by preventing women from entering some field or performing some feat. Here may be found the relationship between maleness and pride; that is, a need for prestige that will outstrip the prestige which is accorded to any woman. There seems no evidence that it is necessary for men to surpass women in any specific way, but rather that men do need to find reassurance in achievement, and because of this connection, cultures frequently phrase achievement as something that women do not or cannot do, rather than directly as something which men do well.

The recurrent problem of civilization is to define the male role satisfac-

[13] Robert Briffault, *The Mothers* (New York: The Macmillan Company, 1927), II, 443.

torily enough—whether it be to build gardens or raise cattle, kill game or kill enemies, build bridges or handle bank-shares—so that the male may in the course of his life reach a solid sense of irreversible achievement, of which his childhood knowledge of the satisfactions of childbearing have given him a glimpse. In the case of women, it is only necessary that they be permitted by the given social arrangements to fulfil their biological role, to attain this sense of irreversible achievement. If women are to be restless and questing, even in the face of childbearing, they must be made so through education. If men are ever to be at peace, ever certain that their lives have been lived as they were meant to be, they must have, in addition to paternity, culturally elaborated forms of expression that are lasting and sure. Each culture—in its own way—has developed forms that will make men satisfied in their constructive activities without distorting their sure sense of their masculinity. Fewer cultures have yet found ways in which to give women a divine discontent that will demand other satisfactions than those of childbearing.[14]

It seems to me that a more realistic appraisal of contemporary theological doctrines of sin and love is possible against this general background, for the prevalent theologies today were created by men who lived amid the tensions of a hypermasculine culture. What is usually called the "modern era" in Western civilization, stretching roughly from the Renaissance and Reformation up to very recent times and reaching the peak of its expression in the rise of capitalism, the industrial revolution, imperialism, the triumphs of science and technology, and other well-known phenomena of the eighteenth, nineteenth, and twentieth centuries—this modern era can be called the "masculine age par excellence," in the sense that it emphasized, encouraged, and set free precisely those aspects of human nature which are peculiarly significant to men. It placed the highest value on external achievement, on the creation of structures of matter and meaning, on self-differentiation and the separation of man from nature. By its emphasis on *laissez faire* competition and economic uncertainty, on scientific and geographic explorations, on the widening of the gulf between family relationships, on the one hand, and the public life of business and politics, on the other—by these and many more innovations, the modern era presented a heightened challenge to men; and, by the same token, it increased their natural sense of insecurity and anxiety. It was a masculine era, too, in the degree to which it devalued the functions of women and children and the

[14] Mead, *Male and Female*, pp. 125-26.

whole reproductive process. It thereby provoked a new restlessness in women, too.[15]

It is clear that many of the characteristic emphases of contemporary theology—its definition of the human situation in terms of anxiety, estrangement, and the conflict between necessity and freedom; its identification of sin with pride, will-to-power, exploitation, self-assertiveness, and the treatment of others as objects rather than persons; its conception of redemption as restoring to man what he fundamentally lacks (namely, sacrificial love, the I-Thou relationship, the primacy of the personal, and, ultimately, peace) —it is clear that such an analysis of man's dilemma was profoundly responsive and relevant to the concrete facts of modern man's existence. Insofar as modern woman, too, increasingly accepted the prevailing values of the age and took on the challenges and opportunities, risks and insecurities of participation in the masculine world, this theology spoke directly to her condition also. And, since the most striking features of modern culture were but heightened expressions of one aspect of the universal human situation, the adequacy of this theology as a description of man's fundamental predicament seemed assured.

As a matter of fact, however, this theology is not adequate to the universal human situation; its inadequacy is clearer to no one than to certain contemporary women. These women have been enabled, through personal experience and education, to transcend the boundaries of a purely feminine identity. They now stand closer to the juncture of nature and spirit than was possible for most women in the past. They believe in the values of self-differentiation, challenge, and adventure and are not strangers to that "divine discontent" which has always driven men. Yet these same women value their femininity also; they do not wish to discard their sexual identity but rather to gather it up into a higher unity. They want, in other words, to be both women *and* full human beings.

Many of these women, who were brought up to believe in the fundamental equality of the sexes and who were given the same kind of education and the same encouragement to self-realization as

[15] This point is discussed at some length by Ferdinand Lundberg and Marynia F. Farnham, m.d., *Modern Woman, the Lost Sex* (New York: Grosset and Dunlap, 1959, by arrangement with Harper & Brothers [originally published in 1947]) .

their male contemporaries, do not really discover until they marry and bear children—or, perhaps, have been forced to admit to themselves that they never will marry—that there are real differences between the masculine and feminine situations which cannot be blamed upon a cultural lag in the definitions of femininity or upon the "selfishness" and "stupidity" of men. It is only at this point, when the ultimate actualization of their specific sexuality must be either accepted or given up for good, that they become aware of the deep need of almost every woman, regardless of her personal history and achievements or her belief in her own individual value, to surrender her self-identity and be included in another's "power of being." And, if she is fortunate enough to bear a child, she very soon discovers that the one essential, indispensable relationship of a mother to her child is the I-Thou relationship. In infancy the very existence of the child depends upon the mother's ability to transcend her own patterns of thought, feeling, and physical need. As Margaret Mead puts it, "The mother who must learn that the infant who was but an hour ago a part of her own body is now a different individual, with its own hungers and its own needs, and that if she listens to her own body to interpret the child, the child will die, is schooled in an irreplaceable school."[16] At a later stage in the child's life, too, the essential relationship continues to be one of love. To take just one example—the least sentimental one, perhaps—the child, when he has learned to talk, is almost constantly absorbed in trying to understand the world around him. It is so full of strange and wonderful and lovely and terrifying things. He is full of questions, and upon his learning the true and adequate answers to them depends the whole process of acculturation upon which the uniqueness of human societies rests. But, in order to answer a child's eager questions, the mother must be able to transcend her own habitual patterns of thought; she must meet the child where *he* is at that moment. It is absolutely impossible to communicate with a young child without in some way abandoning one's own perspective and looking at the world through *his* eyes.

A mother who rejoices in her maternal role—and most mothers do most of the time—knows the profound experience of self-transcending love. But she knows, too, that it is not the whole mean-

[16] Mead, *Male and Female*, p. 284.

ing of life. For she learns not only that it is impossible to sustain a perpetual I-Thou relationship but that the attempt to do so can be deadly. The moments, hours, and days of self-giving must be balanced by moments, hours, and days of withdrawal into, and enrichment of, her individual selfhood if she is to remain a whole person. She learns, too, that a woman can give too much of herself, so that nothing remains of her uniqueness; she can become merely an emptiness, almost a zero, without value to herself, to her fellow men, or, perhaps, even to God.

For the temptations of woman *as woman* are not the same as the temptations of man *as man,* and the specifically feminine forms of sin—"feminine" not because they are confined to women or because women are incapable of sinning in other ways but because they are outgrowths of the basic feminine character structure—have a quality which can never be encompassed by such terms as "pride" and "will-to-power." They are better suggested by such items as triviality, distractibility, and diffuseness; lack of an organizing center or focus; dependence on others for one's own self-definition; tolerance at the expense of standards of excellence; inability to respect the boundaries of privacy; sentimentality, gossipy sociability, and mistrust of reason—in short, underdevelopment or negation of the self.

This list of specifically feminine sins could be extended. All of them, however, are to be understood as merely one side of the feminine coin. For just as man's distance from nature is the precondition of his creativity, on the one hand, and his self-concern, on the other, so does woman's closeness to nature have dipolar potentialities. Her sureness of her own femininity and thus of her secure place in the scheme of things may, if she accepts the feminine role with joy, enable her to be a source of strength and refreshment to her husband, her children, and the wider community. If she has been brought up to devalue her femininity, on the other hand, this same sense that for her "anatomy is destiny" may create an attitude of stolid and sterile resignation, a feeling that there is no use in trying. Again, the fact that her whole growth toward womanhood has the character of an inevitable process of bodily maturation rather than that of a challenge and a task may lead her to dissipate herself in activities which are merely trivial. Yet it is the same lack of creative drive which may make it possible for her to perform cheerfully the thousand-and-one

routine tasks—the woman's work which is never done—which someone must do if life is to go on. Her capacity for surrendering her individual concerns in order to serve the immediate needs of others
—a quality which is so essential to the maternal role—can, on the
other hand, induce a kind of diffuseness of purpose, a tendency toward being easily distracted, a failure to discriminate between the
more and the less important, and an inability to focus in a sustained
manner on the pursuit of any single goal.[17] Her receptivity to the
moods and feelings of others and her tendency to merge her selfhood
in the joys, sorrows, hopes, and problems of those around her are the
positive expressions of an aspect of the feminine character which
may also take the negative forms of gossipy sociability, dependence
on others (such as husband or children) for the definition of her
values, or a refusal to respect another's right to privacy. And her
capacity for forgiving love, for cherishing all her children equally
without regard to beauty, merit, or intelligence, can also express itself in a kind of indiscriminate tolerance which suspects or rejects
all objective criteria of excellence.

All this is not meant to constitute an indictment of the feminine
character as such. I have no wish, certainly, to add to the burden of
guilt which has been heaped upon women—by themselves as well as
by men—for centuries. My purpose, indeed, as far as it concerns
women in particular, is quite the opposite. It is to awaken theologians to the fact that the situation of woman, however similar it may
appear on the surface of our contemporary world to the situation of
man and however much it may be echoed in the life of individual
men, is, at bottom, quite different—that the specifically feminine
dilemma is, in fact, precisely the opposite of the masculine. Today,
when for the first time in human history it really seems possible that
those endless housewifely tasks—which, along with the bearing and

---

[17] "The tendency to identification sometimes assumes very valuable forms. Thus,
many women put their qualities, which may be excellent, at the disposal of their
object of identification. . . . They prefer to love and enjoy their own qualities
in others. . . . There are women endowed with rich natural gifts that cannot,
however, develop beyond certain limits. Such women are exposed to outside influences and changing identifications to such an extent that they never succeed in
consolidating their achievements. Instead of making a reasonable choice among
numerous opportunities at their disposal, they constantly get involved in confusion that exerts a destructive influence on their own lives and the lives of those
around them" (Deutsch, *op. cit.*, pp. 132-33) .

rearing of children, have always been enough to fill the whole of each day for the average woman—may virtually be eliminated; today, when at last women might seem to be in a position to begin to be both feminine and fully developed, creative human beings; today, these same women are being subjected to pressures from many sides to return to the traditional feminine niche and to devote themselves wholly to the tasks of nurture, support, and service of their families. One might expect of theologians that they at least not add to these pressures. One might even expect them to support and encourage the woman who desires to be both a woman and an individual in her own right, a separate person some part of whose mind and feelings are inviolable, some part of whose time belongs strictly to herself, in whose house there is, to use Virginia Woolf's marvelous image, "a room of one's own." Yet theology, to the extent that it has defined the human condition on the basis of masculine experience, continues to speak of such desires as sin or temptation to sin. If such a woman believes the theologians, she will try to strangle those impulses in herself. She will believe that, having chosen marriage and children and thus being face to face with the needs of her family for love, refreshment, and forgiveness, she has no right to ask anything for herself but must submit without qualification to the strictly feminine role.

Perhaps, after all, the contemporary woman who wants to participate in the creative tasks of the world outside her home—those tasks upon which mankind has built all that is distinctively human, that is, history and culture—and yet remain a woman is attempting an impossible task. Perhaps the goal we should set ourselves is to rear our daughters in the older way, without too much formal education and without encouraging them to be independent, differentiated, free human beings of whom some contribution is expected other than the production of the next generation. If we could do this, our daughters might be able to find secure fulfillment in a simple femininity. After all, the division of labor between the sexes worked fairly well for thousands of years, and we may be only asking for trouble by trying to modify that structure.

And yet I do not think we can turn back this particular clock. Nor do I think that the feminine dilemma is of concern only to women. To understand it is important for men, too, not only because it is a loss to every man when a woman fails to realize her full self-identity, but because there is, it seems to me, a growing trend in contemporary life toward the feminizing of society itself, including men as well as women.

To document and explore this trend would require a lengthy exposition beyond the scope of the present paper. I can only refer here briefly to two recent analyses of contemporary Western culture which have impressed me greatly in this connection. Neither of these books—David Riesman's *The Lonely Crowd*[18] and Hannah Arendt's *The Human Condition*[19]—deals with the masculine-feminine theme as such. Yet both of them see quite a recent shift in the fundamental orientation of our present society, one which presages an era as different from what we call the "modern age" as the modern age differs from the medieval. And the analysis of each presents, in its own way, the picture of a society in which the character traits inherent in femininity are being increasingly emphasized, encouraged, and absolutized, just as the modern era raised the essentially masculine character traits to their highest possible power. Lionel Trilling has noted the same trend in our contemporary life and has characterized both its virtues and its dangers with great clarity:

Our culture is in process of revision, and of revision in a very good and right direction, in the direction of greater openness, greater socialization, greater cooperativeness, greater reasonableness. There are, to be sure, tendencies to be observed which go counter to this one, but they are not, I believe, so momentous as the development of the tendency toward social peace. It must always seem ill-natured to raise any question at all about this tendency. It goes against the grain to do so. . . . The American educated middle class is firm in its admiration of non-conformity and dissent. The right to be non-conformist, the right to dissent, is part of our conception of community. Everybody says so: in the weekly, monthly, quarterly magazines and in *The New York Times,* at the cocktail party, at the conference of psychiatrists, at the conference of teachers. How good this is, and how right! And yet, when we examine the content of our idea of non-conformity, we must be dismayed at the smallness of the concrete actuality this very large idea contains. The rhetoric is as sincere as it is capacious, yet we must sometimes wonder whether what is being praised and defended is anything more than the right to have had some sympathetic connection with Communism

[18] New York: Doubleday and Company, 1950, by arrangement with Yale University Press (originally published in 1950) .

[19] Chicago: University of Chicago Press, 1958.

ten or twenty years ago. . . . We cannot really imagine non-conformity at all, not in art, not in moral or social theory, certainly not in the personal life—it is probably true that there never was a culture which required so entire an eradication of personal differentiation, so bland a uniformity of manner. Admiring non-conformity and loving community, we have decided that we are all non-conformists together. We assert the right of our egos to court adventure without danger and of our superegos to be conscientious without undue strain. We make, I think, what is in many ways a very attractive culture, but we really cannot imagine what it means to take an intellectual chance, or to make an intellectual mistake, or to have a real intellectual difference. You have but to read our novels to understand that we have a growing sense of the cooperative virtues and a diminishing sense of the self that cooperates.[20]

It is true that the kind of "selflessness" and "community" described here is hardly what the theologians who identify love with selflessness and community mean when they speak of the redemptive power of love. Yet there is no mistaking the fact that there is a strong similarity between theology's view that salvation lies in selfless love and contemporary man's growing tendency to avoid any strong assertion of the self as over against others and to merge his individual identity in the identities of others. In truth, the only element that is lacking in the latter picture is the theological presupposition of man's inherent sinfulness, the stubborn refusal of the individual human being to give up his individuality and separateness and to unite in harmonious love.[21] But, if this refusal to become

[20] Lionel Trilling, *Freud and the Crisis of Our Culture* (Boston: Beacon Press, 1955) , pp. 50-53.

[21] This presupposition, which from the present point of view is the one saving element in contemporary theology, is nevertheless the real question at issue. I am grateful to Dr. Richard W. Day for pointing out to me the apparent implication in this paper that Reinhold Niebuhr is opposed to the notion that one ought to have "a room of one's own," and for reminding me that Dr. Niebuhr stands with Luther in his exhortation to "sin boldly." It is clear, certainly, that despite his insistence on the absolutely normative character of sacrificial love, Dr. Niebuhr stresses the impossibility of actualizing that norm in history, particularly in the political realm. Beyond this, there is no mistaking the fact that he places a high value on human individuality as such. The difficulty is, however, that he sees the drive to achieve self-differentiation, with its concomitant anxiety and pride, as universally "given" in the structure of human personality and as ultimately more powerful, insistent, and pervasive than the need to relate the self to others in self-denying love. To return to the language of the metaphor, Dr. Niebuhr assumes that everyone *has a* room of his own, and that he is imprisoned in it; the problem is, so to speak, how he is to get out. It is precisely this assumption that I have questioned. I have suggested that there are persons who do not have rooms

selfless is wholly sinful, then it would seem that we are obliged to try to overcome it; and, when it is overcome, to whatever extent this may be possible, we are left with a chameleonlike creature who responds to others but has no personal identity of his own.

If it is true that our society is moving from a masculine to a feminine orientation, then theology ought to reconsider its estimate of the human condition and redefine its categories of sin and redemption. For a feminine society will have its own special potentialities for good and evil, to which a theology based solely on masculine experience may well be irrevelant.

---

of their own, or who, having once had them, abandoned them and became permanent tenants in the homes of others. For such a person, the problem is not how to get out, but how to get in — or how to build a structure around himself which is *both* uniquely his own and a living contribution to the human community.

# CHAPTER 15

# *HUMAN NATURE CAN CHANGE: A SYMPOSIUM**

HAROLD KELMAN, M.D., CHAIRMAN; FREDERICK A. WEISS, M.D.;
PAUL TILLICH; KAREN HORNEY, M.D.

**Discussion by HAROLD KELMAN, M.D.**

HUMAN nature can change. This affirmative proposition prompts many questions and to them a host of possible answers. What is human nature, essentially? We do not assert that man by nature is inherently destructive and only secondary constructive. Nor do we agree that innately he is both good and bad. Rather do we believe that in all human beings there is the potentiality, as a lifelong tendency and direction, to realize and to fulfill his possibilities as a human being and as a particular human being, as circumstances permit.

What has changed? Our knowledge of the psychological, emotional, physical and social nature of man has increased and been revised so that we now hold this optimistic philosophy regarding human beings. What can and have we changed? As physicians of the body and the soul we have helped many individuals to become less sick and more healthy in their relations to themselves and in their social relations. And through these efforts we have helped individuals in the environment of persons analytically treated to change the direction of their life patterns. The trend toward increased sickness has been slowed and even reversed. And the younger members have been helped toward straighter growing to the end of more joy-

* These papers were delivered at a symposium held on March 19, 1952, at Town Hall, New York City, under the auspices of the Auxiliary Council to the Association for the Advancement of Psychoanalysis.

171

ously and productively assuming their responsible places as citizens of a world in which they will live. In short, we have helped potentiality become actuality.

What has essentially changed in human beings as we study man on the canvas of human history? Here again there are many evidences of the change of potentiality into actuality. From a nomadic existence man has changed to community living. From a pathetic reliance on magic to appease or to master physical and animal nature as well as possible malevolent haunting presences inside and outside of himself, man has attained a greater self-confidence and self-dignity through understanding and co-operating with all the aspects of nature. From isolated family groupings, through the sequence of tribes, nations, empires and through the cycles of rise, decline and decay, we now face the prospect of world unity.

How have these changes come about? Through the expression of certain essential human attributes—to name two, conflict and co-operation. Conflict and co-operation are an essential part of life and are essential to living. Looked at this way we do not overfocus on the fact that there have always been wars but also see in proportionate perspective that there have also been periods of peace.

That the world will become one is in the nature of the human evolutionary process. How it will be unified is a matter of the future; whether under a Communist dictatorship, whether under the rest of the world which might become equally totalitarian to accomplish this unification or whether through a long process of hot and cold wars and arbitration ending in a more truly democratic world than we have yet envisaged.

How can we help make this third potentiality an actuality? By work, faith, and understanding our own essential individual human nature and the nature of others; through conflict and co-operation; through a fuller expression of our agreements and differences while fundamentally agreeing that "Life is worth living." This last assertion is the title of an essay by Julian Huxley, a scientific humanist, in which with humility and objectivity he clearly states his credo, with which I agree.

I believe that man, as individual, as group, and collectively as mankind, can achieve a satisfying purpose in existence. I believe this in spite of frustration, aimlessness, frivolity, boredom, sloth and failure. Again I do not believe that a purpose inevitably inheres in the universe or in our existence, or that mankind is bound to achieve a satisfying purpose, but only that such a satisfying purpose can be found. . . . The only faith that is both concrete and comprehensive is in life, its abundance and its progress. My final belief is in life.

The spirit of free expression of agreement and difference, which we on this panel affirm and which we wish from this audience, could not be better stated than in the declaration of the founder of the Dwight H. Terry Lectures at Yale University, who said:

> The lecturers shall be subject to no philosophical or religious test and no one who is an earnest seeker after truth shall be excluded because his views seem radical or destructive of existing beliefs. The founder realizes that the liberalism of one generation is often conservatism in the next, and that many an apostle of true liberty has suffered martyrdom at the hands of the orthodox. He therefore lays special emphasis on complete freedom of utterance, and would welcome expressions of conviction from sincere thinkers of differing standpoints even when these may run counter to the generally accepted views of the day. The founder stipulates only that . . . the lecturers are well qualified for their work and are in harmony with the cardinal principles of the Foundation, which are loyalty to the truth, lead where it will, and devotion to human welfare.[1]

As we search and seek in the spirit of the Terry Lecturers and with the faith of a Julian Huxley, I believe we can help more people to change what can be changed in their nature, help more of potentiality to become more actuality and help make possible a truly democratic unity in diversity in the one world of today and of the future.

### Discussion by FREDERICK A. WEISS, M.D.

Modern man has changed nature; he has transformed atoms into tremendous sources of energy, wide areas of water into land, barren deserts into fertile soil. But when it comes to man himself, time and again we hear the statement, "You cannot change human nature."

To be sure, his powerful changes of outer nature have not transformed the inner nature of man. They cannot and will not do so;

[1] John MacMurray, *The Structure of Religious Experience* (New Haven: Yale University Press, 1936) .

and the magic expectations of those who wish to believe that leads only to an inertia which perpetuates their present condition and makes mankind itself more and more the mere passive object of mechanization and dehumanization. No, the magic solution does not work—not for individual man, and not for mankind as a whole.

Are we then to believe that human nature cannot change at all? This thesis may sound scientific, but it is pseudoscientific; it misuses and misinterprets biological and psychological facts. I think it is characteristic that this statement about the unchangeability of human nature is most often heard in connection with some evidence that seems to deny the very essence of human nature. When people are confronted with acts by which men exploit, hurt or destroy other men; when arrogant, vindictive leaders dominate masses of self-effacing automatons; when demagogues bent on the pursuit of power make scapegoats of other races or nations; then we hear this slogan of defeat and resignation, that "human nature cannot change." It is used to defend their inertia by those whom Lewis Mumford most aptly called the "Society for the Prevention of Change." Had human history been governed by this maxim, cannibalism, head-hunting and slavery might never have been abolished, and our treatment of mental illness might still consist of burning witches and exorcising the devil.

Modern psychology and education, while fully aware of the role of genetic and constitutional factors, have clearly demonstrated the plasticity of human nature and its capacity for change. Children who in an authoritarian social climate are hostile, or inert and paralyzed, become friendly, co-operative and constructive in a democratic climate. Adults are able to change when their motivations shift from goals that are externally, or internally imposed upon them to goals which they really want for their own growth and self-realization.

Psychoanalysis has taught us not only that human nature can and does change, but also how it changes. Freud discovered the tremendous power of unconscious emotions and showed how anxiety and inner conflicts interfere with the free development of human beings. But his assumption that these unconscious, driving forces in man were only "libido" and the "death instinct"—which would leave us only the choice of destroying others or ourselves—resulted in a deeply pessimistic concept of human nature.

Our concept of human nature is a different one. We are convinced of man's inherent potentiality to be human—rather, let us say, to become human—which means to realize himself and to form constructive relationships with his fellow men. Potentiality, however, is not yet realization. Self-realization requires self-awareness and self-transformation.

Pearl Buck recently stated her belief in human nature:

My knowledge of people compels me to believe that the normal human heart is born good. That is, it is born sensitive and feeling. . . . It neither wishes to be killed nor to kill. If through circumstances it is overcome by evil, it never becomes entirely evil. There remain in it elements of good, however recessive, which continue to hold the possibility of restoration. I believe in human beings, but my faith is without sentimentality. I know that in environments of uncertainty, fear and hunger, the human being is dwarfed and shaped without his being aware of it, just as the plant struggling under a stone does not know its own condition. Only when the stone is removed can it spring up freely into the light. But the power to spring up is inherent.[2]

We fully share Pearl Buck's faith in the constructive forces of human nature, and we want to help in removing the stone that hinders human growth. But our analytic experience has shown that it is not enough merely to release a human being from this outer pressure; he must also become freed from the stone within himself. Thus we try to halt the process of inner petrification which makes people rigid, frozen, lifeless and numb; which anesthetizes them to what they really feel about themselves and others, and what they really do to themselves and others. It is this inner petrification that causes people to perpetuate what they believe to be their "unlucky fate."

Freud observed that some persons seemed to repeat earlier experiences all their lives. "Their stories," he said, "give the impression of a pursuing fate. . . . One knows people with whom every human relationship ends in the same way: . . . men with whom every friendship ends in treachery; . . . others who again and again invest some other persons with authority, then overthrow this authority after a given time, only to replace it by a new one; lovers whose tender relationship with women, each and all, come to the same end."

[2] "Roll Away the Stone," in *This I Believe*, ed. Edward R. Murrow (New York: Simon and Schuster, 1952) , Vol. I.

There can be no doubt that these observations are true to life. We all know people whose lives present such perpetual repetition of experiences destructive to themselves and to others. But is this any proof that human nature cannot change? According to Freud the repetition compulsion, a demonic force far stronger than ourselves, induces us to repeat over and over again the patterns of our childhood. To a large extent, it is true, we do create our own "fate," and often this fate appears highly repetitious. But this is not because we are forced forever to repeat infantile experiences, but because we are unconsciously driven by compulsive, neurotic needs. The protective shelter which we built up in childhood as a defense against basic anxiety has become a self-made prison that restrains our freedom and stunts our growth. Yet we are not doomed by our past if we learn to understand its dynamic meaning. Earlier experiences are important, but to delve into the past is by no means constructive if it merely leads the patient to blame all his misery on others—say, on a domineering father or an overprotective mother—it is constructive only in the degree in which it reveals to him the hidden leitmotifs of his life and helps him to change.

As Cyril Connolly, the English writer, says in an essay devoted to Karen Horney's work:

> The battle of life and the part we are to play in it is not decided at the breast or on the pot. . . . Dr. Horney shows that trend of the future which will be in the direction of helping patients to help themselves through an altogether thorough and complete analysis rather than concentrating fatalistically on the therapeutic effects of the discovery of the initial error. We cannot be happy until we can love ourselves without egotism and our friends without tyranny.[3]

What is needed for real change is that emotional insight which stirs us to the very depths of our being and which tells us: "I am no longer doomed by what others once did to me, if I can feel and understand, now, what I myself am doing to my real self and to others. Do I need to be well liked by everyone, like Willy Loman in *Death of a Salesman*? Is it my only goal to dominate and triumph over others, like Willie Stark in *All the King's Men*? Am I relentlessly driven towards success and prestige, without consideration for

[3] *The Condemned Playground:* Essays 1927-1944 (New York: The Macmillan Company, 1946), p. 227.

the rights and life of others, as is Clyde Griffith in *An American Tragedy*? Do I sacrifice the growth of my real self in the service of pride? Do I tear down my real self because it fails to measure up to my idealized image? Do I externalize my own self-hate by degrading others, particularly members of other racial groups?"

The time we live in has become an era of mass anesthesia. Unable or unwilling to face themselves, people seek to anesthetize themselves by their compulsive participation in the race after success and glory, by compulsive eating and drinking, compulsive television, the compulsive use of barbiturates, and compulsive demands for any kind of therapy that will further diminish their self-awareness— hypnosis, narcoanalysis, and shock therapy.

Indeed, a kind of shock therapy is needed. But this need, in "neurotic personalities of our time," is not for any shock treatment which by physical or chemical means *lessens* the awareness of our human feelings. Rather, it is for that deep, emotional shock through which our innermost human nature is powerfully *made aware,* both of our present inhumanity and of our inherent potentiality—and responsibility—to become human. Then, human nature can change.

### Discussion by PAUL TILLICH

The question raised in my mind by the subject of the symposium is the question of human nature, generally. I do not ask whether human beings, individuals or groups can be changed by external events. This, it seems to me, is beyond any doubt. And the questions to be asked, in this respect, are only how deep do such changes go, how can a transitory and a permanent change be distinguished and how can such changes be brought about? It is the daily task of two other members of the forum to work for such changes. Therefore it is quite fit that they deal predominantly with this side of the problem.

But behind their problem a more general problem is waiting for a solution—if there is a solution. This is the problem of "man changeable and unchangeable," which is the title of a very exciting book by my friend, the philosopher at the New School, Professor Kurt Riezler. In this title the question of human nature is clearly and sharply expressed. And this is the subject to which I want to address myself.

The first thing to be emphasized is that human nature could not change if there were not something unchangeable in it. This is easy to understand: absolute change is an impossible notion, because without a subject of which we can say that *it* changes we neither could notice nor measure a change. In our case this "it" which changes is *man*. We do not ask: has man replaced another being or will he be replaced by another being, but we ask: can this nature change, which we call human, and which remains human nature before and after the change? Our question now can be formulated in a precise way: Which are the changeable and which are the unchangeable elements in that which makes man, man?

Those philosophers, anthropologists, sociologists, and psychologists who are inclined to deny anything unchangeable in man usually point to history and the amazing changes in human behavior in every period. They claim that history has already proved the unlimited possibilities of change in human nature. But there is an obvious fallacy in this arguing. They speak of the changes which have happened and still happen in human history: that is, they presuppose in all historical changes that being called man which *has* history. In the context of our experience man is the only being which has history; he is the only being to whose nature it belongs to act and to change within history. If we go back to our animal ancestors, or go ahead to our angelic descendants, both man and history disappear and with them the problem of our forum. But if we remain within human history as we experience it in our own historical existence we can say something about the unchangeable element in human nature. It is that unity of freedom and destiny, of which we are aware in every moment in which we act as men. I do not refer to the obsolete discussion about the freedom of the will but I point to the immediate experience that we are able to transcend that which is given to us in ourselves and in our world. In a somewhat paradoxical formula we could say: the unchangeable element in man is his freedom to change himself and his world. It is not an unlimited freedom. It is embedded in his historical and personal destiny, in the consequences of his past, the given and the self-made ones, in the structure of reality as a whole. In other words: man is finite and his freedom is finite. But as a *finite* being he *has* freedom. Man can be called in the shortest condensation of all his possibilities and impossibilities, "finite freedom." In this basic structure both the unchangeable and the changeable elements are rooted.

*Unchangeable* is his having a centered self which has a world to which it belongs and at which it looks at the same time. This unchangeable structure gives him freedom from both himself and his world and therefore the power of transforming both in the process which we call history. *Unchangeable* is his capability of transcending every given situation by asking questions and receiving demands, by making tools and creating language. Every universal, used in the most primitive language, is an expression of man's universality. It liberates him from the bondage to the concrete situation which, on the other hand, is his destiny. And again it is just this unchangeable structure which makes it possible that man builds a world of tools beyond the given world, that he uses that which is given to him for the creation of cultures and civilizations within the ever-changing process of history in which he creates the new.

*Unchangeable* is man's ability to deliberate and to decide, to receive a stimulus, to take it into the center of the self and to respond in freedom, that is, *through* the center of the self. This gives him the experience of the ought-to-be and of his responsibility for the realization of what ought-to-be. And it is just this unchangeable structure which makes possible the infinite difference of character and the changes of personality structure. The many personality structures are rooted in the *one* structure of personality.

*Unchangeable* is man's freedom to contradict his own nature, to fall away from what he essentially is and ought to be, to try to escape from himself and his true being into sickness in body and mind, into the narrowness of compulsive self-seclusion, into imaginary worlds, into what everybody does and everybody thinks, into self-estrangement and hostility. *Unchangeable* is a voice which reminds him of the split between what he is and what he ought to be, a voice in him which speaks in a thousand voices and sometimes silently, calling him back to himself, producing in him the anxiety of guilt and sometimes the desperate desire to get rid of himself. But equally *unchangeably* he experiences healing powers, coming from the nature in him and around him, from individual helpers and social forces, from the deepest levels of his own being and from the ground of all being.

But here a mistake must be avoided. To heal man does not mean to change the unchangeable in his nature. It does not mean to deprive him of his freedom to contradict himself. It was the fallacy of the progressivistic interpretation of history that it forgot that man remains finite freedom on every level of civilization and that, therefore, he can use the results of progress to destroy them and to destroy himself with them. The risk implied in finite freedom can never be removed, as long as men are neither animals nor angels. In every newborn child freedom gets a new center, life a new chance and spirit a new risk. Neither social institutions, nor education, nor psychological help can change this central element of human nature. Social institutions of the totalitarian type try to transform men into things through terror; education of the adjustment type tries to transform men into easily manageable citizens, psychotherapy of the mechanistic type tries to transform men into well-functioning homunculi or artificial men. But none of them works permanently. On every level freedom breaks through managed perfection. On every level there are people who enter, to use Karen Horney's term, a devil's pact. And the higher the institutional, moral and educational level on which it is done, the more refined are the conditions of this pact. *You can liberate man only to his freedom.* More than this would be less. For man has the unchangeable structure of finite freedom.

It always remains *finite* freedom. *Unchangeably,* man is finite and aware of his finitude. He anticipates his end and this anticipation, which is present in every moment of his life and in every cell of his body, is what one should call his basic anxiety. It is the anxiety which belongs to human nature and which cannot be removed because man's finitude cannot be removed. Man can be liberated from senseless fears and misplaced anxieties. He can take his anxiety upon himself in a courage which says yes to life, in spite of guilt and finitude. Man can be healed, he can be saved. But it is *man* who is healed and saved. It is that being which is both free and finite, and whose greatness and dignity is unchangeably his power of changing himself and of endangering and risking himself in this change.

## Discussion by KAREN HORNEY, M.D.

Those people who are convinced that human nature cannot change usually have not only a static but a pessimistic view of man. In simple terms, their conviction is that man has always been and will always be greedy, envious, cruel, vindictive, and destructive. They usually contend that those who disagree with this viewpoint merely lack the courage to face unpleasant truth, and try to cover it up by a rosy haze of flattering self-deception. Many others consider this a one-sided view. In short, they see in human nature the possibility for good and evil, the latter being expressed in Christian terminology in the symbol of the original sin.

Being in the position to study human beings intimately, we as analysts agree with this latter viewpoint. We see clearly both possibilities, but with one significant distinction. The constructive and destructive possibilities do not stem from the same forces; they are not on the same level; we cannot put them side by side. They are different in origins and different in kind. Briefly, our belief is that the constructive possibilities stem from man's essential nature, from the core of his being, from what we call his real self. Conversely, we believe that man turns unconstructive or destructive only if he cannot fulfill himself—that it is an unfulfilled life which makes him barren or destructive. This belief is not mere speculation, but is based on evidence of three kinds.

1. The first kind can be seen by anyone who keeps his eyes open— it has to do with a child's development. Just as a tree needs certain conditions for its growth, so does a child. If the environmental conditions are favorable, a child develops whatever particular potentials he has. He does so because, like every other living organism, he has the innate urge to grow. These observations are supported by educators and anthropologists.

However, under conditions unfavorable to his growth, his development can easily go astray. Then he may become wary, hostile, withdrawn or overdependent. If, however, his environmental conditions, in the sense of human relationships, change for the better in early years, he loses his wariness, suspiciousness and resumes or embarks upon healthy growth. If the unfavorable conditions persist, a devel-

opmental process sets in—which we call neurotic—which is complicated and essentially unconscious. As a *result* of this neurotic process
he develops all kinds of unconstructive or destructive attitudes, the
main features of which are pride and conceit, unconscious pretenses
and irrational hostility in its many forms like suspiciousness, egocentric callousness, vindictiveness, ruthless ambition.

The conditions under which such a process sets in are manifold
but describable. You could not call the results of this process his
essential nature, any more than you would do so with a tree. If a
tree, because of storms, too little sun, or too poor soil, becomes
warped and crooked, you would not call this its essential nature.

2. The most convincing evidence for our belief stems from our
clinical experiences. We see that a person who is power- or prestige-
ridden, or who is arrogant and vindictive, or who is compliant to the
degree of meaningless self-sacrifices, is *driven* toward such attitudes
or pursuits by powerful or unconscious forces. He cannot but be
aggressive or appeasing: he develops anxiety if he cannot be that
way. The drivenness is what we call compulsive and what in medieval terms was called being possessed by demons—which means, in
other words, it is not what he wants to, but what he must be or do,
determined by inexorable inner necessities, the nature of which are
unconscious. To put it differently and make it more concrete: we
see that a person who is dominating, irritable, and vindictive has
become that way and remains so because, and as long as, he experiences life this way because of all the factors that have driven him
toward a devious development.

3. The third kind of evidence is in the changes that occur during
psychoanalytical therapy. As such a hostile person, for instance,
recognizes how he has hitherto experienced life; as he experiences
his drive for power or his vindictiveness or his using others as means
to an end; as he experiences the compulsive nature and the intrinsic
futility of his drives or attitudes, he begins to change. The change I
am referring to does not consist in better controlling or channeling
these drives. It is far more radical. It involves the giving up of irrational, ultimately destructive drives and of functioning in an increasingly more human and healthy way in the direction of self-
realization.

# CHAPTER 16

## *HOPE*

KARL MENNINGER, M.D.

IT IS from a background of teaching that the topic which I propose to discuss emerged. I would like to warn you not to expect a scientific analysis of it along conventional lines. The subject does not permit of that; we don't yet know enough about it, and it would be presumptuous to make the attempt. I am not reporting a research or a discovery, and it is no dark hour, calling for exhortation or comfort. I write, rather, to the point of focusing attention upon a basic but elusive ingredient in our daily work—our teaching, our healing, our diagnosing. I write of hope.

Long before love became medically respectable, long before Sigmund Freud demonstrated it to be a basic consideration in psychiatry, philosophers and poets and the common people of the world knew that it was essential to our mental health. Perhaps the most beautiful essay ever written was about love and its manifestations in personality.

To that essay is appended a footnote which is often quoted as if it were a summation. True, observed the writer, there are other permanent goods in the world besides love; there is faith, and there is hope. But, he added, "the greatest of these is love." With this concluding phrase most psychiatrists, I presume, would agree. Most of us, I think, would also agree to include faith—the faith that sustains our conviction that what we are doing is worth doing, the faith that our existence has meaning and the faith that our concern for one another reflects the concern of a Creator.

Our shelves hold many books now on the place of *faith* in science and psychiatry, and on the vicissitudes of man's efforts to *love* and to be loved. But when it comes to hope, our shelves are bare. The journals are silent. The *Encyclopaedia Britannica* devotes many columns to the topic of love, and many more to faith. But hope, poor little hope! She is not even listed.

I confess I was astonished to discover this. And yet, I realized that this avoidance of the theme reflected my own attitude. Time was when for this occasion I should have chosen as my subject "Love" or "Hate" or "Conflict" or "Instinct" or "Sublimation" or "Symptom Formation"—but never such a thing as "Hope." It seems almost to be a tabooed topic, a personal matter, scarcely appropriate for public discussion. And yet—since when has psychiatry eschewed examination of our innermost thoughts and feelings? Should we not adhere to our professional habit of self-examination and contemplation? If we dare to hope, should we not dare to look at ourselves hoping?

This is not the way I began to think about the topic. Nor did I come to it fresh from struggles with Kierkegaardian logic, or from brooding over Greek pessimism, or from apprehensiveness concerning the muddled management of unsettled world affairs. It was all in the day's work, so to speak, some preoccupations with the motivations of the young doctors I teach. The miracle of growth has long intrigued me: the growth of the child, the growth of plants, the growth of cultures and the growth of young psychiatrists. I have seen one young doctor after another step forward fresh from his internship or from his military duty, to enter the mysteries of psychiatric training. I have seen these young men approach the abstruse and puzzling material of our field of medicine with resolute courage—let us say, rather, with hope.

But behind the façade presented by these acolytes there are often tumults of conflicting voices, fearful insecurity and bold overselfconfidence. The dramatic picture of psychiatry fascinates them, the reputed resistance to treatment challenges them, the multiplicity of method appalls them. They are assigned to wards filled with vacant or frantic faces, turned now upon "the new doctor." It is usually long after their initiation into the uncanny world of mental illness that they can distinguish the moving process, or would have the personal experience of interaction with a recovering patient.

Nevertheless, the novitiates assail their tasks headlong, sometimes with a *furor therapeuticus*. There is nothing mercenary or aggressive about this. They are not working for money. They are struggling to become effective in a new kind of relationship with patients. Sometimes they go too far, they presume, they expect or promise too much. More often frustration, sad experience, or self-depreciation erodes the confidence required for persistent effort, and the little candle of hope, which for awhile burned so brightly, weakens, sputters and goes out. We see the beginning of a repetition of scenes so common twenty-five years ago—hopeless physicians presiding, passively, over hopeless patients. "Psychiatry," we will hear, "has been oversold. The enthusiasm of inexperience only awaits the disillusionment of time. It is enough if we bestow kindness and wait for the inevitable. Hope is for the hopeless, and for fools."

We would like to think that the young men who pass through our training programs mostly emerge with certain limits put upon their expectations and certain guards upon their implied promises, but with the flame of their hope unextinguished and unextinguishable. We like them to believe that there is no patient for whom something helpful cannot be done. But we also like them to realize that the changes the patient desires in himself, or the physician desires in his patient, may not be the ones which come about, may not even be, in the long run, the changes that it were best to have sought for. It is a responsibility of the teacher to the student, just as it is of the young doctor to his patient, to inspire the right amount of hope—some, but not too much. Excess of hope is presumption and leads to disaster. Deficiency of hope is despair and leads to decay. Our delicate and precious duty as teachers is to properly tend this flame.

I propose, therefore, that we examine this essential constituent of both treatment and teaching. How shall we think of it? Is it something which *deserves* our concern as scientists? Or only as philosophers and poets? Is it only an epiphenomenon of life and the healing art? Do we, perhaps, tacitly ascribe hope to temperament, a sort of fringe benefit deriving from certain fortuitous congenital arrangements of glands and neurons? This is slight improvement upon the humoral theories of sanguinity and melancholy treasured by our forebears. If we ascribe hope, as some psychoanalytic writers have done, to recollections of maternal infallibility and recurrent oral gratifications, what combination of these experiences shall we regard as optimum? Others have seen in hope a prevailing note of fear, a counterphobic denial of the horror and despair born of self-destructive trends or of the immanence of existential doom.

More congenial to my thinking is the ascription of hope to the mysterious workings of the repetition compulsion, the very essence of which is a kind of relentless and indefatigable pursuit of resolution and freedom. I would see in hope another aspect of the life instinct, the creative drive which wars against dissolution and destructiveness. But some will say, with Freud, that this is only our speculative abstractions to supply a model for practical thinking and behavior. Our mythology, he called it.

Here we might pause a moment to consider another mythology about hope. Pandora, it will be recalled, was an agent in the infliction of revenge of mankind by an angry Zeus. Curiosity led to her opening the box from which all the evils now in the world emerged. Biting, stinging creatures flew through the air and attacked mortals; but remaining behind was one good little sprite, man's consolation, Hope. But if Hope was a blessing, why did she remain in the box? And if, on the other hand, she was an evil like the rest, perhaps even the worst evil of all, why did she not fly out with them and begin work?

The Greeks mostly did consider hope an evil. The Greek philosophers and the later Greek literature tended more and more to the view that since fate was unchangeable, hope was an illusion, "the food of exiles" (Aeschylus) and, indeed, "man's curse!" (Euripides). Quotations from Solon, Simonides, Pindar, Thucydides, and others say this in different ways. The Greek feeling about hope is vividly expressed in Anouilh's adaptation of Sophocles' *Antigone*, where, referring to herself, the heroine cries, "We are of the tribe that asks questions, and we ask them to the bitter end—until no tiniest chance of hope remains to be strangled by our hands. We are of the tribe that hates your filthy hope, your docile, female hope; hope, your whore. . . ." [1]

From this, one can see that it was intrepid indeed of Paul, writing to Greek friends, to declare that hope should stand along with love. In this Paul was loyal to his Hebrew heritage (Psalm 42, Isaiah 40)

[1] Which Creon interrupts with "Shut up! If you could see how ugly you are, shrieking those words!" Jean Anouilh, *Antigone and Eurydice: Two Plays* (London: Methuen, 1951).

as well as to his Christian convictions. For while the Jews were, to be sure, people of faith, they were also at all times a people of hope who, despite tribulation, clung to the expectation that the Messiah would come and the world become better. Hence, with the spread of Christianity and the dispersion of the Jews, hope had its missionaries, and Paul was one of them.

Martin Luther, like Paul, shook his fist at Greek fatalism and declared: "Everything that is done in the world is done by hope." Samuel Johnson opined that "where there is no hope there can be no endeavor," and Ralph Waldo Emerson took up the cudgels for hope: it is by one's hope, Emerson said, that we judge of a man's wisdom. "You cannot put a great hope into a small soul," said J. L. Jones,[2] and Tennyson's words, "The mighty hopes that make us men," now echo in our ears.

But many writers have tended to accept (rather bitterly) the fatalistic if not cynical view of the Greeks: "Hope—fortune's cheating lottery, where for one prize a hundred blanks there be" (Cowley, 1647).

"Worse than despair, worse than the bitterness of death, is hope" (Shelley, *The Cenci*, 1819).

"Hope is the worst of evils, for it prolongs the torment of man" (Nietzsche, *Human All-too-Human*, 1878).

I have had some patients who agreed with these writers. Partly that is why they were patients. But when I searched the literature for some kind words about hope, I experienced some uneasiness lest I find that very little (that my colleagues would accept) had ever been said for hope! And very little I found, indeed. But the cupboard proved not to be entirely bare. Particularly Dr. Thomas French, in his five-volume examination of the psychoanalytic process, has dealt extensively with hope as the activating force of the ego's integrative function.

Twenty years ago Mrs. Menninger and I submitted the thesis in *Love against Hate* that hope was the dim awareness of unconscious wishes which, like dreams, tend to come true. We wrote:

There is no such thing as "idle hope." The thoughts and hopes and wishes that we entertain are already correlated to the plan of action which

[2] Jones, J. L., *New Dictionary of Thoughts*. Compiled by Tyron Edwards (Chicago: Standard Book Co., 1956), p. 262.

would bring these about, even though the whole project is ultimately re-nounced as too difficult or too dangerous. . . . This essential identity of hop-ing, wishing, purposing, intending, attempting, and doing is a little difficult for the practical commonsense man to grasp, because for him it makes a great difference whether a thing is executed or only planned or only hoped for. There *is* an external difference, to be sure; and there is an internal dif-ference, too. But internally, (psychologically) from the standpoint of *motive,* there is no difference. There is a difference in the *fate* of the im-pulse, the degree with which it is correlated with reality, inhibited by in-ternal fears, supported by other motives, *etc.*—but the motive force is the same. . . . The hopes we develop are therefore a measure of our maturity.[3]

At that time it seemed to me that education best expressed the hope of the human race. But today I think I see the expression of hope in many clinical phenomena, as well.

Each of us here who has been in practice more than a decade has seen the "hopeless case" recover. And we have sometimes seen, or so it seemed, that a mother's or father's indomitable hope was a factor in this recovery. True, we have also seen hope deferred making the heart sick. But hope must be distinguished from expectation. "We are saved by hope," wrote Paul to some Roman Christians, "but hope that is seen is not hope: for what a man seeth, why doth he yet hope for?"

Nor is hope identical with optimism; optimism always implies some distance from reality, as Marcel points out, so that obstacles appear attenuated. The optimist, like the pessimist, emphasizes the importance of "I." But hope is humble, it is modest, it is selfless. Unconcerned with the ambiguity of past experience, hope implies process; it is an adventure, a going forward, a confident search.

When Doctors Bartemeier, Romano, Kubie, and Whitehorn and I went to the European theater of World War II for my brother Will and the surgeon-general, we arrived at the Buchenwald prison camp a few days after it had been entered by our armed forces. What I remembered most vividly of that terrible place was something we didn't actually see. But we heard it at first hand. The night before we got there, the U. S. Army doctors had given what they called a "smoker" for the physician prisoners they had discovered and re-leased. It was a kind of unearthly medical society meeting. Army

[3] Menninger, Karl, *Love Against Hate* (New York: Harcourt, Brace & Co., 1942), pp. 216-217.

rations were put out as refreshment, with some wine and tobacco, incredibly relished by the emaciated but overjoyed guests. Communication in words was imperfect because of language difficulties, but the spirit was unmistakable. The members of a fraternity were reunited. And in the spirit of the fraternity, experiences were exchanged.

These doctors, prisoners along with all the others, had followed the same routines of 4:00 A.M. rising, shivering roll calls, day-long drudgery on the Autobahn, shivering roll calls again, and finally a cold bowl of thin soup. They were starved and beaten and overworked like all the others, with no reason to expect any other fate than the miserable death and cremation which they observed about them daily.

But now comes the surprise. At night, when the other prisoners were asleep, these thin, hungry, weary doctors got up and huddled together in a group, and talked. They discussed cases. They organized a medical society. They prepared and presented papers. They made plans for improving health conditions. Then they began to smuggle in materials to make various medical instruments. And finally they built, of all things, an X-ray machine! The pieces had to be found somewhere; they had to be stolen, they had to be concealed in the prisoners' clothes; they had to be carried back to the prison on the long, weary marches after work. The guards had to be bribed or otherwise thrown off the scent. But little by little, with the aid of some engineers and electricians among the prisoners, these doctors put together a workable X-ray machine and used it, secretly, at night, in their efforts to ameliorate the lot of their fellow prisoners. This was what dedication to medicine and humanity could do—*kept alive by hope.*

But, someone who remembered may ask, bitterly—what of the thousands who died miserably for *all* the hopes they nurtured? Even here I would not concede that hope had altogether failed. I would believe that hope had sustained them in their martyrdom, and that their hopefulness, however frail and tortured and ultimately defeated, was communicated on down through prison generations to those who were ultimately freed and who brought us the record of this medical miracle. Who can read the eloquent last messages of the condemned as collected by Gottwitzer, Kuhn, and Schneider and published as *Dying We Live,* and fail to catch a spark of hope from them?

Confirmation for the sustaining function of hope in life has recently come from a most unexpected quarter—the psychobiological laboratory. At the annual convention of the American Psychological Association in September, 1956, Curt P. Richter of Johns Hopkins University reported an astonishing phenomenon. It was simply this, that when placed in certain situations which seemed to permit of no chance for escape, even vigorous animals gave up their efforts and rapidly succumbed to death. This was observed experimentally in both laboratory rats and wild rats. "After elimination of the hopelessness feature," reported Richter, "the rats do not die. . . . (Indeed, the speed of their recovery is remarkable). A rat that would quite certainly have died in another minute or two, becomes normally active and aggressive," swimming vigorously for fifty to sixty hours. Richter emphasized that not the restraint alone, nor the immersion, nor the exposure, nor the trimming of whiskers will explain the phenomenon. It is, he insisted, the loss of hope.

Richter added some confirmatory data from other fields and suggested an extrapolation from his laboratory observations to explain the occurrence of sudden death in rabbits, chimpanzees, foxes, raccoons, some birds, musk oxen, otters, mink and even human beings. "Some of these instances," he said "can best be described in terms of hopelessness, all avenues of escape appearing to be closed."[4]

This is not an isolated observation or hypothesis. For example, from a large amount of psychosomatic investigation Engel and his associates in Rochester, New York, consider that what they describe as "helplessness" and "hopelessness" reflect a necessary if not a sufficient condition for the development of organic disease.[5]

And then there is the Queequeg phenomena of "voodoo death" in *Moby Dick,* which Walter Cannon and others have amply substantiated with authentic data from primitive societies. No doubt most of us can recall instances in which the loss of hope seemed to accelerate the arrival of death for a patient. There are many such

[4] Curt P. Richter, "Sudden Death Phenomenon in Animals and Humans." Unpublished manuscript.

[5] A. H. Schmale, Jr., "Relationship of Separation and Depression to Disease (1) A Report on a Hospitalized Population." *Psychosomatic Medicine,* July-Aug. 1958, pp. 259-277.

stories, unconfirmed, of course, but highly suggestive, in the daily press.[6]

All of these things seem to me to support the theoretical proposal that hope reflects the working of the life instinct in its constant battle against the various forces that add up to self-destruction. It would be too narrow to regard it as a form of refined narcissism since, as Marcel points out, there is something essentially unnarcissistic and beyond self in hope. One sees this in the hopefulness, not of the patient but of the physician. How much our patients do for us doctors!

We in Kansas have lived through the experience of a state hospital revival. Although we have built almost no new buildings, and although our admissions have increased tenfold in fifteen years, our once overcrowded patient population has steadily diminished until we now always have available empty beds. We have even closed some wards as unneeded. We are proud of this, and proud that the voters and officials of our state appreciate it, and consider the cost per *stay* more significant than the commonly used cost per day. A distinguished governor visited us for several days, determined, as he said, to "discover the secret." "Our state has more men and more money than Kansas," he said. "Why can't we do these things?"

[6] For example:

BLASTS END MOTHER'S WILL TO LIVE

Twelve days ago, Mrs. Helen E. Hopke lay in her bed fighting to stay alive to see her daughter's wedding.

Incurably ill for the past five years, Mrs. Hopke had been indirectly responsible for the meeting about a year ago of her daughter Rose Marie, 20, and the girl's intended husband, Arthur Woodrow Hudson, 26.

Rose Marie had acted as nurse and housekeeper to her bedfast mother. While buying medicine she met Hudson, a pharmacist in a local drug store. Friends said it was the girl's first romance.

They also said all that kept Mrs. Hopke alive in recent months was the thought of the impending marriage.

The 56-year-old mother heard the couple enter the house laughing and talking about the April 4th wedding. She heard them enter the next room.

Their chatter ended in three blasts from a shotgun.

Police said Hopke, opposed to the marriage, wanted his daughter to continue to care for her mother. He became enraged at reading the wedding notice in the paper, shot the couple then turned the gun on himself.

Rose Marie was taken to one hospital where she is recovering. Her mother was taken to another.

Tuesday night, Mrs. Hopke died.

(*Topeka Daily Capital*, Thursday, April 2, 1959)

He didn't discover the secret partly because he didn't believe what we told him. Many of my colleagues in this audience may not believe it now, either. But we consider the crucial element in the Kansas state hospital program to have been the inculcation of hope. Not in the patients directly, but in the doctors and all those who help them, in the relatives of the patients, in the responsible officials, in the whole community, and *then* in the patients. It was not just optimism; it was not faith; it was not expectation. We had no *reason* to expect what happened, and what still happens, and our faith was only that which all scientists share. But we did have hope.

We had more than hope, you will say; we had had experiences which encouraged hope. But these experiences were themselves based partly on hope, confirming the assumption that hope fires hope. This is not a conscious process, or at least not entirely so. I have wondered if we might perhaps understand the placebo effect in this way, a transmitted hope or reinoculation, as it were? In control research studies of the new drugs, for example, patients who receive only placebos sometimes show much improvement. In one study that I know about, testing an excellent drug, more patients in the group which had only placebos were able to be discharged from the hospital than from the group of those who got the actual remedy (although a larger number of the latter showed marked improvement).

Another phenomenon that is perhaps related to hope is the sudden improvement and even recovery of patients who have been for a long time fixed, as it were, at low levels of organization and regression. A new doctor arrives, or a new aide, and the patient promptly and most unexpectedly begins to recover.[7]

Whatever the explanation offered for such phenomena, to invoke suggestion or coincidence (whatever *they* are) will not suffice. There is more to it. And yet we doctors are so schooled against permitting ourselves to believe the intangible or impalpable or indefinite that we tend to discount the element of hope, its reviving effect as well as

---

[7] But it is also true that just the opposite occurs: A patient on whom intensive efforts have been made fails to respond and is given up in despair, dismissed by his physician or removed to a custodial hospital. We have all frequently seen this result in a prompt improvement and even recovery. Perhaps we could regard this as an awakening of dormant hope by a desperate and unintentional shock-type method.

its survival function. Because of the vulnerability of every doctor to the temptation of playing God and taking the credit for the workings of the *vis medicatrix naturae,* we are necessarily extremely cautious in attributing change to any particular thing and least of all to our own wishful thinking.

There are many sufferers in the world, and there are many who seek to afford them relief. Among the latter there are those who use intuition and magic, and there are those who attempt to derive basic principles checked by experiment and observation, which we call the scientific method. For the former group, healing is more important than truth; for the latter, truth is more important than healing. Indeed, the search for truth, the desire to heal, and the earning of one's living are three persistently conflicting forces in medical practice.

In the daily performance of healing acts, the scales are weighted heavily against scientific truth. Patients long to be deceived. Driven by pain and desperate with fear, they are ready to seize at "straws of hope." They prostrate themselves before the doctor; they queue up in weary, straggling lines awaiting the opportunity to submit themselves to humiliations and new sufferings, or even to hear a few words of reassurance. Besieged by such multitudes of petitioners, often with gifts in their hands, the doctor, knowing his limitations, must try to be patient, kind and merciful—but simultaneously "objective" and honest. The desire to bring comfort, the need to earn one's living, the suppressed longing for prestige and popularity, the honest conviction of the efficacy of a pill or a program, sympathy for the pleading sufferer—all of these throw themselves upon the scales in the moment of decision. Every physician in the world has heard the Devil whispering, "Command that these stones become bread. . . . All these things I will give thee if thou wilt fall down and . . ." And sometimes he falls down. He exploits the patient's hope.

Against such dangers there have been for twenty-five centuries an oath of loyalty, a tradition of humility, and certain maxims of practice. One of the latter is the putting of diagnosis before treatment, empiricism before hope. Even in prescientific days it was indefensible for a doctor not to indicate some comprehension of what one claiming to be a healer was dealing with. For the patient, even a diagnosis offered *some* hope, since it showed that his condition was not unique.

But for the doctor, who was better acquainted with the implications of a diagnosis for which he had no real treatment, the temptation was ever present to neglect diagnosis in the interests of hope, or at least in the interests of treatment.

It should be remembered that there were once many different kinds of competing healers. There were the apothecaries who in 1617 were granted a charter permitting them to sever their two-hundred-year association with the grocers. There were the various trade guilds: the barber-surgeons, midwives, and bone-setters; and then there were the physicians, with their plasters and clysters. All were busy "treating."

Out of this confusion, under the leadership of a gallery of immortals on pillars erected here and there over a wide area, there slowly arose the magnificent edifice of modern, scientific medicine. The elimination of superstition and magic took a century, but the purge strengthened medical science mightily. Thousands of remedies were tested, found wanting, and discarded. Many improvements in diagnostic techniques and instruments were introduced. Treatment, except for the most superficial palliation, was apt to be regarded with great suspicion, while the memory of recent quackery, pretension, and deceit was fresh.

In psychiatry, the efforts of our predecessors to bring order out of the apparent chaos of the phenomena of madness were reflected in assiduous efforts to describe disease entities, to name them, to identify them, to graph them, and to seek for "etiologies." This was the traditional concept of diagnosis and it offered little to justify hope. The broken or misshapen personalities coming under medical observation were described or christened with tens of thousands of names and groupings, painstakingly put together by assiduous workers, only to be discarded by those of a later generation. These old labels, like epitaphs on tombstones, may be read with sober reflections that life is short and the art long, that our grasp of human phenomena is limited and narrow, and that our concepts are ever changing and unclear.

Once diagnosis in the sense of recognizing, naming, classifying and distinguishing between different forms of behavior disorder seemed of fundamental importance. The best psychiatrist in my early days was one who could most convincingly distinguish between some of the many varieties of "paranoia" or "dementia praecox"[8] or "psycho-pathic personality." Some of my colleagues "discovered" new varie-ties of these; I even thought that I did.

Today it seems to me most important that we *not* do that. Our impressive labels only reify and freeze a phase of a process; they mis-represent our modern concepts and they strike a blow at hope, and hence at treatment. Words like *non compos mentis* or "responsible" and "irresponsible" really indicate only whether or not we think an accused person is able to appreciate being executed. "Psychotic" and "neurotic" cannot be competently defined, since what they mean at any one moment depends upon who is using them to describe whom. Many of us have urged their abolition, but they persist as weapons in scientific name-calling. Some colleagues incline to label "psychopathic personality" all patients who admit having broken the law. And surely it is more than a little disturbing to us all to contemplate the results of the recent researches by colleagues Hol-lingshead and Redlich exposing the fact that what one is called by psychiatrists depends to a degree upon what class of society one comes from.

But over and above the matter of social and political and medical misuse of terms, these diagnostic designations belie the progress we have made in understanding the nature of illness. A name is not a diagnosis. It does not determine treatment. Its original purpose, per-haps, was to distinguish between wise and foolish expectations, but its net effect has come to be that of destroying hope.

Today there is a trend away from names, states, and entities, and toward dynamics, relativity, and process. Just as the nature of matter has assumed a new aspect, so the nature of disease has come to be understood differently. The only entities in disease, said Allbutt long ago, are the individual patients, Smith and Jones, in certain phases of their being. "Diseases are not specifics such as cats and mushrooms; they are 'abnormal' *behaviors* of animals and plants." Today we are following Allbutt.

It is the privilege of some of us to be *called* doctors. And if the peculiar phases of existence which Jones and Smith are experiencing lead them to approach us in the belief that we can help them, they

[8] A term introduced ninety-nine years ago by B. A. Morel in 1860 describing the mental condition of a boy of fourteen years.

can then be called patients and their afflictions may be *called* disease. But we cannot discharge our responsibility by "calling." We may not exorcise Smith's afflictions by giving them a name. That is not the basis of our hope, and if it is the basis of Smith's hope, it is one we should not exploit.

It is our responsibility as physicians to instigate some change in the relations of Smith to his environment—directly if possible, indirectly and gradually most likely. To do this we must attempt to understand the man, how he has become what he is, what goes on inside of him, what goes on around him, and how these interact. By observing the internal and external processes we can discover what in his world is good for Smith and what is unbearable, what damage he inflicts upon himself and others, and what potentials within him remain underdeveloped. And here enters hope, for we acquire, thus, a rationale for therapeutic intervention.

This is what we now call diagnosis. It were better to call it diag-*nosing*, to indicate its transitive, continuing nature, its look toward the future rather than toward something static or past. Diagnosing is the first step in a co-operative relation between patient, physician and environment working toward the betterment of a situation, especially as it affects our patient. This is based upon hope, hope implicit in our effort and hope nurtured in our patient.

The practice of medicine today is vastly different from that of a century ago when Samuel Gross wrote, in 1861: "It requires no prophetic eye, no special foresight, to discover that we are on the very verge of one of the most fearful and widespread revolutions in medicine that the world has ever witnessed."[9] That revolution came about but not so soon as Gross expected. Yet it is hard to believe today that there was ever a time when a doctor had to defend himself to his colleagues if he claimed to have cured someone. In those days hope was faint and precious. Today it seems sometimes almost as if hope was considered unnecessary.

The revolution that elevated our medical profession from a discouraged, submerged state to a progressive and confident one was partly the result of new discoveries, and partly from the recognition of psychology as one of the basic medical sciences, along with physics

[9] Quoted by Morris C. Leikind, "The Evolution of Medical Research in the United States," *History of American Medicine*, Felix Marti-Ibanez, ed. (N. Y.: MD Publications, 1958), p. 126.

and chemistry. This came about from the experiences of World War I, and from the discoveries of Sigmund Freud. The latter were introduced into American psychiatry about 1920, the way prepared for them by J. J. Putnam, Ernest Southard, Adolf Meyer, William A. White, A. A. Brill, and Smith Ely Jelliffe.

I cannot describe all of these old friends here, but I must say a word about Southard, because he was my teacher and because above all men I have known, and entirely out of keeping with the spirit of his day, he placed great hope in psychiatry. He said here, long ago, in 1919, *remember:*

> May we not rejoice that we [psychiatrists] are to be equipped by training and experience better, perhaps, than any other men to see through the apparent terrors of anarchism, of violence, of destructiveness, or paranoia—whether these tendencies are showing in capitalists or in labor leaders, in universities or in tenements, in Congress or under deserted culverts. . . . Psychiatrists must carry their analytic powers, their ingrained optimism and their tried strength of purpose not merely into the narrow circle of frank disease, but, like Seguin of old, into education; like William James, into the sphere of morals; like Isaac Ray, into jurisprudence; and above all, into economics and industry. I salute the coming years as high years for psychiatrists![10]

These "high years" really began after Southard died. The public had been alerted by the literary dissemination of the discoveries of Freud and also by the growing "mental hygiene movement." Most doctors had had almost no psychiatry in their medical-school training. Twenty-five years after Southard had spoken those prophetic words—and died—we were in the midst of another World War. There was a shortage of psychiatrists. To enlist interest and recruit doctors, I visited medical schools over the country and talked at length to students, deans, and faculty members. I found that a common objection to entering psychiatry was an impression that our patients "never get well." It is such a hopeless field, they said. Penicillin and the other miracle drugs are more definite and exciting than the dreary wards of state hospitals, filled with silent, staring faces.

We can see, now, that these students had been shown the wrong side of psychiatry, its failures rather than its successes. But one thing struck me then which has remained in my mind indelibly. I per-

---

[10] "Cross Sections of Mental Hygiene, 1844, 1869, 1894," in *American Journal of Insanity*, 76:91-100, October, 1919, pp. 110-111.

ceived vividly how hopelessness breeds hopelessness, how the non-expectant, hope-lacking or "unimaginative" teacher can bequeath to his student a sense of impotence and futility, utterly out of keeping with facts known to both of them! Surely even these misled students knew that *some* psychiatric patients recover, even if they didn't know that the vast majority does so. But like their teachers, they adopted some of the very symptoms of their patients: hopelessness and goallessness. Physicians in state hospitals at that time did not expect their patients to recover, and were a little surprised when recovery occurred. Some superintendents quite unabashedly announced (published) recovery rates of 5 per cent per year!

This experience only reinforced my conviction that hope, that neglected member of the great triad, was an indispensable factor in psychiatric treatment and psychiatric education.

At the end of the war, veterans requiring continued psychiatric treatment began returning to this country in large numbers, and at the same time the physicians who had seen these phenomena of stress and overstress develop and recede were demobilizing. Many of these doctors now sought to learn more about this psychiatry which seemed so important in understanding these cases. During the first few months of its existence, the Menninger School of Psychiatry received over six hundred applications. Other training centers were similarly flooded.

Some of them no doubt came into psychiatry because of an awareness of their own threatened disorganization and the dim realization that this human-all-too-human tendency was one against which penicillin and heart surgery and all the discoveries of modern medicine offered no protection. By Freud, discoveries of quite another sort had been made and knowledge of them had slowly become common property. These discoveries promised no miracles, no instantaneous cures; they did not seem to justify hope. In fact, Freud was frequently accused of a devastating pessimism. Surely hope has rarely entered medical science through so narrow and tortuous a crevice. But it did enter and its rays transformed the face of modern psychiatry in our lifetime. A whole new viewpoint in medicine developed, one that gave authority and technique to efforts at systematic self-scrutiny, a kind of extended and continuous diagnostic case study.

In a way it seems curious that the psychoanalytic process, which is so obviously diagnostic, has generally come to be called treatment. Diagnosis is the hopeful search for a way out; but the setting forth on the way which one discovers and the unflinching persistence in making the effort—*that* is the treatment; that is the self-directed, self-administered change.

The psychoanalytic treatment method is a great discovery but this is not what changed psychiatry. It was the new understanding that psychoanalytic research gave us concerning men's motives and inner resources, the intensity of partially buried conflicts, the unknown and unplumbed depths and heights of our nature, the formidable power each of us holds to determine whether he lives or dies. It was the realization that we must encourage each individual to see himself not as a mere spectator of cosmic events but as a prime mover; to regard himself not as a passive incident in the infinite universe but as one important unit possessing the power to influence great decisions by making small ones. Wrote William James:

> *Will you or won't you* have it so? is the most probing question we are ever asked. We are asked it every hour of the day, and about the largest as well as the smallest, the most theoretical as well as the most practical things. We answer by *consents* or *non-consents* and not by words. What wonder that these dumb responses should seem our deepest organs of communication with the nature of things! What wonder if the effort demanded by them be the measure of our worth as men![11]

"Ye shall know the truth and the truth shall make you free," said another wise One. For this emancipating truth, Freud searched not in physics or chemistry or biology, but in the tabooed land of the emotions. From the Pandora chest of man's mind, full of harmful and unlovely things to be released upon a protesting world, there turned up—last of all—Hope.

Selfishness, vengefulness, hate, greed, pettiness, bitterness, vindictiveness, ruthlessness, cruelty, destructiveness and even self-destructiveness—all these are in us. But not only those. Invisible at first, but slowly pervasive and neutralizing came love, and then—perhaps because of it—came faith, and then hope.

Love, faith, hope—in that order. The Greeks were wrong. Of

[11] *The Principles of Psychology*, New York: Dover Publications, 1950, p. 579.

*course* hope is real, and of course it is not evil. It is the enemy of evil, and an ally of love, which is goodness.

Freud's great courage led him to look honestly at the evil in man's nature. But he persisted in his researches to the bottom of the chest, and he discerned that potentially love is stronger than hate, that for all its core of malignancy, the nature of men can be transformed with the nurture and dispersion of love.

This was the hope that Freud's discoveries gave us. This was the spirit of the new psychiatry. It enabled us to replace therapeutic nihilism with constructive effort, to replace unsound expectations—first with hope, and then with sound expectations.

This is what it did for us, for psychiatrists. And for our patients—miserable, apprehensive, discouraged, and often desperate—what can we do better than that? What can we do better than to dispel their false expectations—good and bad—and then light for them a candle of hope to show them possibilities that may become sound expectations?

And we who are teachers—can we do better by our eager young seekers for the keys to wisdom than to help them sharpen the accuracy of their expectations without extinguishing the divine fire?

But there are many people in the world who are neither our patients nor our students, and who are nonetheless filled with great apprehensiveness, partly from ignorance and mistrust of one another. They are afflicted with great suffering which all our discoveries have not ameliorated, and awed by vast discoveries which none of us fully comprehend. Some of them look to us for counsel, to us whom they have so highly honored and so generously rewarded with prerogatives and opportunities. They are our friends, our brothers and sisters, our neighbors, our cousins in foreign lands. For these people—for them and for ourselves—are we not now duty bound to speak up as scientists, not about a new rocket or a new fuel or a new bomb or a new gas, but about this ancient but rediscovered truth, the validity of Hope in human development—Hope, alongside of its immortal sisters, Faith and Love.

# CHAPTER 17

## *THE IMMORTALITY OF MAN*

### MARGARET MEAD

WITH DISCUSSION BY PAUL TILLICH, WALTER M. HORTON, AND ELMER G. HOMRIGHAUSEN

As THE study of the cosmos has broadened man's sense of the universe in which he lives, the words of the Psalm, "The heavens declare the glory of God; and the firmament sheweth his handiwork," have taken on very different meanings for the speaker in 1600, 1800, and today. As the study of the fossils of the earth and of the changes in living forms have given new meaning to the condensed statements of creation of earlier times, so too we may expect the comparative study of the ways in which human beings have attempted to understand man as a being with a soul or spirit somehow separate from its corporeal abode to add new dimensions to our understanding of man's search for immortality. Each great religious system has carried within its explication the limitations imposed by the state of knowledge of its interpreters. While we may say that the very meaning of the word "prophet" is that his inspiration transcends the limitations of time and space and the state of man's knowledge within which the prophecy is made, the inspiration must nevertheless be couched either in words of tremendous generality and universality or else in the homely figures of speech of those who listen, and then such a phrase as "in my Father's house are many mansions" loses its universality when the image is constructed with marble floors or tile roofs. Men will differ in their preferences for the bleak sweep of an infinity in which there is no familiar shape or color, or for some particular evocation which is within their narrow experience. Meanwhile we may easily lose sight of the extent to which our present most lofty conceptions of man's place in the universe are limited and narrowed either by the provincialisms of Euro-American traditions or by the obstreperous materialism of a young scientific development.

Anthropological materials—that is, a comparative discussion based upon records of other, particularly of other more primitive, cultures—should be able to give us the means whereby we may assess the special character of our own historically limited approach to the question of immortality, and so deepen and widen our perception of the scope of the question. When Americans think of immortality, they think of survival after death, of some other sphere or plane, and of the persistence of personal identity. And indeed at first glance, it would seem quite difficult to think about immortality at all except in terms of these three ideas.

Yet each of these three—to us—essential aspects of immortality can be thought of, have been thought of very differently. Let us take first the period of immortality, which we think of as beginning at birth, or at conception, and stretching onward forever. But there are people who are more concerned with pre-existence, as we would have to phrase it because of the importance which we attribute to this single existence on earth. For them the pre-existence of the soul before entering on a human life may be as crucial as is the afterlife to us. In the folk beliefs of Eastern European Jews, the soul was believed to have existed since creation, waiting to be born, and just before birth an angel would take it on a journey through all time and space and then, at the moment before birth, would give it a blow which wiped all trace of this knowledge from memory. Among the Palestinian Arabs, angels brought earth as well as a soul at conception, and the being so formed spent its early life traveling toward the place from which the earth came, for there its life would be ended. This interpretation gives a new and concrete poignancy to the words of the church burial service, "Dust thou art and unto dust thou shalt return." Perhaps even more widespread than the beliefs in immortality which conceive of a single sojourn in this world are those in which the human soul is conceived of as returning again and again. Some peoples see this return as a simple repetitive cycle which has always gone on since the beginning of the world and in which a man is reborn in one of his descendants—sometimes in the descendant who bears his name, sometimes only in someone in a designated generation. There are, of course, the elaborations of these ideas in the great Eastern religions, in which the soul may enter lower forms than man and lives many lives, rewarded or punished for the way each life is lived by the nature of the next incarnation until, finally purified, it may escape the burden of further incarnations.

The second item in our picture of immortality—continued life in another sphere—has also many modifications. Many peoples think of the souls of their ancestors as staying near them, near their graves, or near the houses in which they have lived, or guarding the boundaries of ancestral lands, watching over the health and welfare of living kindred. In these beliefs, death introduces another state of being, but the person lives on, disembodied, within the familiar earthly scene. Or when the next world is thought of as somehow in some other place—in the sky, within the earth, beneath the sea, or towards the sunset—this may be conceived of as a condition of continuous, unchanging bliss, as when the Polynesian chiefs go to become pillars in the house of the gods, or as a state of frozen ecstasy, of eternal adoration of the Godhead, or as a world filled with events which will govern later incarnations, or as a world in which reward and punishment are differentiated. It seems to be a widespread characteristic of human beings that they are able to think more imaginatively about a Hell than about a Heaven, for while a desired next world may be pictured in terms of selected luxuries from this world or the details may not be specified at all, the tortures of the damned have been conceptualized over and over again with zest and vividness. It may well be that one measure of man's growing spiritual maturity, through the centuries in which his knowledge of the universe is deepened by exploration and experiment, will be a beginning ability to think as creatively about good as, in the past, he has thought about evil.

And third, there is the question of the persistence of identity. Our sense of personal identity is so strong that is seems inseparable from the idea of immortality. Yet many peoples see the problem quite differently. The Balinese have an Indonesian version of Hinduism and believe in a form of reincarnation within the same family life in an endless recurrence, from which escape is possible only for rajahs, for whom great ceremonies can be made, and for an occasional dedicated virgin worshiper. Souls, in an indeterminate number for each person, are reincarnated in great-grandchildren, and if a great-grandfather meets a great-grandchild on the street he must pay him a penny, for he has no right to be alive at the same time. When someone dies in Bali, no one weeps. Only for an infant of a few months is a mother permitted to weep, and the relatives, as they dig the grave, are permitted to reproach it, "The next time you come, stay longer and at least eat rice with us before you go." The burial ceremonies include ritual practices to make the body more beautiful in the next incarnation, but all sense of personal identity disappears. One may compromise one's next incarnation either on this earth or in the dim purgatory where the dead await the next incarnation. A long run of bad luck may be blamed on debts that one of one's souls contracted during its stay in the other world, and people will say, "I am having bad luck this incarnation." Or, in giving to a beggar, they may remark, "I would not dare not to give to him. Who knows when I may not be as he? We all take turns." And a mother will say to a son who shows a sudden interest in gambling, "The reincarnated soul in you must have been a great gambler!" But it is all quite impersonal for there is no individual identity involved. This lack of a sense of identity is so marked that no one can describe the looks or manners of a person who died only a short time before. The body dies completely; the souls join other souls and return.

But the disposal of the body is a terrible problem for the Balinese. In ceremony after ceremony they seek to eliminate it finally. In the full cycle, there is first burial or a long period of keeping and guarding the corpse and then cremation. From the ashes, the bones are picked out and are reconstituted in the form of the skeleton, are dressed and laid out again in a miniature village in the graveyard; the souls, in the form of little figures carried by young girls as if they were babies, are taken home to the household temple, are given refreshment, and then are returned to the bones. Then the bones are pounded to ashes and are deposited in special containers which again represent human form. These, in turn, are burned and the resulting ashes are taken down to the shore and sent out to sea in tiny canoes. Forty-two days later, a new representation—this time with no material link to the old body—will be reconstituted to represent the souls, now become part of a household pantheon to whom their descendants pray. So breaking the tie with the body is a condition of keeping the tie to the souls, but the sense of identity is only ceremonial.

In sharp contrast were the beliefs of the lagoon-dwelling people of the Admiralty Islands as recently as 1929. Here, souls, which came into being at conception, led their most vigorous and powerful lives immediately after death when a male became the overlord of the household of his immediate kin. His skull was kept in the rafters and, through diviners and mediums, he made his wishes known, rewarded and punished his kin for sins of omission and commission, and wreaked havoc among neighbors with whom they became involved in economic disputes. But his reign, during which he married and sometimes had ghostly children, lasted only as long as he was able to protect the living males in his household from the malice of other ghosts; when the next male died, he was deposed, his skull was thrown out, and he became a homeless, malicious inhabitant of the lagoon, first a member of a set of anonymous kin ghosts, then a sea slug and finally, after a few generations when all memory of his period on earth was gone also, he ceased to exist. When the Manus decided to become Christians, they pitched all the skulls of their guardian ghosts into the sea, deposing at once all of their regnant dead. Today they have a new culture which has incorporated many western ideas, a local version of Christianity at present blessed by no Mission, and an eager desire to multiply and become as numerous as the Americans who streamed, a million strong, through their islands during World War II; and they have invented the idea of reincarnation. Finding it wasteful to leave the souls of infants in heaven—as the Mission taught them—they now pray to God to send them back in reincarnated form. Thus, in the space of twenty-five years, they have moved from an extreme view of the mortality of highly identified individuals who were given a brief afterlife which was followed by annihilation, through an acceptance of orthodox Christian beliefs in an afterlife, to a new version of reincarnation.

A third relationship between immortality and identity is illustrated by the Iatmul of the Sepik River, a New Guinea mainland people, among whom reincarnation follows names and goes down in family lines. An Iatmul man will be telling a story about some semimythical ancestral figure who bore the same name as the storyteller; in the middle of the tale, he will shift from the third person to the first and say, "I was on the prow of that canoe," and, as he speaks, he will stamp his foot on the floor of the house. The Iatmul sense of identity has a dreamlike impersonal character in which role and individual existence are separated; a twelve-year-old boy, asked to tell the story of his life, will start to relate the events of childhood and then suddenly will be heard to say, "And then I married a woman of Angoram and had three children and the eldest was named . . ." Without noticing it, he has passed himself and gone on into a future which is as clear for him, because it is equally clearly defined socially, as is his past. So the Iatmul will relate elaborate events filled with the details of appropriate conversations and acts— which careful research shows never occurred at all—in the sense in which we, with our sense of actuality anchored in an irreversible, directed universe, would say that an event had occurred.

The persistence of identity not only is tied up in various ways with role, kin position, name, and the body—especially the less corruptible parts of the body, the bones—but it is related also in many different ways to the conception of the continued existence of the soul either as beneficial or harmful to the survivors or as the primary concern of the individual himself. Characteristically, in societies where ideas of the religious development of the individual are crude and rudimentary, beliefs about the soul reflect a concern with the living and the terms of their grief. Human grief has many components—anger at being forsaken, guilt over hostile acts which have been left unatoned for and unforgiven, a passionate desire to capture and keep the memory of the departed, a desire to be rid of the reminder of one's own mortality. Different peoples have taken parts of this complex and have elaborated them. Among the Bagobo of the Philippines, in an area of the world where multiple souls are common, the people distinguish a good soul and a bad. At death the bad soul becomes a demon who feeds on the dead body, tearing it with its fingernails, and the good soul goes to a heaven where "the rice is of immaculate whiteness, and each grain is as big as a kernel of corn; the camotes are the size of a great wash pot, and every stick of sugar cane is as large as the trunk of a cocoanut palm." So people can make offerings to the good soul and attach to it all their positive feelings about the dead, while their negative feelings go into hatred and fear of the bad soul.

Some people emphasize only the hatred and fear, and go through elaborate ceremonies to separate themselves from the dead, deceiving the soul so that it will never be able to find its way back, cutting the throat of the corpse in a violent attempt to do away with the dead finally and forever. Within the tradition of Christian mourning, only the positive feelings are emphasized; people weep for the dead as deeply and unambivalently loved, and those who harbor hatred and resentment feel guilty because of the inappropriate emotions which they must repress. Many primitive peoples have developed ritual exercises to ensure a proper display of agonized grief, such as cutting off a finger at the death of a relative. Grief so displayed may also be an essential propitiation, for the dead are expected to take revenge for unexpressed negative attitudes which the excessive mourning only masks.

Whether it is a question of banishing the dead or of keeping them close, the form of immortality is closely tied up with the role of the living. However, persistence of identity may also be envisaged as a personal goal, expressed either in a desire for continued identity— even in the same body—in the afterlife or in alternative technically secular forms in which the individual craves or is accorded immortality through the continued repercussions on earth of his acts while alive. These secular forms of immortality—through historic acts, generous bequests, or artistic or scientific creativity—appear to present a kind of negative counterbalance to literal and vivid expectations of immortality in another world. Visions of heaven become pallid and abstract as a man plans to live through his children— "the only immortality we have"—through buildings and discoveries, paintings or books, that bear his name. Conversely, a preoccupation with one's spiritual life and a belief that the main task of men on earth is "to colonize heaven," as an English bishop phrased it, tend to be accompanied by a negative attitude to the things of this world, including fame and creativity. But the line is seldom clear. A Burmese scholar once told me about the destruction of his life's scholarly work in a bombing during the war. "It is bad," he said, "for history, but good for me, as it detaches me from this world." And in England, a recent study by Geoffrey Gorer shows that one out of seven people believe in some sort of reincarnation, because, they rationalize, one life doesn't give one a fair chance.

Thus, whether identity is to be cherished or escaped from, whether this life on earth is an intermediate state, a beginning or a recurrent episode in man's existence in the universe, whether, at death, the emphasis is upon the personal spiritual fate of the individual or upon the bereaved, whether the tie to this world is expressed in a belief in the resurrection of the body or in the persistence of a man's contribution to human culture, men's views of immortality become a framework within which earthly ways of life are judged and changed, lived and abandoned. A long life on earth is important to those who are concerned with taking a fully developed personality into the next world where all further development will cease and only eternal rewards and punishments remain. But the briefest sojourn as a day-old infant may be sufficient to attain a place in another world in which development is possible. The Soviet Communists, who have proclaimed their militant materialism, speak of a place in history, as a man fulfills the role assigned to him by history and so attains a sort of immortality—in history—with burial in the Red Wall. Modern medicine and public health practices flourish among those peoples for whom a long life in this world is a principal value; they are harder to introduce among peoples for whom the earth is a passing prelude to an impersonal eternity.

When the International Astronautical Congress met in Rome, Pope Pius XII blessed interplanetary exploration, within which man would work out new relationships to God and His Universe. As we widen our sense of man's potentialities through our widening knowledge of the cosmos, the question of the immortality of man may be expected to widen also and to take on new forms.

#### Discussion by PAUL TILLICH

Margaret Mead's article about the immortality of man shows clearly two things; first, that there is rather universally a belief that man's being is not limited to the stretch of time between birth and death, and second, that this belief expresses itself in many different forms, not only in the high religions but also in the very primitive ones. It is always a deterrent to theological arrogance if the theologian is forced to realize that central ideas of his own religion are not strange to other religions and that the symbols in which these ideas are expressed vary immensely in all religions, including his own.

The Christian theologian—on Protestant ground—must, in view of these facts, first ask what is the meaning of the belief in immortality if the Christian message is interpreted as an answer to a question implied in man's existential situation. It would be rather inadequate if he discussed the problem of immortality as being the question: What will happen to man after his death? There is no theological answer to this question, since the question itself contradicts the human situation, as does the question: What has happened to man *before* his birth? The "before" and the "after" subject man endlessly to the structure of temporality. But man, in the Christian view, comes from the eternal and goes to the eternal; and he can experience the eternal in every moment of time. Man's existential situation implies the awareness of his finitude and, at the same time, the quest for the infinite to which he feels he belongs and from which he feels excluded. Out of this awareness arise the symbols of immortality. In spite of their variety and absurdity in content, they are existentially meaningful. They are absurd if taken as descriptions of something that will happen in a future time, as for instance, shortly after death; they are meaningful if taken as symbols of man's sense of belongingness to the eternal.

The assertion that the various symbols of immortality are meaningful does not imply that they are equally adequate to the human situation. On the contrary, they express fundamentally different and often contrasting relations of man to the eternal. On this point, theological criticism must start, for this point has bearing on the whole of religious experience. It is decisive whether immortality is understood as the return of the individual to the transcendent One in a union which is anticipated in mystical experiences, or whether it is understood as the participation of the individual in the divine life which is the life of love. And if the latter alternative is accepted —as it predominantly has been in the Western world—it is decisive whether one thinks of the immortality of a spiritual part of man, called "soul," or of the total man, dying totally and being resurrected totally. The second alternative is the classically Christian valuation of love. But, of course, it is more absurd than even popularized Platonism, if taken literally. A Christian motif which in Protestanism has not been taken seriously enough is the question of a possible development of the individual after death. The doctrine of reincarnation gives an answer, but—as Margaret Mead rightly points out—an answer which cannot account for the very thing for the sake of which it has been given: the identity of the developing self. In the doctrine of purgatory, the Roman Church attempts to answer the question of a developing self after death, and Protestant theologians have talked about a "state between" temporal existence and eternal life. Perhaps one should be satisfied with the answer that eternal life is *life*, and therefore not static but dynamic, and that it transcends the three modes of time, reaching back into the past and ahead into the future and experienced (as the Gospel according to John indicates) in the present: the eternal now.

### Discussion by WALTER M. HORTON

I have been asked to comment, from the theological point of view, upon this fascinating and thought-provoking article by Margaret Mead. In the field of anthropology her name is a name to conjure with; and to all that she says concerning the divergent concepts of immortality among various peoples, I would only ask the reader's most respectful attention. As she rightly remarks, all such anthropological studies help us to "assess the special character of our own historically limited approach to the question of immortality, and so deepen and widen our perception of the scope of the question."

My first theological comment is on the conception of *prophetic inspiration* at the very beginning of the article. I am in agreement with Dr. Mead when she says that the word "prophet" implies some sort of higher vision transcending the environment and thought-world in which the prophet lives; yet every prophet who tries to express his vision must either use terms so general that they suggest "the bleak sweep of an infinity in which there is no familiar shape or color," or else use terms drawn from his own limited range of experience and knowledge, which are bound to fall into "provincialisms" unconvincing to those born and raised in other cultures.

The problem she raises with regard to concepts of immortality is exactly analogous to the one noted by Paul Tillich[1] with regard to concepts of God: they are either so *"ultimate"* that they are remote and vague, or so *"concrete"* that they threaten to involve us in childish anthropomorphism and idolatry.

The only way out of this dilemma, in both cases, is through a candid recognition of the inevitable place of *symbols* in religious life and thought. Drawn as they necessarily are from the cultural context in which each prophet lives and speaks, these symbols must be expected to vary from culture to culture, and thus to give a first impression of complete relativism to one who surveys them *all together*, as the cultural anthropologist does. If I understand Dr. Mead, she does not regard this first impression as fully true. A symbol drawn from a particular culture may have meaning and validity for other cultures, *if viewed in its deeper intention rather than in its specific form.*

Religious prophets have often been quite conscious of the inadequacy of their words and thoughts to express the full meaning of their visions. The Apostle Paul, certainly an inspired prophet if there ever was one, claiming insight into hidden divine mysteries through the revelation of the Spirit (I Cor. 2:7-16), nevertheless can say, "We know *in part* and we prophesy *in part*. . . . we see in a glass darkly" (I Cor. 13:9, 12). All that he tells us about bodies terrestrial and celestial, in another chapter (15) of the same epistle, must therefore be read with the superscription: "partial, symbolic, aiming at more than a mortal man can say in human speech." Let fanatics interpret prophecy to mean that one can calculate "the day and the hour," or that the streets of heaven are paved with literal gold; the prophets themselves know better. They know that knowledge is symbolic, and they do not press particular symbols as though they were photographic copies of what "eye hath not seen" (I Cor. 2:9).

This leads to my second theological comment. The three prevailing Western ideas which Dr. Mead selects for comparison with quite different ideas in other cultures (1) "survival after death" in (2) "some other sphere or plane" and (3) "persistence of personal

---

[1] *Systematic Theology,* (Chicago: University of Chicago Press, 1951), Vol. I, pp. 221 ff.

identity," are more universal ideas in their intention than such obviously symbolic ideas as streets of gold and gates of pearl. While there are symbolic elements here too, which may be nonessential, theologians would distinguish these nonessentials from other elements which are organically bound up with the central revelation which is the "light of all their seeing."

Western theologians cannot afford any longer to treat primitive and Oriental religious ideas of human destiny as too absurd for seri- ous consideration. Yet they are bound to test all ideas of immortality by their conformity or nonconformity to the central revelation of God and man in the Old and New Testaments, *unless they are prepared to accept some alternative revelation as profounder and truer than this.* The great issue that runs through fully half of the variant views described by Dr. Mead is whether life is a "wheel of rebirth," as so persistently and systematically taught in the mystical religions of the East, or whether, as the Bible teaches, it is a drama moving toward a significant outcome, in which every least individual plays some significant part, for good or ill. One cannot say this is a matter of indifference, or that these different views are symbolic of the same truth; one is compelled to choose between the two outlooks, as they lead to seriously different ways of living.

Such a choice need not imply a total rejection of the cyclic wheel- of-rebirth concept. Life does obviously have its rhythmic recurrences and repetitions—day and night, summer and winter, birth and death, and birth again. In some religions, these are the ultimate framework of interpretation. In our religion, they are surface phe- nomena, beneath which is the "increasing purpose" of a God who transcends this world, and offers each individual creature of his a significant part in the making of a new and better world. Though we know in part and see through a glass darkly, such a God can be trusted to preserve the life and identity of all who put their trust in him, not only in this sphere we now inhabit, but also in the higher sphere which he inhabits. Anthropology can challenge pro- vincial and naïvely symbolic expressions of this faith, but cannot shake the major and minor premises on which it is based: (1) that God transcends this world, and (2) that he has an individualized, never-failing love for all his creatures, such as Christ showed to the least, last, and lost among his contemporaries.

My last theological comment is upon Dr. Mead's remark that "men's views of immortality become a framework within which earthly ways of life are judged and changed, lived and abandoned." This connection does exist, and gives present importance to all such views. It also permits us to judge (in part) between rival revelations by their pragmatic consequences. Psychical research may some day give scientific evidence of the existence of a sphere within which human identity survives after death. Some consider that valid evidence of this is already at hand; but until such proof is more widely accepted, we shall have to judge between rival views of final destiny by the "earthly ways of life to which they lead." "Wheel-of-rebirth" views lead to a kind of fatalistic acceptance of repetition in nature, which Western science and technology, by *changing* nature's immemorial ways, have shown to be invalid. Medieval "otherworldliness" led to a neglect of the opportunities of this life, while modern secularism often leads man to spend his dreams and hopes upon temporal goods which cannot permanently satisfy a creature in whose heart God has set eternity. Since every culture has an implicit religious faith at its core, the total life of this culture is a kind of explicit exhibition of the implications of this faith. While each culture seems natural and logical to its own adherents, the clash of cultures with which our world resounds today is sifting out the weak and impermanent elements in all of them, and revealing the elements fit to stand in the future world-order. Those who believe in the eventual triumph of God's providence and grace should not hesitate to expose their theological concepts to this conflict and sifting.

### Discussion by ELMER G. HOMRIGHAUSEN

I find Dr. Mead's article very interesting and challenging. Coming from a recognized anthropologist, her remarks issue from a lifetime of careful and firsthand observation gleaned from various cultures.

Her major thesis is that man's conception of immortality is conditioned by the cultural context in which he finds himself. Now that Euro-American traditions regarding immortality are confronted with new views of science and the comparative conceptions of other religions, perhaps "the question of the immortality of man may be expected to widen also and to take on new forms."

Yet, the three popularly accepted ideas of immortality held by Americans—survival after death, of some other sphere or plane, and of the persistence of personal identity—have been differently conceived by other peoples. Even in the so-called Christian tradition, immortality has been variously conceived. Dr. Mead gives us some rather detailed interpretation concerning these variations.

I find these varying conceptions not only interesting but indicative of a serious concern about immortality on man's part. I would not discount or ridicule these earnestly held traditions. They indicate to me the age-old attempt on man's part to deal with the real and tragic event of death. All religious leaders and traditions have wrestled with the problem of man's "end" in this life. And they have worked out answers to the great questions: Does death end all? Does man have an immortal spirit? What is the relation of the spirit to its pre-existence? What is the relation of the spirit to the body? What is life like beyond death? What is the relation of immortality to the community? Is bodily life real or only a shadowy existence?

These and many other related questions have plagued and challenged the race from the beginning. Of only a few things can we be more or less sure: There is a mystery about life and death; death is not a welcome event; man wishes to transcend his end; man's conceptions about his future state are confused and varied. In some ways, man feels that he does live on, but it is hard to tell whether he *wishes* to persist beyond death or whether he *must* persist. It seems to be evident that what man is in life has much to do with what he will be after death. The meaningfulness of life in this world is closely related to the desirability and state of life beyond death!

Of course, immortality has been variously conceived in the West. Right now, one of the most significant emphases in Christian theology is the unity of man's life. There has been a strong reaction against the Greek body-spirit dualism in favor of a strong psychosomatic unity which is found in the Bible.

Man is a unity. The Greek emphasis upon immortality is also

being challenged in favor of the emphasis upon the resurrection of the body. The so-called persistence of man's spirit—as though it could be dissociated from his life in this world—is questioned. It casts aspersions on the body which God has made and which, for the "new being in Christ" is called the temple of the Holy Spirit.

A strong emphasis upon the Incarnation of the Son of God also gives this human pilgrimage a new dignity. The new man in Christ is not just a renewed spirit but a man renewed in the totality of his life and relationship.

Not a little emphasis is being given to the relation of faith to health these days. Incidentally, this point of view is championed by scientists in their conception of "matter." All this has led some theologians to go beyond the so-called immortality of the individual person. Few biblical interpreters will maintain that the images of heaven in the Bible are to be taken literally. Those images represent the only possible framework or context in which the hope of man in the Gospel could be stated. There is no way by which the future state of life could possibly be fully portrayed in terms of time and space.

It is not without reason that the ecumenical movement at its Evanston Assembly in 1954 centered its thought on the Christian hope. Little was said in that Assembly about mere personal immortality. Rather, this hope was directed towards mankind and towards the world. As one theologian put it: "We are no longer interested in little hopes. We are interested in the one big hope!"

Even the hopes of immortality which were largely interpreted in secular terms have been challenged. For what hope is there for a peaceful world? Progress for mankind? A better world for future generations? Now progress, it is maintained, is an undeniable fact! But is immortality to be interpreted in terms of the immortality of man in this world?

Yet, the alternative is not to "leave it all behind" and concentrate upon personal immortality. Individual persons are bound up in the bundle of life; they are parts of one another. Is the great hope of mankind and of the world to be consummated only in personal persistence after death?

More and more, the future of man's life is conceived in terms of a hope in God who is almighty and gracious. Hope of the future is not in man at all. It must be grounded in the Grand Context: God. And it is given assurance through the bearer of that hope who is Jesus Christ. In him, Man has been manifest, the Man who is the hope of everyman. This Man is the goal of all history. This Man is identical with the kingdom of God, says Emil Brunner. And this hope is not some far-off destiny only; it is a present living and working reality in faith even though imperfect. And in this hope is the hope of all mankind and of the whole world. *Immortality* is based on man's potentiality for immortality; *resurrection* is based on God's will and power to create and redeem life.

There seems to be less of a desire on the part of Christian theology today to portray what life beyond death will be. If it is a resurrected life, it will bear continuity with this life-in-the-body, but it will be a transformed and remade life. A new life. Heaven is not a prolongation or magnification of earth. Eternity is not extended time. It will not only be one of personal identity but of corporate identification. It will be the "city of God."

There is less of an emphasis in Christian circles on the secular joys of heaven in our time and more of an emphasis upon the fulfillment of those higher joys of the Spirit which men may know in and through Jesus Christ. The quality of life we now may know in this world through Christ is the *real basis* for the Christian hope. For why should anyone wish "immortality" of something which in this world is undesirable?

I think that much of so-called "Christian immortality" is little more than a kind of secular hope by which men hope to survive death. More and more this kind of secular hope has become questionable. Perhaps that is why so many people have lost their interest in immortality. Who wants it if it is nothing but more of what they now know? They long deeply and sincerely for the Great Hope! They want something new! And it is only as this becomes a living conviction that people today will live real lives in this world in the "power of the resurrection" that worked in Jesus Christ. By such a power they will be able to transform life and change it. A church composed of such believers will become a social cell of redemption in the world.

However, if men continue to force hope for the survival of death merely on the basis of the secular good and hopes they know, I am afraid that immortality will be not only a rather undesirable thing, but perhaps even a demonic thing! If I *must* persist beyond death, and if I have nothing but a dreary hope set within a tragic life, it is a terrible thing to contemplate the future.

I confess that science has made all our little hopes rather insignificant. Its conception of the unity of life, the dynamic nature of matter, the living nature of society and cosmic forces, should arouse even Christians out of their cribbed and cabined conceptions of "immortality" into a whole new vision of the living hope of human and world redemption in cosmic terms. Perhaps science may again shake even Christian thinking about death and life into becoming serious about the grand concern of the Bible for the human race. For the biblical revelation breaks through the provincial to the cosmic.

# CHAPTER 18

# *A THEOLOGY FOR MODERN MAN*

## WILLIAM HAMILTON

PAUL's Epistle to the Romans is peculiarly appropriate for the development of a theology for the Christian layman, because it takes seriously what I believe to be *the* question that he is beginning to put to the church. The layman is being rediscovered today in all sorts of dishonest ways: as a potential political pressure group, or as an untapped source for the administrative work of the church. But if the layman at work in the world is the chief concern of the church; if the church's main business is to speak to the layman at his work, and not to invite him into the church buildings to busy himself there, then a theology that claims to be appropriate for something more than the theological schools must try to speak to the real questions he is asking.

What answer does the epistle give to the questions that are now occupying men's minds? What, if any, is the theological question of modern man? Rudolf Bultmann has put it this way, and I think he is right: "How is a Christian existence possible in this world when one, in both his work and pleasures, shares in its culture, its tasks, and its worldly goods?" [1] The layman's theological question, in other words, begins as an ethical question, and if we demythologize Bultmann's formulation we get something like this: "What is the will of God and how can I do it?'

Therefore let us approach Romans by beginning with this question. The layman is legitimately dissatisfied with many of our current answers, and so Romans may enable us to set both the question and the answer in proper focus.

[1] In his preface to the new edition of Adolf Harnack, *What Is Christianity?* (New York: Harper & Brothers, 1957) p. xi.

218

## On Doing the Will of God

"I appeal to you therefore, brethren, by the mercies of God, to present your bodies as a living sacrifice, holy and acceptable to God, which is your spiritual worship [or reasonable service]. Do not be conformed to this world but be transformed by the renewal of your mind, that you may prove what is the will of God, what is good and acceptable and perfect" (Rom. 12:1-2).

This is the point in the letter where Paul faces our problem, and it marks a decisive stage in his argument. Look at the "therefore" in the first verse. On what basis does he make his appeal? What does "therefore" point to? Because of the whole argument of the early chapters, man's obligation is to offer himself to God, rejecting the form of the world. Why? Because he has been and is now being formed by Jesus Christ, who is the will of God. And just what is the argument of the early chapters? All men are sinners, Paul has declared, religious and secular men alike (Gentiles and Jews, as he puts it), and all deserve condemnation (1:18-3:20). But their lot is not hopeless, for salvation has been offered to all men (3:21-8:39). And, after a digression on the problem of Israel's rejection of Christ in the light of God's plan (in Chapters 9-11—a very poignant personal concern for him as a Jew), he makes his appeal. Because of the gift of salvation in Jesus Christ, the problem of the will of God can now be presented to the man in Christ.

Because of the great act of salvation in Jesus Christ ("by the mercies of God"), man is to present his body—his whole complex life, physical, intellectual, spiritual, moral—as a self-offering of gratitude and obedience. Do not, he says, take the form of the world for the form of your life. The will of the world is never the will of God, though the world is eager and anxious to impress its form on your life. You have been given, he argues, a form to put over against the form of the world. You, your mind, every part of you, has been transformed by God's act in Christ, and now all you have to do is to manifest, to show forth, to "prove" this form or will of God in the life of the world.

What does it mean to do the will of God, then? Dietrich Bonhoeffer has said some helpful and practical things at this point:

The first demand which is made of those who belong to God's Church is not that they should be something in themselves, not that they should, for example, set up some religious organization or that they should lead lives of piety, but that they shall be witnesses to Jesus Christ before the world.[2]

This means that we cannot be satisfied that we have answered the question about the will of God merely by saying that we should be good, or say our prayers, or transform the world. To be a witness to Jesus Christ is identical with doing or proving the will of God. Jesus Christ *is* the saving act that God has done for man; Jesus Christ, then, is the form of the life that I must stand for in the world. To prove the will of God, to witness before the world for Jesus Christ, will never come easily. But in any specific situation, the one possibility is there, "very deeply concealed beneath a great number of available possibilities." [3]

Man cannot simply identify the will of God with love. For he does not know what love is apart from Jesus Christ, apart from what he did and said, and from what God did through him. Nor can man, Bonhoeffer says,

. . . prove what is the will of God simply from one's own resources, from one's own knowledge of good and evil; on the contrary, only that man can do this who has lost all knowledge of his own of good and evil and who therefore abandons any attempt to know the will of God by his own means, who lives already in the unity of the will of God because the will of God has already been accomplished in him. Proving what is God's will is possible only on the foundation of the knowledge of God's will in Jesus Christ. Only upon the foundation of Jesus Christ, only within the space which is defined by Jesus Christ, only "in" Jesus Christ can man prove what is the will of God.[4]

This is not an easy passage to get clear. But it is certain that Bonhoeffer is saying that our answer to the will of God must be very largely given by an investigation of what God has already done for us in Jesus Christ. This is the significance of Paul's "therefore" in Romans 12:1: because of God's saving act in Christ, therefore, the Christian man is free to reject the forms that the world presses upon him and to choose instead the form of Jesus Christ, who him-

---

[2] *Ethics* (New York: The Macmillan Company, 1955), p. 69.
[3] *Ibid.*, p. 161.
[4] *Ibid.*, pp. 162 ff.

self *is* love, who himself *is* all of the will of God we can ever claim to know. To understand, to claim, and to make visible, our allegiance to him is to prove or to do the will of God in the world.

## Salvation: Past, Present, and Future

The question about the will of God is thus a question about Jesus Christ. (Ethics is Christology, theology would say.) And the question about Jesus Christ is in turn a question about the total act of salvation. (Christology is soteriology plus eschatology, to use the jargon again.)

This is why we must turn from 12:1-2 to the central argument of the epistle in Chapters 1-8. What is the clearest way of setting forth this argument? Is there a single key idea that can bring it to life? Is there really order and coherence here? I suppose I belong to a postwar theological generation which was virtually saved for the Christian faith by the message of justification and forgiveness in Romans 1-8. Is justification by faith the true key? Or have we perhaps been too inclined to read Romans through the eyes of Martin Luther, especially through the eyes of his 1513 discovery of the righteousness of God?

Does Calvin provide a better clue? He is certainly clearer than Luther that justification includes a real and active righteousness.[5] We are justified, Calvin declares again and again, by being united with Christ. Union with Christ is for him the real key to Romans. We are not punished, he says, because we are guilty of Adam's sin; we are guilty of our own sin. "But we are restored to salvation by the righteousness of Christ in another way; for it is imputed to us, not as though it were within us, but because we possess Christ Himself with all his graces, given to us by the bountifulness of the Father." [6]

Albert Schweitzer, agreeing with Calvin, also sees the mystical being-in-Christ as the clue, a more significant one than the theme

[5] "We cannot be justified freely through faith alone without at the same time living holily. For these free gifts are connected, as if by an indissoluble bond, so that he who attempts to sever them does in a manner tear Christ to pieces." *Commemtary on I Corinthians* 1:30. Cf. *Institutes*, III, 3, 1.

[6] *Commentary on Romans*, 5:17.

of justification by faith. Schweitzer points out that Paul uses both themes: he works mainly with justification in Romans 3:1-5:21, and then goes over the same ground again in 6:1-8:1 with the union with the death and resurrection of Christ as his main theme. This confusion of themes, Albert Schweitzer says, is the reason that the epistle as a whole makes what he calls such a confusing impression on the reader.[7]

But we need not choose between justification and union with Christ. There is a way of setting forth Paul's basic structure in Romans 1-8 that will do justice to both positions. For Paul's key idea is *salvation*. The gospel is for him "the power of God for salvation to everyone who has faith" (1:16). Indeed, what God has really given to us is a *story of salvation*, with Christ as the key or meaning of the story. The story begins before Christ, and stretches on to the present and beyond. A. M. Hunter has a convincing defense of salvation as the theological key to Paul's thought, and points out that salvation is both a past act, a present reality, and a future hope.[8] So let us try to use this scheme to unlock the meaning of the Epistle to the Romans.

Perhaps we can make the idea of salvation as a story, with a past, present, and future, a little clearer if we put to ourselves a question that many of us have been asked before: "Are you saved?" Is there a decisive Christian answer to this? Surely the first and most important part of the answer is "yes." And if our questioner, as is often the case, goes on to ask us when and where, we ought to have no hesitation in replying: "On three o'clock in the afternoon, on the first Good Friday on a hill outside Jerusalem." The objective reality of the gospel of salvation is the first thing that needs to be stressed, especially in response to those who would seek to make our experience the center of the picture. The Christian view of salvation is first of all a fact about God, and what he did in the life, death, and resurrection of his Son. We have been saved; it is a past event, completed, once-for-all.

But this is not the whole story. Paul saw salvation as something richer than a past event which the believer remembers or partici-

[7] *The Mysticism of Paul the Apostle* (New York: The Macmillan Company, 1931 and 1955), pp. 225 f.

[8] *Interpreting Paul's Gospel* (Philadelphia: The Westminster Press, 1954), pp. 21 f. I am greatly indebted, throughout this article, to this admirable book.

pates in. It is a cosmic story that begins with God, dips into history, and ends, as it were, with God again, in the future. To become a Christian, to be "in Christ," is really nothing else than to take that whole story as our story. We see that the past part of the story is part of our past; what was done once, on Calvary, was done for us. We see that the present part of the story involves our present existence in a very radical way. And we see that the story has a future that goes both beyond our present and beyond our historical life altogether. When someone says that the eschatological framework of the New Testament message has been recovered in recent years, what is really meant is this: we are learning to see Christianity as primarily a story with a plot, and we grasp our role in that story when we decide that the whole story is for us.

Let us try to understand, by referring to the Epistle to the Romans, the precise meaning of the story of salvation—past, present, and future.

> For in this hope we were saved (Rom. 8:24).
> For man believes with his heart and so is justified, and he confesses with his lips and so is saved (Rom. 10:10).
> Since, therefore, we are now justified by his blood, much more shall we be saved by him from the wrath of God. For if while we were enemies we were reconciled to God by the death of his son, much more, now that we are reconciled, shall we be saved by his life (Rom. 5:9-10).
> Besides this you know what hour it is, how it is full time now for you to wake from sleep. For salvation is nearer to us now than when we first believed (Rom. 13:11).
> Therefore, since we are justified by faith, we have peace with God through our Lord Jesus Christ. Through him we have obtained access to this grace in which we stand, and we rejoice in our hope of sharing the glory of God (Rom. 5:1-2).

Note how in these passages salvation as past, as present, and as future, all blend together. "We were saved"; "we were reconciled to God by the death of his son"; "we have obtained access to this grace in which we stand"; something has already happened. But something is even now in the process of happening: "man believes . . . is justified . . . confesses . . . and so is saved"; "we are now justified . . . we are reconciled"; "we are justified by faith"; "we have peace with God." And yet, we wait, we look for, we hope: "in this hope"; "much more shall we be saved by him from the wrath of God"; "shall we be saved by his life"; "salvation is nearer to us now" (but not yet here?) ; "we rejoice in our hope of sharing the glory of God."

Now of course Paul knows what he is doing here; this is not confusion or bad grammar. The thing that God has done, is doing, and will do for man in Christ is all of a piece. Justification points perhaps to the past character of the story; union with Christ perhaps more to the present reality. But the story as a whole is really Paul's central concern, and the precise relation between the three parts is really the problem of Romans and the clue to the modern question we have put to Paul.

Bultmann agrees that the essential message of the epistle is contained in the temporal tension it maintains.

After the section 1:18-3:20 has demonstrated that before the revealing of "God's righteousness" both Gentiles and Jews stood under the "wrath of God," the thesis of righteousness now established by the occurrence of salvation in Christ is represented in 3:21-31 and the Scripture proof of it is offered in 4:1-25. For the Jew, with whom Paul is debating in all these arguments, the assertion of the present reality of eschatological righteousness could only appear absurd; for where, he could ask, are the blessings that were to be given along with righteousness? Where is "life"? Are not sin and death still present realities?

Paul replies in chapters 5-8. In chapter 5 he endeavors to demonstrate that eschatological life, though a matter of hope, is, nevertheless, in a certain manner already a present reality. Further he shows in 6:1-7:6 that even sin has lost its domination for the justified. Then, after a digression (7:7-25) has discussed the significance of the Law in the history of salvation, chapter 8 is the conclusion; it deals once more with freedom from sin (8:1-11) and from death (8:12-39), pointing out again the peculiar double character of salvation: future, yet already present.[9]

And both based, we should add, on the past reality of the salvation act in Christ.

When we think of our salvation as a past event, we look back to the life and particularly to the death of Jesus Christ on the cross. Paul makes use of a whole network of metaphors to analyze the past and present effect of this event. In Romans, he sometimes

[9] *The Theology of the New Testament* (New York: Charles Scribner's Sons, 1951), Vol. I, p. 279. The translation is slightly altered.

draws on the language of the slave-market and speaks of our redemption or being set free (3:24, 6:18, 8:2). Sometimes, in the language of the courts, he describes our being justified, acquitted, set into a right relation with God (1:17, 3:21). In other places he uses the idea of reconciliation (5:10 f.). All of these figures are pressed into service to explain the release from the law and from sin that God made possible for man. Without Christ, man was lost in his sin, without access to the righteousness of God. Now, in Christ, God has set man on his feet before his face.

By faith we bear witness to what God has done. Faith is our obedience, our trust (like that of Abraham, in Chapter 4), our actual participation in the benefits of this past event. Most of all, for Paul, faith is the recognition that Christ's death was for me, for my sins.

This past part of the story, however, ends but does not begin with the cross. The cross is itself the climax of an age-long story of God's righteousness confronting sinful men. In Romans, Paul sets the meaning of the cross against the background of the whole Old Testament: creation, fall, preparation, fullness of time. Much of the language that Paul uses to describe a man's sin, man's false religion, man's false reliance on himself, is derived from the Old Testament. So it is not surprising that Luther could declare that the whole of the meaning of the Old Testament could be found in this epistle.[10]

Salvation for Paul, however, is not only a past event, finished and over; it is a present and progressive thing, happening even now. Paul describes this present occurrence in many different ways: as life in the Spirit (7:6, 8:4-5), as life or being in Christ (6:3, 8:1), as a new creation, as participation in the corporate reality of Christ's body (12:4 f.). The Christian ethic for Paul, therefore, is really the way one describes the quality of this new dynamic present, and it is an ethic of love. If by faith we participate in the past event of salvation, love is the way we respond to the present gift, even now being offered. Looking at salvation this way, we are not so much saved, once-for-all, as in the process of being saved.

Sometimes this "love" is called a fruit of the Spirit that God now works in us; sometimes it is a reflection of the love of Christ; some-

[10] In his 1522 Preface to the Epistle to the Romans, *ad. fin.*

times it is a reflection of the love of God that was shown in the death of Christ. Love, the Christian ethic, can never be derived from one particular part of the Christian story; not simply from Jesus' words, nor from the doctrine of man, nor from forgiveness, nor from the church. The Christian ethic, the theologians say, is an eschatological ethic, which simply means that the character of the demand of love placed on us here and now derives from the whole story of salvation in Christ, and not just from some special part of it. Paul's "therefore" in Romans 12:1 was his transition from theology to ethics; and he had to presuppose the whole sacred story, past, present, and future, before he could tell his Roman readers what their ethical responsibility was. We have been saved; and we are in the process of being saved. Salvation is a past and a present thing.

But it is a thing of the future as well: "we shall be saved." When we look at our own lives, we are not so much impressed by our being saved as by our still needing to be saved. Here, our faith and love are weak; in hope we point to the time when we shall see face to face. The future of the story is unknown, but only partly. For this future is an extension of the known past and present, and we have the decisive clue. When Lord Peter Wimsey assembles the suspects in the Duke's library in the next to the last chapter, all the clues are in the hands of the reader. He has not read the final chapter, but if he is a true devotee he will already know enough to be able to figure it out. The Christian exists perpetually in the next to the last chapter of the salvation story. The end of his own life is only the end of the next to the last chapter. But he does have the clue that enables him to know something about the end. If faith is the means of our relation to the past; love to the present; hope is the way we "know" the future part of the story. The future is partly known because we know the past part, and we know him who gave us the story as our own. It may have been that our forefathers knew too much about the future part of the story; but it may be equally true that we have been too timid and too unknowing today. We do know the one thing that we need to know. God, who has acted in Christ, is now acting in him and in the Spirit, and he is Lord of the future. If we are willing to fall into his hands now, we can never fall away. If it is a fearful thing to fall into the hands of the living God, it is a difficult thing to fall out of them.

### Salvation for What? Faith, Love, and Hope

We began by saying that if we really want to know more about the will of God, we must press back to know more about Jesus Christ. And Paul, we have seen, refuses to say anything about Jesus Christ that does not at the same time point to the whole story of salvation, of which our Lord is the key and the meaning. Salvation is a story; it has a past, a present, and a future. This story has a clue, a plot, and a means by which we locate ourselves in the midst of it. But in order better to understand how we are to move our way along this story, we must look more precisely at the three ways we have discerned for making our response. In just what way are faith, love, and hope, our proper responses to the gift of salvation?

### *1. Faith*

For I am not ashamed of the gospel; it is the power of God for salvation to everyone who has faith, to the Jew first and also to the Greek. For in it the righteousness of God is revealed through faith for faith; as it is written, "He who through faith is righteous shall live" (Rom. 1:16-17).

. . . Christ Jesus, whom God put forward as an expiation by his blood, to be received by faith, . . . It was to prove at the present time that he himself is righteous and that he justified him who has faith in Jesus (Rom. 3:25-26).

Notice the precision of these two passages. In the first, faith is called the way we receive the righteousness of God, the condition for the new "life" that righteousness brings. In the second passage, the righteousness of God is defined as the act of God in the cross of Christ. Faith, then, is the way man receives the cross.

Paul's use of faith here surely makes questionable the many loose ways we have often used the word. "Faith in man," we sometimes call for; or "faith in America." Whatever truth there may be in the intended meaning of these phrases, they do not use faith in a Christian sense. It even seems clear that "faith in God" is not a

fully satisfactory phrase, for our faith is directed to—or better, responding to—a particular act of God, the death of his Son Jesus
Christ. Let us put this another way. Faith can be defined as response to grace; and grace is not a generalized truth about God, it
is "*a single deed* which takes effect for everyone who recognizes it as
such and acknowledges it (in faith) . . . . God's deed of grace consists
in the fact that He gave Christ up to die—to die as a propitiatory
sacrifice for the sins of men." [11]

Faith, then, is a specific human decision in response to a specific
act of God in Christ. The status of faith as a decision of man cannot be qualified even if it is also the case that the prevenient grace
of God is what makes the decision possible. When we make the
decision, we can understand only it as God's gift. But it is still a
decision that he has empowered *us* to make. [12]

In terms of our three-fold understanding of salvation, faith can
be described as our decision about the past part of the story. Faith
means that I decide that the New Testament events leading up to
the death of Christ are events in my life, not merely in someone
else's. Faith does not primarily mean that I affirm that God exists
as an historical entity (for he does not), or that Jesus certainly said
or did this or that (for he may not have). Faith is a decision about
the cross. Not just that it happened; but that it happened for me.
More exactly, it is saying that when Christ died something happened that affected my despair, my sin, my death.

But if faith begins with a decision about the past part of the
story, about the cross, it does not end there. If the first decision of
faith is the affirmation that Christ died for my sins, the second
decision of faith is an extension and inference from it. If in the
first place I have said that the facts reported about Christ are true
and that these facts represent the grace of God for me, I now can
go on to say that therefore God can be trusted and I can commit
myself to him completely. If my sin can no longer be an obstacle
between me and God, then nothing can separate me from him and
he can wholly be trusted, in the present and beyond into the unknown future. So if faith is grounded on a completed act of God
in the past, it is at work in the present and spills over into the

[11] *Theology of the New Testament, op. cit.,* p. 289.
[12] Cf. *Ibid.,* p. 330.

future, so that it becomes almost indistinguishable from hope. Both Romans 1:17 and 10:10 suggest this.[13]

But ordinarily Paul has another way of describing our response to or participation in the present part of the story of salvation.

## 2. Love

Let love be genuine; hate what is evil, hold fast to what is good; love one another with brotherly affection; outdo one another in showing honor (Rom. 12:9-10).

Owe no one anything, except to love one another; for he who loves his neighbor has fulfilled the law. . . . Love does no wrong to a neighbor; therefore love is the fulfilling of the law (Rom. 13:8-10).

Love is the Christian's posture before the present, but it never derives its content from the present world. Its content and shape come from the reality we have grasped by faith, from the character of God given to us in the cross of Christ. The direction of love comes from faith: it is to go outward to men in need. And the form of love is from faith; its form is that of God's love, of the servant, of humility. We love because, through faith, we received God's love. This love is identification, humility, judging only by refusing to judge, not waiting to be summoned but loving before we have been asked. This is how love feeds on faith; we can faithfully live in the present part of the story only when we have traversed the past.

But love not only points backwards: it judges our present imperfect love and lovelessness, and it points forward to the content of our hope. Here, we who are being saved, know how we ought to love, but we cannot so love. Then, when we shall know God as clearly as he now knows us, we shall also love him and our neighbor as clearly as he now loves us. Between the past and the future, between the perfect love of the cross and the fulfilled love of everlasting life, stands the present demand of love now. Our present love, insofar as it is ours, is a love that fails. But it is a failing love that is loved now by the unfailing love of God.[14]

[13] Cf. *Ibid.*, pp. 290, 314 ff., and references there.

[14] Bultmann points out that Paul can call love the "greatest" because in love "the possibility opened up by 'faith' and 'hope' becomes reality in concrete existence." *Ibid.*, pp. 344 f.

## 3. Hope

For in this hope we were saved. Now hope that is seen is not hope. For who hopes for what he sees? But if we hope for what we do not see, we wait for it with patience (Rom. 8:24-25).

Hope, then, is the way we participate in what we are to become, in the part of the story we have not yet read. We have pointed out that faith gives us the conviction of the trustworthiness of God. So knowing this about him, we know something about the future. We know that the future will not be without God, even if we do not know the form or quality of his presence beyond our death. When Paul says that neither death nor things to come can separate us from the love of God, he is saying that God is Lord of the future. When we move into our historical future, God will be there before us. When we move through our death into a "future" that is unknown, there is one thing that is known, and this takes away the dread: God will be there; he can be trusted, for he will not turn his back on those who trust him. So hope feeds on faith, and our dealing with the unknown future part of the story depends on our dealings with the part that is past. Bultmann puts this nicely: "This 'hope' is the freedom for the future and the openness toward it which the man of faith has because he has turned over his anxiety about himself and his future to God in obedience." [15]

### Salvation from What? Sin, Suffering, and Death

This is my argument up to now. We can best approach Paul's presentation of the gospel in the Epistle to the Romans by looking at the total story he tells about God's dealing with men. This, we have seen, is a story with a plot; it has a past, a present, and a future; and the "virtues" of faith, love, and hope, are the means

---

[15] *Ibid.*, p. 320. In Rom. 9-11 when Paul deals with the problem of the hope of Israel, we are not surprised to find the solution worked out in terms of God who is already known to faith. Here again hope feeds on faith. There is a practical sense in which hope may be said to feed on love, in which our knowledge of the future depends on our understanding of love in the present. Have we not sometimes felt that the death of a truly loving person is in itself a kind of unanswerable argument for the reality of eternal life?

by which we relate ourselves to the different parts of the story. Each part is related to the other; each part needs the other for its full understanding.

But if God "saves" us *through* and *for* faith, love, and hope, he also saves us *from*. Our argument would be neither complete nor faithful to Paul's analysis, if we did not take one further step. We are "saved" *for* and *through* faith, love, and hope; but we are also saved *from* sin, suffering, and death. Faith (not virtue) is the weapon we have against sin, for faith is nothing else than the conviction that Christ died for our sins. Love is our weapon against suffering: partly that suffering in others elicits our sluggish love; partly that when we suffer we see something of the meaning of God's suffering love for us; partly that to undertake the burden of responsible human love for one another is always to be willing to enter into suffering: "There must be sorrow if there can be love." [16] And hope is our weapon against death; not that we do not die, but that death is not the end, and we are not afraid. Let us look at sin, suffering, and death, a little more carefully.

## *1. Sin*

What shall we say then? Are we to continue in sin that grace may abound? By no means. How can we who died to sin still live in it? (Rom. 6:1, 2) .

There is therefore now no condemnation for those who are in Christ Jesus. For the law of the Spirit of life in Christ Jesus, has set me free from the law of sin and death. For God has done what the law, weakened by the flesh, could not do: sending his own son in the likeness of sinful flesh and for sin, he condemned sin in the flesh . . . (Rom. 8:1-3) .

Paul never claims that the man in Christ can expect to be without sin, suffering, and death. But something decisive has been done. What is it? Do you remember a few years ago, before the Salk vaccine was perfected, how parents of young children used to approach the polio season? Every decision to go to the beach or to the circus was made, if at all, with real anxiety. With the coming of the vaccine, a whole bloc of fear was removed from the minds of millions. The disease was not removed; but its power to cripple and kill was. This is exactly what Paul claims for the gospel of salvation, the Christian story. Sin, suffering, death are still here, and claims to be

[16] This is the final line of W. H. Auden's "Canzone."

able to escape them are vicious. But one thing has been changed; they have no power to cripple or to kill: that is, they can no longer destroy man's relation to God.

A good bit of Paul's time in Romans is given over to his analysis of the reality of sin. All men are involved, both Gentile and Jew (1:18-2:24) ; sin is universal. Sometimes he treats this as an empirical fact, sometimes he tries to explain it (as in 5:12-19, where he traces it to Adam). Even the man in Christ knows the struggle against sin (Rom. 7:7-25). But as we look at the transition between Chapters 7 and 8 in Romans one thing is clear. If sin has been a leading character in the story of salvation up to the cross, after this event it no longer plays a major role. With the coming of Christ, it is there, but in the shadows. It is present, but it no longer has the power to determine the outcome of the story.

And faith is what God has given us to make good his victory over sin. Faith as the decision that Christ died for me brings forgiveness, justification, release from the guilt of the past sin I bear. Faith as the decision about the eternal trustworthiness of God here and in the life to come brings participation in the new life in Christ, and the growing conformity to his life that can mean a victory of humility over pride.

Love and hope are related to the war against sin too. For the love that faith has made possible for us, a consuming love reflecting the terrible love of the cross, is what draws the sting of sin. And our hope points us beyond to the corporate life, only dimly shadowed here, in which sin will no more be seen. In a way, we are more sinful than ever before as Christians, for we are obliged to extend the range of our responsibility for actions we have not ourselves committed. But we are free from sin in a new way too, because of our trust in a God who can both accept us as sinners and remake us into his own image.

## 2. Suffering

When we cry, "Abba! Father!" it is the Spirit himself bearing witness with our Spirit that we are children of God, and if children, then heirs, heirs of God and fellow heirs with Christ, provided we suffer with him in order that we may also be glorified with him. I consider that the sufferings of this present time are not worth comparing with the glory that is to be revealed to us. For the creation waits with eager longing for the revealing of the sons of God: for the creation was subjected to futility, not of its own will but by the will of him who subjected it in hope; because the creation itself will be set free from its bondage to decay and obtain the glorious liberty of the children of God. We know that the whole creation has been groaning in travail together until now; and not only the creation, but we ourselves, who have the first fruits of the Spirit, groan inwardly as we wait for adoption as sons, the redemption of our bodies (Rom. 8:15b-23).

Suffering, here is *the* mark of the present age. It is not explained by Paul and he does not claim that the story of salvation will lay bare for man "the cosmic meaning of suffering in general, but in the suffering that strikes his own person he finds a question addressed to himself and a new possibility of his life."[17] Suffering, we may say, dominates the Old Testament part of the story. And it is so much a part of the gospel account of Jesus' life that an early creed could sum up the significance of that life in the phrase "suffered under Pontius Pilate." On Calvary, the character of suffering, so to speak, makes its last bid to be the hero of the tale, and it almost succeeds. For a moment we suspect that its success has been complete, and then we see that it has been a total failure. And from the resurrection until today, it is in the shadows. It is still present; and it can still do all that it could ever do to us. But now we can do more against it than we could ever do before. Since Christ, in a way, we suffer more, not less. For again, we are affected by a wider range of tragic events than before. But suffering cannot destroy us.

Love is our response to the present reality of suffering. It is almost true to say that suffering is the truest form of love for the present age. Love responds to suffering and is moved into action by it; the one who loves must be willing to suffer if it is truly God's love that he is reflecting.

Faith and hope also speak to our present suffering. Faith has made available to us the grace of God who has participated in and shared our suffering through the death of Christ. The cross will always be the key to our answer to the "problem" of suffering, so much a part of our present lives. If this death was God's will for a fallen world, perhaps something like this may also be said about our suffering; though Jesus accepted his fate as coming from God

[17] Bultmann, *Theology of the New Testament, op. cit.*, p. 349.

only after he prayed that the suffering might be averted. In the cross, faith reminds us that rebellion and resignation are both parts of our present response. And hope points to our conviction that God, in his perfected kingdom, will accept our lives, deepened and shaped by suffering, and bring us to his presence in perfect joy.

### 3. Death

Therefore as sin came into the world through one man and death through sin, and so death spread to all men because all men sinned . . . so one man's act of righteousness leads to acquittal and life for all men. For as by one man's disobedience many were made sinners, so by one man's obedience many will be made righteous. Law came in, to increase the trespass; but where sin increased, grace abounded all the more, so that, as sin reigned in death, grace also might reign through righteousness to eternal life through Jesus Christ our Lord (Rom. 5:12, 18b-21).

For we know that Christ being raised from the dead will never die again; death no longer has dominion over him. The death he died he died to sin, once for all, but the life he lives he lives to God. So you also must consider yourselves dead to sin and alive to God in Christ Jesus. . . . When you were slaves to sin, you were free in regard to righteousness. But then what return did you get from the things of which you are now ashamed? The end of those things is death. But now that you have been set free from sin and have become slaves of God, the return you get is sanctification and its end, eternal life. For the wages of sin is death, but the free gift of God is eternal life in Christ Jesus our Lord (Rom. 6:9-11, 20-23).

For I am sure that neither death, nor life, nor angels, nor principalities, nor things present, nor things to come, nor powers, nor height, nor depth, nor anything else in all creation, will be able to separate us from the love of God in Christ Jesus our Lord (Rom. 8:38-39).

We live, Paul says, in a world in which death is somehow at home. The world of sin seems to fit with a world in which there is death. The wages of sin is death, not perhaps as an exact payment, but at any rate we seem to deserve to die. We have lost the meaning of life, and there is nothing left to us but death.

Yet—however deserving we are, however we may feel that often death is a kind of release, it is not a natural thing. We do not contemplate the death of loved ones easily; we do not think of our own death without pain and misgiving. This is still a world that has, for each of us, death as the end of one part of the story. We all will die. The promise that we shall not die is the Platonic hope; it is a lie, the first lie recorded in the Bible.

For Paul the Christian hope is not a hope that we will be spared death. It is a hope of life through death. It is the hope, the conviction, the faith, that God will not break the relationship he has given us in Christ through faith. We are not the immortal ones; the relationship we have laid hold of by faith, that is what is "immortal" in Paul's vision of hope. What we might say is this: the basis for hope in Paul is faith and love. There is no independent proof for eternal life here; the Christian hope is intelligible only as part of the whole story, the partly unknown, partly known extension of the past and present parts which we do in fact know.

Hope is grounded on faith, for faith has opened us to a God who forgives us, a God who will not let us go, however deep our sin and doubt and despair may be. Faith has enabled us to know that here and now sin, doubt, and despair cannot separate us from God. So we go on to say, on the basis of the known thing, that neither can death separate us from him, even though it may separate us from one another.

Perhaps we may add that hope is also grounded on love. Our ability to love one another is the only truly permanent thing we know in this life. When we allow our vocations, even our religious vocation, to dry up our capacity for open, uncoercive, and free loving-relations, we are emptying ourselves of the one pointer to eternal life that is given us here.

When we see sin, suffering, and death against the background of the whole story that Paul sketches out, and when we see that this story is our story, that what happens in it happens to and for us, then these enemies no longer need be obscurers of God but may actually become pointers to him.


## Conclusion

This great story that Paul sets before us is really the clearest way I know of describing what being a Christian means. The church has no other business but to illuminate that story. Its preaching, its sacraments of baptism and the Lord's Supper, its prayer, and its service, all act it out in different ways. There is something happening here. The act of God's salvation in Christ is, as it were, going on right now. The story illuminates just what this action is; it tells us what it gives us, it tells us what it overcomes, and it tells us what to do. There is no short cut to the problem with which we began: How can I know and do the will of God? The will of God, we said, is Jesus Christ. The will of God is the whole story that centers around him. Today, here and now, our doing the will of God in our work, in our solitude, in our homes, will be inadequate and sentimental if the doing does not spring from this total story. As Protestants, we have no required answers to our questions about the will of God except one: be sure you use all your human powers to understand the situation in which you are to act, and then be sure you use all your human powers to bring your participation in the will of God to bear on that situation. To find the will of God is not to look outside for some forgotten rule or principle; it is to look at your present existence as a man of faith. What have we been given, according to Paul? Through the death and resurrection of Jesus Christ, we have been given the ability to be open to the living God himself. He holds us in his hand, and only our denial of him can sever this bond. He has made us free men in Christ, free from our-selves, free from worry about what others think of us, free from anxiety about how our personalities are getting along in the eyes of someone else. Free in this sense, because he alone determines who we are. Thus freed by him, we can turn to our common lives and fight for this freedom for all men, bearing witness especially where that witness is not gladly received. For under God, bound to his Son, nothing can hurt us, nothing can shake us, nothing can make us timid, for nothing now "will be able to separate us from the love of God in Christ Jesus our Lord."

# CHAPTER 19

# CONCLUSION:

# THE DIALOGUE ON MAN'S NATURE

## SEWARD HILTNER

EVERY serious interpretation of man's nature contains an "ought," even if its content is only that man should be what the facts appear to report. And every "ought" about man eventually attempts to ground its interpretation in an "is," even if the real "is" be regarded as fathoms removed from appearance. Taken together, these points may serve as a focus through which the current dialogue between theology and psychology on the nature of man may be examined.

The first point asserts that any interpretation or understanding of man, if it is not frivolous, always at least implies, however minimally or tacitly, something normative. With theological views of man this requires no argument. No matter what man appears to be, he ought to be different in at least some important respects. In Judaism and Christianity he is, sometimes despite appearance, always sinful and requires to be saved. In some other religions he is seen as impeded by desire, from which he needs release. In still others he is regarded as ignorant, lazy, or hypocritical—from all of which conditions he needs escape. Salvation, release, escape—all are ways of considering man's "oughtness."

All other serious views of man, we contend, also contain "oughtness." This may be in a minimal degree, and it may be only implicit, but it is always present. The man who, in Sigmund Freud's view, is caught in neurotic internal conflict, will be more truly man if he assimilates the experience of the past which produced this conflict and thus permits the conflicting forces to meet in real combat on the same level. "Man," he wrote, "cannot remain a child for ever." However limited and implicit, this is an "ought."

According to Carl Jung, man is caught in a crossfire between the social forces that would make him into a "persona" or mere mask on the one side, and deep unconscious forces which, if allowed to dominate, would engulf him on the other. Few men, he held, can take a purely solitary path in their movement toward "individuation" and "selfhood." Most must be guided by the institutions of culture, especially religion. But when religion fails in this function, as Jung believes is characteristic of our day in the West, then individual men must move on their own. The "ought" in this account is obvious, even if but few men can do what "man" ought to do.

Is the inevitability of an "ought" applicable also to interpretations of man that emerge from scientific investigations of one kind or another? The answer is yes. Man becoming obese because of resentment against deprivation of love is man implicitly resolving either to get love or to get along without it. Man revealed as projecting father-images into gods or political leaders is, implicitly, man resolving either to let religion and politics alone or to vote for the proper god or president.

We must warn against the false conclusion that any kind of report about man is necessarily also an interpretation of man. The late Alfred C. Kinsey tried hard to make only a report about American sex behavior and not also an interpretation. He failed in part because some unintended interpretations crept into his account. Some scientific reporters are more successful. The factors that influence what man perceives, for example, may be studied and reported on with no necessary implication about precisely what he ought to perceive among the viable choices. But even such a scientific reporter can not succeed in confining himself to reporting unless he is aware of the possible interpretative implications of his data. He need not note or discuss them. But if ignorant of them, his report is likely also to be at least an implicit interpretation.

Some existentialist interpretations of man might appear to be an exception to our argument, but we believe not. Even the contention that meaning in life consists only in acknowledging life's lack of meaning is an "ought" statement. And he who asserts the merit of acknowledging life as absurd must speak from some hypothetical basis that is not wholly absurd. When these modern Stoics are serious, as Sartre is, every "is" statement implies an "ought." It may be tentative, limited, qualified, or implicit, but it is still present, provided there has been something beyond sheer reporting about man. Such reporting is a high and difficult art, unto which few attain. Thoughtful interpretation is of course even harder.

Our second point is that every "ought" about man attempts, eventually, to ground itself in an "is." For scientific interpreters this seems obvious. If all men everywhere have two eyes, two ears, and one nose, then the interpretation of man includes the same organs in the same quantity. When, as is usually true, the statistics are less uniform, then the interpretation may lean, on the one side, toward cultural relativism which is a form of nominalism, or it may lean, on the other side, toward a search for a "common human nature" despite surface differences, this being a kind of realism in the Platonic sense. The difference lies in the level at which phenomena are viewed. In both instances, however, the implications for "oughtness" are grounded in convictions about "isness."

It may make an enormous difference in the scientist's interpretation of man if he is nominalist or realist, cultural relativist or "common human naturist," observer of the more obvious or of the more subtle dimensions of human behavior. But it seems plain that, provided he ventures an interpretation at all even by implication, he rests his case for the "ought" on his understanding of the "is." No self-respecting scientist can defend an "ought" apart from its rootage in an alleged "is."

Although different on details, the same thing is true of theological interpretations of man. In most of these the "ought" is more obvious and explicit. The "ought" in theology is ordinarily more like a ceiling, or maximum while the scientist's explicit interpretation is more nearly like a floor, or minimum. But the obtrusiveness of the "ought" in theological statements should not blind us to their inevitable grounding in alleged "isness."

Most theological views contend that man as he exists or appears to be—in his sin, desire, ignorance, and the like—is to be distinguished from man in his true nature or "isness," whether this is understood in the perspective of past, present, or future. Adam, the Noble Savage, or "first man" is viewed as having a true nature quite different from that of the presently obvious sin, desire, or ignorance, and as demonstrating no incongruity between the true or essential and the actual or existential natures. Projected to the future, there is man immortal or resurrected, or society as a new kingdom of re-born men, or man in Utopia, when all present and past pains and contradictions and divisions shall have disappeared and man has become his true self. In the perspective of the present, man under certain conditions is seen as redeemed (or at least starting his re-demption journey) from sin, desire, or from ignorance. Even though the same contemporary conditions may exist within and about him, man reconceives his citizenship as being more real (past, present, and future) in another world (at least metaphorically speaking) than in that of obtrusive actuality, and he has a passport about his new nature and new belongingness.

The history of religions demonstrates immense differences in the level at which "isness" is perceived as real or essential or unques-tioned. The allegedly higher "ought" of monasticism, for example, was not set forth in ignorance of the strength of man's sex drives. Instead it was held that the "ought" of allegiance only to God could overcome the sexual-drive *level* of "isness." Thus monastic commit-ment could testify to another level of man's "isness" felt to be purer or deeper. Right or wrong, and for how many people under what conditions, a phenomenon like monasticism demonstrates a highly complex dialectic between "oughtness" and "isness." As always, a deeper "isness" was finally appealed to.

If Christianity had not believed in an original Adam from whose true nature there was a fall, or in man made as free and in the image of God, it could not have alleged that man is corrupt at the core of his selfhood, or even "totally depraved." Without the vision of some "isness" beneath obtrusive actuality, the "ought" of man's na-ture could not have been brought in judgment upon the actuality. Here also the relationship between various levels of "isness" and "oughtness" is both subtle and dialectical. But the case for "ought" is finally asserted to rest upon the deepest understanding of "is."

The allegation that every claim of "oughtness" attempts to ground itself in its best understanding of "isness" does not of course mean that the "isness" appealed to really is or that this "isness" consti-tutes the basic motivation behind the "oughtness." There are *a priori* elements in every attempt at interpretation. Any serious inquiry, however, whether theological or scientific, ought to test even the *a priori* dimension of its "oughts" against its best understanding of the deepest "isness." Thus our argument, while not denying the presence of *a priori* considerations in the interpretations of man, believes that serious inquiry involves both acknowledgment of these assumptions and explicit attempts to re-examine them in the light of the deepest understanding of "isness."

When we are dealing with interpretations of man, it is false to associate science with man's "isness" and theology with man's "oughtness," whatever may be the differences between science and theology at any point including their conceptions of "isness" and "oughtness." In both science and theology the "ought" and the "is" are interlaced and in tension in subtle and complex ways. Keeping this in the back of our minds as a kind of methodological model may, we believe, aid us in understanding recent developments in psychology and theology, and the emerging dialogue between them concerning man's nature. Our discussion will concentrate on developments in the United States.

## No Dialogue in 1900

When the present century dawned, there was no great controversy between scientists and theologians on the nature of man except for the dregs of the "special creation" conflict focused on Darwin. Since the reactionary theologians have long since been convicted of error on this question, not only because they denied valid scientific evidence but also because they had misread the biblical account of creation, this was, therefore, a false issue about man on which lagging theologians had simply to bow to scientific reporting. There were, to be sure, some conflicts between scientists and religionists about aspects of man's nature, such as whether or not he is immortal. But there was no open arena of general controversy concerning man's nature.

This is far from saying that science and theology agreed. What they did was to pay attention to man from points of view that appeared to be quite different, with little or no convergence of their findings and hence without the potentiality of conflict. Both physical and biological science, except on their growing edges, were materialistic and mechanistic and reductionistic with a grimness and rigidity long since qualified or discarded within those disciplines themselves. A good deal of nineteenth-century theology found little threat in this unless it appeared explicitly to trespass upon man's "spirit," and then proceeded to "spiritize" spirit away from its holistic Christian intent.

A good revelation of general nineteenth-century attitude was the way in which physicians and clergymen made alliance against Mary Baker Eddy and Christian Science. Perhaps clergy as well as doctors were concerned over her renunciation of medicine, and perhaps some doctors as well as clergy were bothered by her metaphysics. Both agreed, however, that she was wrong in alleging an inherent and internal relationship between psyche and soma. Yet on this last and most fundamental point, both have subsequently been proved wrong.

Different ways of looking at man are not likely to provoke controversy (or serious agreement either) until or unless each acknowledges some kind of "village green" of interest and concern. An idealistic view of man in religion, and a materialistic view of man in medicine, for example, might exist side by side without real controversy so long as they felt they were examining entirely different things. The actual situation in 1900 was not quite so simple as here pictured, for the thought of many leaders was already pointing ahead toward what would make controversy necessary, and dialogue possible, in our century. But the over-all fact is, nevertheless, that the century opened without basic controversy and wholly without dialogue. Since no dialogue is either possible or necessary without controversy, we shall turn to examine the developments in psychology and in theology that produced, first, controversy, and now, hopefully, the beginnings of dialogue.

## Psychological Views of Man

In the sense we now take for granted, the psychological and social sciences were mere toddlers at the century's beginning. Psychology was new as an independent discipline, had barely begun experimental work, knew little if anything of personality in the modern sense, and was being seriously applied only in relation to religious phenomena (William James), to industry (Münsterberg), and to education (John Dewey). There was no clinical psychology at all, little social psychology based on direct observations, only the beginnings of developmental psychology (in G. Stanley Hall), and little vision of a comprehensive future psychology except in the towering mind of James.

The related disciplines of sociology and cultural anthropology were just on the threshold of modern-type field studies. Most of psychiatry was simply general medical care of, and institutional housekeeping for, psychotic persons. Freud's great work, *The Interpretation of Dreams,* was published precisely at the turn of the century, but it would take years before it should become influential.

Seen in the light of this sketchy survey, what psychology has accomplished in the intervening half-century plus ten is astonishing. Viewing psychology in the more general sense as involving all the fields of psychological study and application, the development in professional numbers is simply prodigious. The American Psychological Association, for example, now has more than eighteen thousand members, and the American Psychiatric Association is not far behind. The increase in professional personnel since 1900 must be measured in terms that approximate a hundredfold. Here everything is onward and upward at least in terms of numbers.

But something even more significant than growth in numbers has been true of psychology in our century. To cite an astute observation by Harry A. Overstreet, "The characteristic knowledge of our century is psychological." No doubt the growth in numbers of professional personnel in the psychological disciplines is paralleled or exceeded by that of electronics engineers, atomic scientists and technologists, and magazine editors. Yet important as their work may be to society, it is not their knowledge but that of the psychologists that has infiltrated the internals of modern man. For good or for ill, this seems to be fact.

The seminal clue to the new psychology was given by Sigmund Freud. Understanding man's conduct, he found, required attention to previously neglected dimensions and phenomena—to what he called the "unconscious" (which, however, affects behavior) and to things like dreams, slips of the tongue, and sexual development in children. It was his work that gave major impetus to the development of clinical psychology and psychiatry, and for much in social work. His key opened the door for developmental psychology, now so crucial in education. It has aided the anthropologists and sociologists to understand the dynamic interrelatedness of the patterns of culture. All modern psychologies, due to Freud, are "dynamic" in that they see human beings as energetic but open systems of tension, conflict, and equilibrium, the forces within which go far below what can be seen on the surface. They differ widely of course in the extent to which they agree or disagree with Freudian thought as an entire psychology.

The numerical growth of psychology still continues, but in other respects it is centering down. The initial and exciting early and prophetic era is now giving way to a kind of priestly period. More common canons and criteria are generally acknowledged than ever before. Yet the vitality of the prophetic period is still present, even if tamed and humbled in face of the vast areas still to be explored. There seems to be less imperialistic rashness but more bold experimentation. Extreme positions are not absent, but their advocates are seldom either followed or excommunicated. The movement as a whole seems to have attained enough maturity to welcome the extremes as useful admonitions against the rut of priestly institutionalization.

In a prophetic period the number of "rebels" is likely to exceed that of "organization men." But it is also likely to have among its greatest leaders those who were rebels only with great reluctance, who simply had to break through conventional modes of thought and inquiry in order to pursue the object of their concern. The ordinary rebel, quite in contrast, may "play" with what he attacks. The leader who is a reluctant rebel is quite different. And although he may pursue his investigations as relentlessly as ever, he may, perhaps unconsciously, try to avoid being too queer or too rebellious by reverting to a methodological position that his logic would have him transcend. This may do odd things to his view of the "isness" and "oughtness" in man.

This view of the reluctant rebel applies par excellence to Freud.

He did not set out to rebel but to contribute to science and to the solving of some of the riddles of the universe. Of his discovery of the place of sexuality in neurosis he wrote, "I was not prepared for this conclusion and my expectations played no part in it." Even in terms of what a scientist should properly report, he had to be reluctantly rebellious against the conventions. His first published reports were accused of giving too few data. When publishing his first long case, later on, he wrote, "Whereas before I was accused of giving no information about my patients, now I shall be accused of giving information about my patients which ought not to be given." The Freud who was devoted to science had, nevertheless, to alter the meaning of the science to which his devotion was given. It is small wonder that, even when his implications led elsewhere, he should have felt the security-pull of the simpler, more deterministic, and more biologically materialistic views of his nineteenth-century scientific background.

The psychologist of today who simply assumes a view of man that is deterministic, naturalistic, or reductionistic is very different from Freud. Freud, finding the implications of his discoveries leading away at least from the nineteenth-century forms of those "isms," felt compelled to anticipate and repudiate charges that his view of man was speculative, mythological, antibiological, or mystical. In doing so, he went back to a notion of science that is far more dubious than his brilliant discoveries. Most of his discussion of human freedom, for example, simply undercuts (rightly) man's illusion that he is capable of arbitrary choices. But psychoanalysis demonstrated, and Freud faithfully reported, what genuine increase in freedom looks like and even one way to bring it about. Whatever determinism may mean, it must mean something, after Freud, that is more complex than what came before.

Albert C. Outler has pointed out correctly that the naturalistic and deterministic assumptions lying behind much of modern psychology have their roots in the eighteenth century, as carried over into scientific thought of the nineteenth century. It seems to us, however, that the dynamic reasons for a Freud to adhere to such assumptions are quite different from those motivating a modern psychologist who seems to take the same position. A pioneer who makes enormous advances in knowledge, and then does not quite succeed in transcending the methodological structure from which he began, is understandable. A modern who simply takes the whole *corpus* of the pioneer as *textus receptus* requiring no reconsideration and no wrestling is, whether he knows it or not, a kind of organization man.

There seems now to be a greater consensus among psychologists about their view of man than at any previous time in our century, and this view includes more factors of greater complexity. There are many varying views, including extremes, and the "standard deviation" from the consensus is no doubt large. But it may be worthwhile to suggest some of the factors that seem to be approaching consensual status, even if they have not all quite made it. Logical positivists, social conditioners, determinists, existentialists, social relativists, and even dogmatists aside and to the contrary notwithstanding, we believe the following statements are increasingly characteristic of psychologists' views of man.

Man should of course be studied as objectively as possible from a psychological perspective, but attention to him in his subjectivity (as initiator) is also necessary. Man has a dynamic and influential unconscious, or something like it, but he needs to relate this to an ego that is not merely epiphenomenal. Psychic illness in man is at root a compromise formation, and its meaning can be understood only if both dynamisms are considered—the thrust to defend what needs defense even if the available means are poor, and the vicious-cycle momentum of the defense pattern once formed. Psychic illness is more widespread than most people believe, but so are the potential psychic and social resources to combat it. Persons whose actions cannot be socially trusted should indeed be under social restraint, but the therapeutic and research efforts to rehabilitate them should be unremitting. It is true that many men become psychically ill because their conscience is too rigid or distorted. But at least as much social difficulty comes from insufficient development of conscience as in so-called "sociopathic personalities." Men are more bound than they realize, but they can be helped toward the capacity to exercise greater freedom especially by the patient and painful "working through" of the ways in which they are determined. The freedom that results may still be socially and ethically ambiguous; but since it is less ambiguous psychologically, it is likely to be more plus than minus by social standards. Both love and aggression operate in man and at deep levels. Love is to be encouraged in socially acceptable forms. Aggression, even if not holding quite the same intrapsychic status as love, nevertheless is to be channeled rather than extirpated. Most men, at some time in their lives, may profit from some degree and kind of therapeutic intervention, and for many, such action may spell the difference between psychic life and death. This list is somewhat biased toward therapeutic psychology, which seems legitimate because of the focus of our immediate concern.

## Theological Views of Man

Theology in this century has undergone almost as much revolution as psychology. The fact is less apparent on the surface. The same Bible, the same creeds, and the same basic ceremonies and rites are to be seen. The obtrusiveness of these tends to conceal the amount of change that has occurred.

When this century began, American theology had yet to fight out the battle of modernism versus literalisms of various kinds, even though this contest had already been won in principle through acceptance by most theologians of at least some forms of scientific criticism of the Bible (through textual study, archeology, linguistics, history, and the like). Nonliteralism had to win, not only for the sake of contemporary relevance but also for that of fidelity to the biblical intent. Adam and Eve, for instance, were prototypes not persons, and what tempted them was more slinky and seductive than the serpent used to symbolize it. Jonah was the tragic antagonist in a drama of divine love, not a historical personage who reversed the technique of angling. The biblical account of the resurrection of the body is not a biological prediction of reincarnated cells but a confession of ultimate trust in the God who is revealed through the whole life and work of Jesus Christ. This general procedure is now often called "demythologization."

Many forces operated to effect the victory of modernism in the sense in which we have defined it. Historical study of the Bible played a large part. So did the movement to find the implications of the gospel for man's social and institutional life. So did the fact that an increasing proportion of clergymen attended graduate theological schools. So did the new attempts to make religious education relevant for persons at different ages. So also did the courageous leadership of various persons, perhaps especially Harry Emerson Fosdick, who refused to concede that he believed "less" than the literalists.

By the time the nonliteral view had won the victory in the nineteen-twenties, except for mopping-up operations like the Scopes trial, the scene seemed free for a "liberal" advance in theology. The war to end war had been fought and won, and there was a League of Nations to keep the peace. Charity was increasing along with the stock market. Science and technology could continue to decrease illness, poverty, crime, and prejudice. Theology should ally itself with all men of good will, and encourage the use of new findings and possibilities for human good. To be sure, man was still a sinner and he would continue to do wrong things, but too much talk about sin could discourage man from moving ahead. The Bible was still important for its high ethical vision, its magnificent literature, its picture of the perfect man Jesus, and the Word that could still lead men to the kingdom of God; but it was, after all, written by primitive peoples in primitive times, and the parts that showed those peoples always in political hot water or economic depression were not quite relevant to us.

The theological reactions against this kind of "liberalism" began in Europe, in part because the sheer tragedies and catastrophes of life were much sharper and more pervasive. The havoc of the war was not only the widespread casualties in central Europe but also the subsequent inflation that wiped out the securities of the middle class and which led eventually, through weakness and despair, to Hitler. The tottering legs of the League of Nations were more visible anywhere than here, where a combination of isolationism in international relations, apparent prosperity in economics, and gullibility in ethics prevented a clear view.

The first sign indicating that our world was not so different from that of the Bible was the depression of 1929. Then came the prophetic figure of Reinhold Niebuhr who, more than any one else, showed theology what it must do in this period that had closed out "liberalism" with the depression. It is folly and faithless, he said, for Christian ethics to enunciate the Beatitudes, urging men to live up to them as far as they can. No man can live up to them. The standard they present is humanly impossible although as a standard they are absolute. The pietistic diversion of Christian energies from the great issues of nations and institutions simply permits blind or demonic forces to gain control. Christian concern must begin not with verbally advocating love as if it were a simple possibility, but with striving proximately and fallibly but determinedly for justice. Niebuhr's thought was of course far more complex than this; but his beginning with social ethics, and then moving to deeper reconsideration of the biblical and theological foundations for understanding man was both a cause of the general movement in the same direction and also a symptom of it.

Then came World War II, nuclear fission, the movement of the Soviet Union and more recently of China into the status of rival powers to the United States, the rise of peoples all over the world, and most recently the rapid decline of esteem for the United States all over the globe. Since World War II, theology has been predominantly "neo-orthodox." Positively, this movement has attempted to retrace and to rediscover the depth of the Christian message in order to meet the newly revealed depth of man's need, while omitting the literalisms that had once clouded the meaning of that message. At its negative worst, it must be confessed, this movement sometimes acted as if reading the Book were a substitute for hearing and heeding the Word, or as if beating the breast about sin could replace critical encounter with culture. As a strategic and realistic retreat to acquire fresh energies and a sense of direction, this movement has been very important. In the long future it will probably be regarded as like the prophet's forty-day retreat into the Wilderness. Since a large number of American Christians including clergy have never even skimmed through a desert on a weekend, the thrust of this movement is still important. But the prophet, unlike the hermit, did after all return from the Wilderness to take up his task anew in the midst of the world.

Even among those who have been leaders in this attempt to recover the distinctiveness of the heritage, there are rising doubts about whether the rediscovered message is being rendered intelligible to modern man and relevant to modern culture. True, it must be protected from distortion. But it is a talent to be opened to the world not hidden in the ground. They call for theology to engage in genuine dialogue (which is not mere agreement) with the disciplines of modern culture. Convinced that the gospel is the clue to understanding both man and God, they nevertheless believe that clue alone does not contain man's whole task.

It has been said recently that the arena of controversy within contemporary theology does not include the doctrine of, or teaching about, man. It is true that there is widespread agreement on fundamentals. Man was and is created by God in his "own image," and is therefore free, not a puppet; and capable of love, not essentially a monad or isolate. Man has, however, both individually and through culture, sinned—both rebelled and fallen short—in such fashion that his actual situation indicates isolation and estrangement from his own (God-) intended nature, from his fellows, and from God. Both the prototypical image of man's "essential" or true nature, and the power of grace that can rescue man from sin, come from Jesus Christ the Savior. Grace is brought to man through the Word and the sacraments, which are also connected in some way with nature, although convictions differ on how and to what degree. The power that sets man on the redemptive path is not his own; but the man who is renewed or "sanctified" may and must exercise freedom and responsibility as he could not before, even though he is not free of sin. He is a new creature in Christ, a New Being, no longer the Old Adam who fell.

There are among theologians some disagreements about man, and much would have to be added to make even a summary complete. But the real controversy within theology about man concerns method. Theologians are split right down the middle about whether, if at all, the findings of the cultural disciplines like psychology affect in any crucial way the theological understanding of man. There is no argument about the importance of these disciplines within the sphere felt to be proper to them, for example, medicine's dealing with sickness. But is any such knowledge important to theological understanding and construction? Or is it, even when it is accurate and far-reaching, simply prolegomenon to theology in the same sense that knowing a language is prerequisite to theologizing, but the language selected need not affect greatly the content of the theology?

Positions like Karl Barth's regard any wisdom that may come from the cultural disciplines as purely preliminary. In contrast, positions like Reinhold Niebuhr's believe such knowledge is important and worthy of systematic study; yet the findings are felt to be related to theology only externally. Paul Tillich goes further, holding not only that theology must take psychology seriously but also that no relevant modern theology can deny the contributions that psychology has made to it. In this sense, psychology does affect theologizing internally as well as externally. To Tillich, nevertheless, such insight seems finally to be only about man's "existence" and not also about his "essence." My own position is that psychology is to be seen not only as a cultural discipline developing its own autonomous categories and findings without hindrance and from which we may learn, but that there is also a "psychology" that is a proper branch of theology, and which pursues itself in dialectical interaction both with the other branches of theology and with the cognate cultural disciplines. To my position, the stand on psychology as a cultural discipline is like that of Tillich; but my position on psychology as a theological discipline shows it to be internal to theology itself, hence as potentially revelatory of man's "essence" as any other branch of theology. My position is not statistically widespread, but neither does it seem to draw the charge of heresy.

## The Dialogue

Since this book manifestly attempts to encourage real dialogue between psychologists and theologians, it is especially important to make the honest confession that comparatively little true dialogue has taken place or is now going on, and that even most of this book itself falls short of genuine dialogue.

This does not mean that open general enmity or suspicion is present as it tended to be twenty or thirty years ago. Each group has accepted the fact that the other is here to stay, and tends now to see certain pragmatic gains the other has brought or may bring. All theologians are grateful for what psychiatry and psychology have done for the mentally ill, including persons with psychoneuroses, and for the hints about how the clergy, too, may properly help people. In their turn, psychiatrists and psychologists generally recognize the mental health values that may inhere in church fellowship, in clergy who are sympathetic but not gullible father-figures, in religious rituals that relieve rather than increase feelings of guilt, and in religious ethics when they provide some structure and discipline, but without rigidity and perfectionism. Such mutual acceptance and appreciation has certainly grown. And there is now a gratifying trend to interpret the other group according to its best and not its worst representatives, in contrast to an earlier period when "psychiatrists" might be accused of advocating sexual promiscuity or "clergymen" of inducing neurotic guilt feelings.

There is also an increasing interest that moves beyond the pragmatic. The wide response, for example, to the program of the Academy of Religion and Mental Health shows that the increased desire to learn about the other and to co-operate with him is growing, and is not confined to any single type of group. On the face of it, the desire to learn and to co-operate seems evident among more clergymen than psychologists, but it is increasing among both groups. All this is more than pragmatic, more than prudence, more than "good business." But it is not in itself dialogue. Real dialogue requires also some knowledge of the other's field of learning and some acknowledgment of its kinship (in some basic respects) with one's own, in sufficient depth to prevent encounter from degenerating into either premature agreement or categorical separation. Unless the interest does reach the stage necessary for dialogue, it might result in a more sophisticated version of the nineteenth-century parallelistic relationship between physicians and clergy.

What will happen when and if there is true dialogue between the kind of psychology and the kind of theology that have been described? It seems very likely that commonality will be found on some convictions the nature and depth of which may surprise both sides, that the need to disagree about other things will be clarified, and perhaps most important and most baffling, that concerning other things confusion will continue about both content and method. Yet confusion of this kind is never quite what it was before. It becomes the new focus of new dialogue. Dialogue of this kind is to be enduring and not swallowed up, for example, by an eschaton along about 2061.

What can now be done, on both sides, to increase the amount and the quality of dialogue between psychologists and theologians on the fundamental question of man's nature? Certainly the first is to use available opportunities to overcome ignorance. Not long ago, for example, I was invited to meet with an able group of clinical psychologists. When I arrived, they said I should feel free to discuss what I wished, but admitted they had constructed a question on which they would like some light. This question was about the nature, meaning, and transformation of what they called "man's sinful experience." I replied that I liked the question and would try to deal with it, and assumed that what they wanted me to get around to eventually was the distinction between "true" and "neurotic" guilt feelings. But since they had mentioned "man's sinful experience," I said it seemed to me wise to begin by trying to convey the basic intention of the doctrine of sin in the Jewish and Christian traditions, since the notion of "man's sinful experience" suggests that a distortion of that intention is already in evidence.

This phrase suggests that sin is something done by bad people, and that "sinful" is one kind of experience as over against other kinds. On the contrary, I continued, sin is just as much about good people as about the bad, and is an ingredient in all experience. So far as time and my knowledge permitted, I then developed this case both historically and constructively. Discussion that followed was very deep-reaching and penetrating, and was a good deal more than their questions and my replies. In the midst of this it suddenly occurred to me that this able group of young professional psychologists, armed as they were with Ph. D.'s, had nevertheless never before heard a serious analytical exposition of the meaning of sin that tried to separate its intent from the moralistic and legalistic accretions. Twice I stopped to ask if they wanted to get on to the matter of guilt. The first time I was simply waved back to the subject of sin, but on the second occasion the chairman said, "We already know about guilt. You keep on about sin." I cannot imagine having such a discussion ten years ago. The implication of this story is not that all sincere attempts to dispel ignorance will succeed equally, but that the presence of such ignorance should always give the signal to attempt communication, albeit modestly and on request only.

The story is also a reminder that the level of discourse in such encounters must be appropriate to the kinds of knowledge a particular group does and does not have. For example, this psychologist group was able to grasp and deal creatively with the dynamic meaning of sin far more quickly than any group of theological students I have met. Hence any "talking down" or "going slow" with them on this point would have impeded our dialogue. On the other hand, they were factually ignorant of the Bible, Augustine, and Luther, and what contemporary theologians say about these. Any attempt on my part simply to apply my own criteria of sophistication, to flatter them by assuming that they knew all about the Bible, Augustine, and Luther, and to avoid giving basic information they wanted and did not have, would also have held up our discussion. In general, what each group knows, and what each group is ignorant about, is different. A sensitivity to these differences so that there is neither "talking down" nor "flattering highbrowism" can help dispel ignorance in a way that will make dialogue possible.

A second way in which real dialogue may be promoted is to let the "ground rules" evolve out of the interaction instead of being imposed with secret disadvantage to the other. For example, the theologian who insists that the discussion begin with the articulation of fundamental presuppositions about man is "fudging" on his own side. This is not because of the content of his, or of the other's, presuppositions, whether they are the same or different. It is rather because the type of training he has had has probably enabled him to deal more easily, but not always better, with presuppositions directly than has the training of the psychologist. Of course, eventual discussion at this level is needed. But it may be a poor place to start unless theologians are so fearful of the outcome that they must put psychologists initially on the defensive.

Psychologists may also "fudge" in setting the ground rules. For example, they may ask that theology be defined with a kind of item-by-item uniqueness which, if answered in terms of the question, will distort the concern and the method of theology. It cannot be said too often, with William Temple, that God is interested in many things besides religion. Or again, psychologists are generally very much better equipped, technically, to deal with case studies than are theologians (although this is not inherent in the nature of the two callings). On the other hand, just because they have done so much technical learning about case studies of one kind or another, psychologists are more likely than theologians to have many arbitrary conventions about what a case study is. If psychologists set case studies as the beginning point of the dialogue, this may be excellent, provided the genus case study is not necessarily confined to a particular form and pattern. The hero of *The Catcher in the Rye* may, for these purposes, be as important as Mr. Teen.

Finally, real dialogue can be aided if one can recognize, even in advance of specific discussions, that there are deep and organic connections between the views of man that have emerged in psychology and in theology, even though it is necessary to burrow beneath the obtrusive in order to discover these affinities. It is no accident that the Soviet Union regards Christianity and psychoanalysis as being of the same order; for beneath the differences that are all too obvious to us, it senses correctly a common respect for individuality and for the human person. To it, psychoanalysis seems too mythological and not sufficiently materialistic. It is true that some of the presuppositions with which modern psychology has developed rest in a kind of naturalism and reductionism that theologians must reject. But historically, in a longer view, these mostly arose in reaction against some fixated orthodoxy that was strangling inquiry or appearing to make it unnecessary. The fact is that the deeper presuppositions about valuing the human person, without which modern psychology could not have taken the course it has, are derivative from the imprint of Judaism and Christianity upon Western culture. Let us lose sight neither of the proximate differences nor of the deeper affinities.

## The "Isness" Beneath "Oughtness"

We argued at the start that every serious interpretation of man's nature, whether psychological or theological, contains at least a limited and implicit "ought," and that every such interpretation eventually tries to ground itself in an "is." Indeed, it is these two facts that make it possible to use the understanding of "man's nature" as a possible point of meeting and dialogue. No position is so naïve as simply to equate man's "isness" with obtrusive actuality.

Both psychology and theology are metaphorical miners. Both seek ore that cannot be handled by strip-mining. Both believe that "is-ness" has some kind of depth.

Yet even here there is a difference which, if unrecognized, can impede real dialogue. To theology, depth means ultimacy. To psychology, it connotes either complexity or early origin. All the meanings are legitimate and important, but they should not be confused. And if any of the three meanings of "depth" is so pursued as to exclude the others, the consequence is a particular kind of bias or distortion. For example, if man is thought of with so much of the bias of ultimacy that everything proximate or preliminary or actual is denigrated, the psychological result is to "spiritize" man, and the theological result is for him to be swallowed up rather than to be redeemed by God. If only man's complexity comes into the foreground, then there may be no vision of what gives him a common humanity and makes him man as well as a man. If he is seen as simply extrapolated developmentally from his early origin, then his uniquely human capacities, many of which do not become evident early, may be depreciated to epiphenomenalism. Precisely in a clarification of the different meanings of depth, each of which contains a different order of relating "oughtness" to "isness," may fruitful dialogue go on.

Whatever may be different about the content, both psychologists and theologians who present serious interpretations of man tend to use a similar structure in relating "oughtness" to "isness." They both think of (1) man who was, essentially or basically, or who might have been, under favorable conditions; (2) man who exists or is in actuality, with real difference between this condition and what is essential or potential or desirable; (3) man who may, through certain processes and by certain powers, be released at least to move in a direction different from, and superior to, that which characterizes him in actuality. This common structure of the relation of "oughtness" to "isness" may also be a point of departure in dialogue.

Still another point from which dialogue may move profitably is that at which the professional concerns of psychologists and theologians coincide at least in part. "Professional" is used here as against the scientific, theoretical, or intellectual concern for general knowledge and truth. While the "professional" draws upon such knowledge, it focuses on the convergence of all relevant knowledge to help the particular human person. Professional as well as scientific concerns are present in psychology and in theology. And especially at the points where they coincide may they be provocative of dialogue.

Finally, it is strange but true that both psychology and theology approach the study of man indirectly as well as directly; that is, sometimes each of them studies something else first. In theology, this is clear. The real question of man's nature, it contends, can be answered only by seeing man in relation to God. Man's true nature, therefore, is what God created man for, and what his will for man is. In psychology, something similar is true in terms of method. The recollections of adults may tell some things about childhood that children cannot tell, even though children may tell other things about childhood on which adult recollection is slippery. The study of psychically sick persons has told much about well people which, at least initially, could not be garnered from studies of well people, even though both kinds of studies are now necessary and fruitful. Psychology is a bit inclined to depreciate its use of indirect methods, while theology is inclined to shout so loudly about its indirect method that it conceals the shrewd direct observation of human behavior which also underlies its statements. Here is a methodological similarity in relating "oughtness" to "isness" that may also be a promising point for dialogue.

## Some Nasty Questions

If taken up *seriatim*, posed acidly, with no previous development of a sense of common interest, the following lists of questions—from psychologists to theologians, and from theologians to psychologists —might well prevent any discussion at all, dialogue or otherwise. For the questions are intended to be sharp and searching to the point of mercilessness. No honest or thoughtful man on either side will say that he can answer them clearly and without struggle.

But if they are so dangerous, and may cause bad feeling, the reader may ask, Why include them? The answer is that we shall have genuine dialogue only as the mutual asking and speaking to just questions of this type becomes possible without resulting in bad feeling. In that sense, the questions are included not as agenda but as criterion. When, as, and if discussion at this level can be maintained, then there is real dialogue. Everything that comes before is predialogue.

*Psychologist to Theologian.* 1. In your view of the essential or prototypical man, you surely do not mean that Adam existed in actuality, do you? In fact, if Adam had stayed on in innocence and laziness in Eden, would he not have been something other than a man? Doesn't this mean that his "fall" was a movement into humanness and therefore a kind of "rise" from his earlier prehumanness? Further, since you seem to accept the principle of evolutionary development for both race and individual person, isn't it false to try to see how man may become better by looking backward? And if you want to let Adam alone, and deal only with Jesus Christ as the true man, how can you do that since you regard him as both God and man? Do you secretly want men to be gods? Or if just the human aspect of Jesus Christ is to be the prototype for true man, then by which criteria do you say what we take and what we leave? Are we to be celibate, use spittle for healing, try to walk on water? Where do you draw the line, and on what grounds?

2. You seem to say that the actuality of man's trouble lies in his sin, that he sins because he is free but that his freedom does not enable him to avoid sin. Frankly, does that make sense? And if you think you can avoid the danger by introducing original as well as actual sin, then doesn't sin become something other than free decision by people, and therefore is no longer sin? And how is it you seem to think you have diagnosed everything adequately once you have talked of sin? Aren't you curiously uninterested in differential diagnoses? But how can you pay serious attention to individual persons and their troubles without differential diagnosis? Of course there is a kind of spelled-out differential diagnosis in Roman Catholic moral theology, but it is put in purely behavioral and not motivational terms. Shouldn't you Protestants begin to have a differentiated account based on motivation? Or if you don't, aren't you just doing more subtly what you've done before in revivalism? And anyhow, is sin the whole of the problem? Does a youngster

whose mother did not love him, and who now can love no one, simply get chalked up as "sinner"?

3. Are you really correct in thinking you know just what a man, extricated or redeemed, should look like? Aren't saints likely to be untouchable and inhuman, or a bit neurotic in the way they repress things? Frankly, isn't your redeemed man likely to be the same old reprobate, motivationally speaking, but perhaps with a better object of identification than he had before? Isn't his belief in God still a dependency reaction that he ought to have outgrown? Isn't his faith in Christ a little cowardly because he dare not confront the Father outright? And isn't his belief in the constant presence of the Holy Spirit a bit reminiscent of unassimilated homosexual tendencies? Even if it is granted that redemption or salvation in the Christian sense sets a man's feet on a positive path, how do you help get him there? If you reply that God does it rather than you, then why bother yourself at all? If you have something to do with it, why don't you show us some specific studies that contain the kind of fact and analysis we can examine? Isn't it strange that you've shown us little or nothing of this kind, except of an anecdotal nature? Could it be that you're afraid to get down to cases?

*Theologian to Psychologist.* 1. Isn't there a kind of Noble Savage in your view of man's original nature? Of course you don't believe that the Noble Savage ever literally existed, but how does your view of the baby happily suckled at his mother's breast really differ? If you reply that you know the baby will soon have to deal with separation from the mother, and that, in mastering the new conditions, the infant will begin to develop an ego, an interest in play, and many other things, do you mean to imply that all this is a kind of "fall"? Is the long course of development, containing many hardships and renunciations, a kind of backward movement, a price paid for civilization, while something more fundamental in the child would be better served otherwise? Is the suckled child more human than the later child who has learned, or been forced defensively, to think? Further, do you believe that scientific investigation alone can tell you what the favorable conditions are for rearing a human being? No matter if you want to put such conditions only negatively, as what a child ought *not* to experience, on what grounds do you say so? What values do you want to protect by your understanding of child-rearing conditions, even minimal conditions? On what grounds do you affirm them?

2. Do you believe that virtually all of man's troubles and sufferings are of the nature of sickness or illness? If so, what do you mean by illness? Of course, you mean humanitarian concern for the sufferer, and attempts to discover the nature of his particular trouble so that ways of extrication may be found; but what else do you mean? Do you imply that he, as a subject, has no kind of responsibility for confronting and dealing with his condition? If you don't mean that, then precisely what is the nature of his responsibility? Further, if you rest so much on the notion of illness, does that mean you regard healthy man as perfect man? If man's actual condition involves more than deviations from health, however, what else do you include? Granted that you have a differential diagnosis of illness, why do you not extend this method to all kinds and causes of trouble, if any exist beyond illness? Why not a differential diagnosis of all kinds of troubles, including the kind you yourself have even if you have been psychoanalyzed? Beneath your differential diagnoses, do you not have a notion of man as ambiguous, trying for one thing (perhaps safety against attack) and bringing forth another (illness)? If that is so, is your thinking not a kind of Gnosticism, implying that if man had more of the proper kind of knowledge he would not get himself into such messes?

3. Of course you rely on a wide stock of medical, psychological, and social resources to help a man move out of his existing pathological condition toward something better, but what are your criteria for telling when he is better? Is it when he suffers less? If so, what about painless cancers, paranoid conditions, and sociopathic personalities? Is it that he becomes more mature? If so, is there really anything especially psychological or scientific about your understanding of maturity? Or if learning to love is better, by what standard do you say how much love is good and of what kind? What about productivity in art or work, and why isn't this just obsessionalism? Further, what, if anything, do you have to say about persons who have the kinds of troubles in which you do not specialize, like poverty, prejudice, pride, or smugness? Do you believe they too need to be "healed"? Finally, suppose you have done a therapeutic job on a man, so that he is freer, more mature, more loving, more

productive, or whatever you think appropriate, in other words more a true man than before by your criteria. Is he not, then, more capable of damage to the world, as well as of more potential benefit to the world, than he was before? If you think he is likely to do more good than harm, on what grounds do you base this prognosis?

# CONTRIBUTORS

Seward Hiltner is Professor of Theology and Personality, Princeton Theological Seminary, Princeton, N. J.

Edith Weigert, M.D., is a psychoanalyst and training analyst of the Washington Psychoanalytic Society, Washington, D. C.

James I. McCord is president of Princeton Theological Seminary, Princeton, New Jersey.

Paul W. Pruyser is Associate Director, Department of Education, The Menninger Foundation, Topeka, Kansas.

Paul Tillich is University Professor, Harvard University, Cambridge, Massachusetts.

Carl R. Rogers is Professor of Psychology and Psychiatry, University of Wisconsin, Madison, Wisconsin.

Bernard M. Loomer is Professor of Philosophy of Religion, The University of Chicago, Chicago, Illinois.

Walter M. Horton is Professor of Theology, Graduate School of Theology, Oberlin College, Oberlin, Ohio.

Hans Hofmann is Associate Professor of Theology, Harvard University, Cambridge, Massachusetts.

Howard L. Parsons is Professor of Philosophy and Chairman of the Department of Philosophy and Religion, Coe College, Cedar Rapids, Iowa.

The late Willard L. Sperry was Dean of Harvard Divinity School, Cambridge, Massachusetts.

Noel Mailloux is president of the Center for Research in Human Relations, Montreal, Canada.

Franz Alexander, M.D., is Director of the Psychiatric and Psychosomatic Research Institute, Mount Sinai Hospital, Los Angeles, California.

Elliott Dunlap Smith is Provost Emeritus, Carnegie Institute of Technology, Pittsburgh, Pennsylvania.

Randolph Crump Miller is Professor of Christian Education, Yale Divinity School, New Haven, Connecticut.

Valerie Saiving Goldstein is instructor in religion, Hobart and William Smith Colleges, Geneva, New York.

Harold Kelman, M.D., is President of the American Institute for Psychoanalysis, New York City.

Frederick A. Weiss, M.D., is a lecturer at the American Institute for Psychoanalysis, New York City.

The late Karen Horney, M.D., was Dean of the American Institute for Psychoanalysis, New York City.

Karl Menninger, M.D., is Chairman of the Board of Trustees of The Menninger Foundation and Chief of Staff, The Menninger Clinic, Topeka, Kansas.

Margaret Mead is Associate Curator of Ethnology, American Museum of Natural History, New York City.

Elmer G. Homrighausen is Dean of Princeton Theological Seminary, Princeton, New Jersey.

William Hamilton is William Newton Clarke Professor of Christian Theology and Ethics, Colgate Rochester Divinity School.